Presuppositionalism:

A Biblical Approach to Apologetics

Paul S. Nelson

FOREWORD

This book is a compilation of sermons, lectures and articles related to the subject of Christian apologetics. The sermons were preached from the pulpit of Sovereign Grace Baptist Church in Morgan Hill, CA. The lectures were delivered under the auspices of the Pacific Institute of Religious Studies (P.I.R.S.) and the articles were published in the *PIRSpective* theological newsletter.

The position of the writer is unabashedly *presuppositional*. Simply stated, I hold the inspired word of God to be absolute in authority over all reasoning and knowledge. It is the ultimate standard for the interpretation of all reality – including the universe and all facts of nature. The enterprise of apologetics cannot ignore, devalue or exempt itself from this great and grand presupposition of the Christian faith. The virtue of apologetics lies in its loyalty to Scripture. If our approach to apologetics is not scriptural, it will not be pleasing to God or blessed of Him.

There are essentially two basic approaches to Christian apologetics: evidential (including classical) and presuppositional. The difference between the two approaches is the place one gives to Scripture. In evidential apologetics, one begins outside of Scripture with evidences and facts, reasoning to Scripture. Scripture cannot be used as an authority until you have proven its reliability. Hence, Scripture becomes a hypothesis to be proven by evidences and not embraced as the actual truth of God. It must be subjected to independent human reasoning and the scientific method. At best, the truth of Scripture is only a probability; therefore Christianity can only be probably true. This exalts human reasoning as ultimate and man as autonomous. It puts God on trial and his word sits in judgment of unregenerate man. Do not think for one moment that unbelieving thought is neutral or unbiased toward God. To argue strictly from evidences without the presupposition of Scripture is to betray the Lordship of Jesus Christ and the authority of his word.

In presuppositional apologetics, God and his word are presupposed to be absolute and ultimate. This is the first and overshadowing presupposition for a truly biblical approach to apologetics. There is no higher authority for man in knowledge and reasoning. God is absolute and his revelation comes to man with absolute authority; it is the inspired, infallible, inerrant, and all-sufficient word of God. God's word is absolute because God is its author, and therefore, it is the final criterion and standard for all truth and knowledge.

Dr. Oliphint of Westminster Theological Seminary (Professor of Apologetics) tells the story of one of his students attending a conference on defending the faith. The keynote speaker began with the statement, "This year our topic is apologetics, so you really won't need to have your Bibles with you." It was not meant to be flippant; it was a statement describing the method of apologetics. Ultimately, this is where evidential apologetics will take us. Something is seriously wrong when we are trying to defend the faith without the Bible.

PSN

CONTENTS

CRITICAL TEXTS

FOR

PRESUPPOSITIONAL APOLOGETICS

1. A CALL TO APOLOGETICS
(1 PET. 3:15)

1 Peter 3:15 But sanctify the Lord God in your hearts: and *be* ready always to *give* an answer to every man that asketh you a reason of the hope that is in you with meekness and fear.

The charter text for Christian apologetics is 1 Peter 3:15. The following article discusses five aspects of Christian apologetics taken from this text: *A Universal Call to Be Ready, The Purpose of Being Ready, Defending the Hope in Us, Commitment to the Lordship of Jesus Christ* and *A Spirit of Humility*.

A UNIVERSAL CALL TO BE READY

In the above text Peter exhorts, "Be ready always to give an answer to every man that asketh." It is an urgent command and call to all Christians to be prepared to engage in defending the faith. The sense in the Grk is to be *perpetually* prepared (ἕτοιμοι ἀεὶ), at any time and all the time. Every believer must be ready to give an answer, not just the experts and professionals, not just philosophers, scientists, and theologians, but every Christian. Negligence in this duty is not an option. It is a moral necessity for every Christian to be continually ready to engage in apologetics.

THE PURPOSE OF BEING READY

The purpose of being ready is to "give an answer to every man that asketh." The Grk word for "answer" is ἀπολογία. This is a technical term denoting the argument a defendant makes before a judge in a court of law, responding to an accusation (Acts 22:1;

25:16).[1] Etymologically, ἀπολογία is a compound word derived from the preposition ἀπο meaning "from," and λόγιον (diminutive of λόγος) meaning "utterance" or "speech." Thus, it indicates speaking from a certain position or persuasion. Our English word *apologetics* derives from the transliteration of this Grk term. Theologically, *apologetics* means to defend the faith. The Christian is to be always ready to give his defense, to present his case for the hope that is in him.

Peter exhorts his readers to "answer" (ἀπολογία) from a *reasoned* position, i.e., to give a "reason" for the hope that is in them. The Grk term employed for "reason" (λόγον) denotes logic, not logic in its formal or symbolic sense, but as a consistent rationale.[2] Defending the faith is a *reasoned* defense, a consistent rationale of our hope that is in Christ Jesus. Every Christian must be prepared to intelligently articulate and rationally defend the doctrinal content of the Christian faith.

DEFENDING THE HOPE IN US

Defending the faith, as presented in 1 Pet. 3:15, is a response to an unbeliever's question. More specifically, it is responding to a question about the "hope" in us. The Grk term for hope is ἐλπίς, which means "expectation." Hope is the expectation of something invisible and unseen (Rom. 8:24). Literally, it is "the in-you hope" (τῆς ἐν ὑμῖν ἐλπίδος). Every Christian possesses hope in Christ: hope of salvation, the resurrection, heaven and eternal life. These are not probabilities, but certain realities. Although this hope is outwardly invisible, yet it is manifested in the life of the believer.

What prompts an unbeliever to ask a Christian of the hope he possesses? Godly living! Living an obedient life before God is very

---

[1] R. C. Lenski, *First Peter*. Peabody, MA: Hendrickson Publishers, 1998, p. 150. Commentary on the New Testament.

[2] K. S. Oliphint, *The Battle Belongs to the Lord*. Phillipsburg, NJ: P&R Publishing, 2003, p. 34.

conspicuous to the unbeliever. A Christian is not of this world, and it should be evident in the life. We are the light of the world, and are commanded to "Let your [our] light so shine before men, that they may see your good works, and glorify your Father, which is in heaven" (Matt. 5:16). The sanctified life of a Christian is convicting to the ungodly. It is a witness and testimony to the unconverted that inevitably draws out his curiosity. If you live a godly life, be prepared to be asked about the hope that is in you. Our Christian conduct has apologetical implications.[3]

Christians will be ill-treated by the world. The historical background of 1 Pet. 3:15 is persecution and slander directed against the good behavior of Christians (v. 16). Peter tells these Christians that their good conduct, under such abusive conditions, will cause their slanderers to be ashamed.

COMMITMENT TO THE LORDSHIP OF JESUS CHRIST

The Authorized Version[4] reads, "Sanctify the Lord God in your hearts." However, from the better Grk manuscripts,[5] it is actually "Sanctify Christ as Lord in your hearts" (κύριον δὲ τὸν Χριστὸν ἁγιάσατε ἐν ταῖς καρδίαις ὑμῶν). "Lord" is placed forward in the word order for emphasis: "As Lord! – Christ, sanctify in your hearts." Here, the apostle Peter stresses the lordship of Jesus Christ in the work of apologetics. The verb "sanctify" (ἁγιάζω) means to set apart, to separate.[6] The aorist imperative form of the verb denotes obeying

---

[3] Clifford B. McManis, *Biblical Apologetics*. Bloomington, IN: Xlibris Publishing, 2012, p. 82.

[4] Commonly known as the King James Version.

[5] The Authorized Version follows the inferior variant "the Lord God" (κύριον δὲ τὸν Θεὸν) found in the later uncials (K, L, P). Τὸν Χριστὸν is better supported by ℵ, A, B, C, Ψ, 33, 614, 1739, vg and others.

[6] The noun forms ἁγιασμός (translated holiness and sanctification) and ἅγιος (translated holy or saint) depict the same basic meaning of separation unto God.

with determination. The Christian apologist must be wholly committed to the lordship of Jesus Christ.

Further, the apologist is commanded to place Christ as Lord "in the heart." The term "heart" (καρδία) in Scripture is variously used: sometimes for the mind and understanding, sometimes for the will, sometimes for the affections, sometimes for the conscience and sometimes for the whole soul. Generally, it denotes the whole soul of man and all his faculties: intellect, will and affections. In particular, the heart is the place where self-consciousness functions – the center of man's reasoning, thinking and understanding. Therefore, to sanctify Christ as Lord "in the heart" is to bow to Christ's lordship in all reasoning and thinking, i.e., the entire world of thought. The goal of apologetics is to "bring into captivity every thought to the obedience of Christ" (2 Cor. 10:5).

The Christian must submit to the absolute authority of Christ's word in the work of apologetics. The word of God must be established as the absolute standard of all truth and knowledge, and asserted as the ultimate reference point for all reasoning. To seek to prove the reliability of God's word by evidences is to commit intellectual treason, defying the authority of Christ's word. It would promote man's reasoning above Christ's authority, and put man in judgment of God's word. God, the Lord Jesus Christ, is the author of the word of God. He is Lord. There is no higher authority! Hence, the Christian is obligated to presuppose Christ and his Word in the activity of apologetics. It is upon this imperative, to sanctify Christ as Lord, that defending the faith functions.

This means that apologetics is not neutral. To assume neutrality in interpreting any evidences would be to relinquish the lordship of Christ, whose Word alone is the absolute standard for all truth and reality. Christians must refuse to think or reason according to the

12

secular mind-set of the world, and their apostate epistemology.[7] Neutrality is a delusion because everyone has presuppositions that are held to by faith. The unbeliever has his presuppositions and a corresponding worldview that is antithetical to the Christian's. Likewise, the Christian has his presuppositions and is commanded to reason from Christ's word as the ultimate authority.

Some might object that you are coming to the unbeliever with a biased point of view. The unbeliever has his biases as well. Is there any neutral ground where both can be objective in interpreting evidences? My answer is neutrality is a myth. Everyone is inherently biased. It is a delusion to think that man can be neutral in his interpretation of evidence. We all have our presuppositions that dictate our interpretation of reality. The unbeliever would have the Christian give up the lordship of Christ and his Word in order to adopt his ungodly worldview[8] – all under the guise of being neutral and objective.

The Christian apologist must account for the fact that all unbelieving thought is under the power of the noetic effects of sin. The term *noetic* is from the Grk word νους, which means "mind." The noetic effects of sin refer to the effects the Fall had on the mind and intellectual faculty of man. The Fall had a drastic effect on man's reasoning capacity and his ability to understand reality. As a result, natural man is born with a false theory of knowledge. He exchanges the truth of God for "the lie" (Rom. 1:25) and lives in a world of self-deception. His thoughts are overcome by moral corruption (Gen. 6:5), futile reasoning (1 Cor. 3:20; Rom. 1:21) and intentional suppression of the truth (Rom. 1:18). The Bible characterizes natural man's depraved mind as having his understanding darkened (Eph. 4:18; Rom. 1:21), groping around in darkness (Acts 17:27), walking in the

---

[7] Epistemology is the theory of knowledge. It seeks to answer questions about the nature of knowledge, what we know and how we know it.

[8] A worldview is the sum total of one's presuppositions. It can be divided into three categories: metaphysics, epistemology, and ethics. See Chapter 10.

vanity of his mind (Eph. 4:17), hostile to God in his mind (Rom. 8:7) and an enemy of God in his mind (Col. 1:21). In short, man's reasoning ability has become totally depraved because he is spiritually dead. He has become destitute of the truth because of his hatred of God. He is noetically blind and spiritually insane. He constantly suppresses the truth in unrighteousness (Rom. 1:18). His mind-set is hostile to God and cannot be neutral in his thinking.

The reality of the noetic effects of sin correlates directly to the unbeliever's inability to truly know anything.[9] Consequently, one's apologetic method must take into account the total depravity of man's intellectual faculty. Natural man is incapable of reasoning objectively without bias against God. Intellectual neutrality is impossible because of the sinful nature of man.

However, the unbeliever blindly claims intellectual autonomy in order to interpret the universe without reference to God. He naturally will make himself ultimate in determining truth and reality. It is the propensity of the unregenerate heart to exalt itself against the knowledge of God. The unbeliever's fallacious epistemology would do away with God in every respect, and determine for himself what is true and what is false. It is the expression of a corrupt nature.

In light of what we have said about the noetic effects of sin, it should be obvious that there is no neutrality. There are no neutral interpretations of evidence. We cannot assume unregenerate man will be intellectual unbiased in his reasoning. Quite the contrary, he will be biased against God in the interpretation of evidences because he is an enemy of God and spiritually dead. Therefore we cannot begin with an alleged neutral ground outside of Scripture and reason to Scripture. It is a capitulation to the unregenerate's worldview and forces the Christian to use the world's apostate epistemology. To assume neutrality would be to give up the ultimate and absolute

---

[9] See Chapter 9, *The Noetic Effect of Sin and an Apostate Pou Sto*, pp. 151-178.

standard for all truth and reality – the word of God. It would relinquish the Lordship of Christ over to man's reasoning. The Christian is called upon and commanded to reason from Scripture as his ultimate authority.

In our text, the apostle Peter demands an unreserved allegiance to the lordship of Jesus Christ. Christ's lordship stands above and beyond all other authorities. Our starting point in reasoning with the unbeliever must be Christ and his Word. Peter's command is "sanctify the Lord Jesus Christ." Christians must refuse to think or reason according the mind-set of the world. It would be immoral to do so. We do not have the right to set apart God's word in any of our thinking.

A Spirit of Humility

Finally, we note that 1 Peter 3:15 also speaks of the spirit and attitude in which we are to defend the faith. The Christian apologist must adorn himself with two things, "meekness and fear." "Meekness" (πραΰτητος) denotes humility and a gentleness of spirit. "Fear" (φόβου) can mean either fear of Christ (as it did in 1 Pet. 1:17; 2:18; 3:2), or it can mean reverence and respect for others. Both are true. Christians are to reverence Christ when they engage in the work of apologetics. This is part of sanctifying Christ as Lord in our hearts. Christians are also to give due reverence and respect to men. All human beings possess the dignity of being made in the image of God. Therefore, they are to be treated with respect and in a becoming manner suitable to that dignity.

It is essential to conduct apologetics in an atmosphere of mutual respect. We are not to be parading our knowledge, or to be arrogant, rude and disrespectful. We are not to be contentious. Being belligerent and obnoxious does not do any good for the cause of Christ, and only serves to irritate and provoke. We are representing Christ and his gospel. As Christians, we are to exhibit grace in our speech. *The servant*

15

of the Lord must not strive; but be gentle unto all men, apt to teach, patient, in meekness instructing those that oppose themselves; if God peradventure will give them repentance to the acknowledging of the truth (2 Tim. 2:24-25).

2. DEFENDING AN OBJECTIVE BODY OF DOCTRINAL TRUTH (JUDE 3)

Jude 3 Beloved, when I gave all diligence to write unto you of the common salvation, it was needful for me to write unto you, and exhort you that ye should earnestly contend for the faith which was once delivered unto the saints.

Jude 3 is an extremely important text for apologetics because it identifies what the Christian must defend. Before we consider how to defend the faith, we must know what we are defending. Therefore, it is essential to first define the object of our defense. Jude 3 gives us a clear description of *the faith* every Christian is called to defend.

BACKGROUND FOR JUDE 3

Jude was writing in the context of a perilous situation. Intruders had "crept in unawares" and infected the churches with destructive teaching.[10] The seducers were propagating a form of antinomianism and "turning the grace of God into lasciviousness" (v. 4). Their doctrine led to an immoral lifestyle, which Jude characterized as "ungodly." He says, "It was needful for me to write unto you and to exhort you." He was compelled to write because of the urgency of the threat. False teachers had infiltrated the church and were deceiving many. It was an internal threat; the seducers were among them. Jude points them out as "spots in your feasts of charity, when they feast with you, feeding themselves without fear" (v. 12). The necessity of writing this letter is emphasized because action was needed. Indifference, passivity and procrastination would lead to their spiritual

---

[10] Most commentators identify the seducers as adhering to a primitive and libertine form of Gnosticism.

ruin. The gospel witness was at stake and the need to do apologetics was urgent.

Jude asserts his purpose for writing the letter by exhorting his readers "to earnestly contend for the faith." "To earnestly contend for" (ἐπαγωνίζομαι) describes the act of defending the faith. The Grk term ἐπαγωνίζομαι means to struggle on behalf of. It is an intensive form of ἀγωνίζομαι from which we get our English word agonize. It only occurs here in the N.T., but was commonly used to denote athletic contests or military battles. In our text, this strong metaphor probably has reference to a wrestling match, or some other athletic contest. Whether athletic or military, one thing is for sure; this imagery describes apologetics as a rigorous fight and intense struggle. The grammatical form of the verb "to earnestly contend" is a present infinitive (ἐπαγωνίζεσθαι), indicating that the Christian struggle is continuous. We can never let our guard down. There will always be those that oppose the faith, and every Christian, sooner or later, will be called upon "to fight the good fight" (1 Tim. 6:12; 2 Tim. 4:7). The need for apologetics is urgent in every generation.

WHAT IS "THE FAITH"?

When Jude exhorts his readers to earnestly contend for "the faith," he is not referring to a Christian's personal faith in Christ, but rather to the content of faith. In the Grk, "faith" possesses a definite article (τῇ πίστει) and is objective. Jude is referring to a definite body of truth that was articulated at the time of the apostles. This construction (τῇ πίστει) is used numerous times in the N.T. to refer to a system of doctrinal truth. The apostle Paul refers many times to "the faith" as the recognized system of doctrinal truth (Gal. 1:23; 6:10; 1 Cor. 16:13; 2 Cor. 13:5; Phil. 1:27; 1 Tim. 3:13; 4:6; Tit. 1:13; 2:2). Other N.T. terms used to describe this objective body of truth include "the doctrine" (1 Tim. 4:6, 16; 6:1, 3), "the apostle's doctrine" (Acts 2:42), "the sound doctrine" (1 Tim. 1:10; 2 Tim. 4:3; Tit. 1:9; 2:1), "that form of doctrine" (Rom. 6:17; 2 Tim. 1:13), "the doctrine of

Christ" (2 John 1:9), "the deposit" of truth (1 Tim. 6:20; 2 Tim. 1:14), "the message" (1 John 1:5; 3:11) and "the tradition" (2 Thess. 3:6). These terms indicate that during the time of the apostles and N.T. authors there was a clearly defined and authoritative system of Christian doctrine; a definite theology derived from Scripture that was the true expression of the Christian faith.[11] Clearly, "the faith" is the objective body of truth that Christians believe. This is what Jude exhorts his readers "to earnestly contend for."

Furthermore, Jude describes "the faith" by use of a participial phrase, "once-delivered-unto-the-saints." In the Grk, this participial phrase is sandwiched in between the definite article "the" and the noun "faith," functioning as an adjective. Literally, it is "the *once-delivered-unto-the-saints* faith." The participle calls our attention to three elements of the body of doctrinal truth collectively referred to as "the faith": 1) *revealed once for all*, 2) *handed down to us by God himself*, and 3) *entrusted to all Christians*.

First, the apostolic body of truth that Jude makes reference to was revealed "once for all" (ἅπαξ), i.e., it was completed by Christ. "God, who at sundry times and in divers manners spake in time past unto the fathers by the prophets, Hath in these last days spoken unto us by his Son..." (Heb. 1:1-2). The faith we defend is founded upon the completed work of Christ – his death and resurrection. The inspired writing down of this revelation (Scripture) is complete, never to be altered, supplemented, changed, subtracted from or added to. To do so would be to deny the inspiration, authority and sufficiency of Scripture. Any new doctrine inconsistent with this system of truth is a falsehood and should invoke all Christians "to earnestly contend for the faith."

Second, God himself has *handed down* this objective system of truth. Jude uses the term "delivered" (παραδίδωμι), which literally

---

[11] R. Reymond, *A New Systematic Theology of the Christian Faith*. Nashville, TN: Thomas Nelson Publishers, 1998, p. 878.

means "to hand over." It denotes entrusting someone to keep and take care of something. The definitive body of truth designated as "the faith" has been transmitted from the apostles to "the saints." God himself is the source of this body of doctrinal truth. It is not of human origin. The apostles did not concoct it; we are defending truths given to us by God himself. Therefore, if God has committed it to us, then our defense of it is credentialed with divine authority. We are the ambassadors of Christ (2 Cor. 5:20).

Third, this apostolic body of truth is entrusted to all Christians. Jude uses the term "the saints" (τοῖς ἁγίοις), which denotes all Christians. Defending the faith is not just for biblical scholars, pastors, or teachers; it is the duty of every Christian to defend the faith. All believers and every N.T. church must safeguard the purity of sound doctrine. We must keep the gospel pristine and free from all human innovations and any other worldly pollution. We are entrusted by God to preserve this body of truth for future ages. In our generation we have seen the onslaught of pragmatism, secular philosophies of church growth, and worldly entertainment pervert the worship of God and the gospel message to the point of blasphemy. Christians need to rise up and defend the faith against such evil practices and restore the scriptural, God-centered and reverent worship of God.

We also note Jude's reference to "common salvation" in v. 3. What does Jude mean by "common salvation"? It must be taken in conjunction with "the faith once delivered unto the saints." "Common" (κοινῆς) means that which is common to all believers. Paul uses this term in Tit. 1:4 to describe our "common faith." There can be no common salvation (or common faith) without a definitive body of truth. Our "common salvation" is the salvific doctrines articulated from the Word of God. This is the common salvation we share.

DEFENDING AS A COHERENT WHOLE

From our text we learn that Christianity is to be defended as a coherent whole. We must defend the system of truth contained in Scripture as a unit. Thus, it is apparent that systematic theology is more related to apologetics than any other discipline.[12] One must go to Scripture to know the content of the Christian faith, comparing Scripture with Scripture,[13] collating, deducing and framing doctrinal statements.[14] Scripture alone determines the content of "the faith," and the business of systematic theology is to set forth the system of truth presented in Scripture. The biblical doctrines of God, man, Christ, salvation, the church and eschatology are all interrelated and interdependent. Together, these doctrines define Christian theism[15] as a coherent whole.

We must not try to defend the faith by seeking to prove isolated historical facts that are separated from the coherent system of truth presented in Scripture. Cornelius Van Til stated, "It is impossible and useless to seek to defend Christianity as an historical religion by a discussion of facts only."[16] The historical events of Christianity did not occur in a teleological vacuum isolated from the purpose of God. Facts are not brute and we must not separate them from the Creator who gives all facts their true meaning. It is the triune God of Scripture who pre-interpreted and foreordained all facts before they ever were. Thus, man can only interpret facts by aligning his thinking with the word of God, and thus *thinking God's thoughts after him*. It is futile to try to defend the faith by attempting to prove historical facts simply by

---

[12] C. Van Til, *Christian Apologetics*. Phillipsburg, NJ: P&R Publishing Co, 2nd Edition (William Edgar editor), 2003, p. 23.

[13] This has reference to a principle of interpretation known as "the analogy of faith," which is the principle of allowing Scripture to interpret Scripture.

[14] R. Reymond, *A New Systematic Theology*, p. 878.

[15] *Christian theism* is the belief in the triune God of the Bible as a coherent worldview. It presupposes the absolute authority of Scripture.

[16] C. Van Til, *The Defense of the Faith*. Phillipsburg, NJ: P&R Publishing Co, 1967, p. 7.

evidences. These events will surely be misinterpreted unless viewed from the perspective of the whole council of God.[17] Are we defending isolated facts such as the resurrection of Christ, or are we defending Christianity as a coherent whole? Our defense of the faith should not be piecemeal; we are defending the Christian theism of Scripture.

For example, suppose you are able to prove from evidences a miracle of Scripture such as the virgin birth or resurrection of Christ, what will it accomplish? The scientist cannot and will not admit to a supernatural act such as a miracle because he is fully committed to his naturalistic worldview. It proves nothing more than something unusual took place. To him, you have simply expanded his realm of possibility to a previously unknown phenomenon. In due time, with the advancement of science and technology, the scientist believes it will eventually be fully explained by natural processes. The scientist's belief system will not allow him to view this world as under the sovereign control of God.

Ultimately, facts of history are interpreted by one's worldview or belief system. The apologist's task is to expose the fallacy of a secular worldview, and to show that rationality is only possible through Christian theism. Only the Christian can properly interpret facts of history because he presupposes the theism of Scripture. Scripture provides the only basis for a true understanding of reality; therefore any defense of Christianity must be based upon the authority of Scripture. We must be careful not to compromise the authority of Scripture and the coherent system of doctrine that flows from it when defending the faith.

In summary, we have identified what the Christian is to defend in the work of apologetics. In the words of Jude, it is "the once-delivered-unto-the-saints faith," i.e., the doctrinal system of truth contained in Scripture. It is the coherent unity of doctrine that expresses the

---

[17] R. Reymond, *The Justification of Knowledge*. Phillipsburg, NJ: P&R Publishing Co, 1976, p. 9.

biblical worldview of Christian theism. We must defend the faith as a package deal.[18] In this context, we can define apologetics as the vindication of Christian theism.[19]

---

[18] G. Bahnsen, *Pushing the Antithesis*. Powder Springs, GA: American Vision, 2007, pp. 43-44 (Gary DeMar, ed.).

[19] C. Van Til, *Christian Apologetics*, p. 22.

3. THE SPIRITUAL WARFARE OF APOLOGETICS (2 COR. 10:1-5)

2 Corinthians 10:1-5 Now I Paul myself beseech you by the meekness and gentleness of Christ, who in presence am base among you, but being absent am bold toward you: [2] But I beseech you, that I may not be bold when I am present with that confidence, wherewith I think to be bold against some, which think of us as if we walked according to the flesh. [3] For though we walk in the flesh, we do not war after the flesh: [4] (For the weapons of our warfare are not carnal, but mighty through God to the pulling down of strong holds;) [5] Casting down imaginations, and every high thing that exalteth itself against the knowledge of God, and bringing into captivity every thought to the obedience of Christ.

Apologetics is spiritual warfare. Indeed, any assault on the truth of the Christian faith is a declaration of war. In this vivid passage, the apostle Paul likens defending the faith to warfare, or more particularly to the siege of a fortified city.

As in any military battle, there are two opposing sides. Paul is describing a conflict between the wisdom of the world and the wisdom of God; he uses very strong military metaphors to do so. The conflict is not against people, but against thought patterns, philosophies and human reasoning. There is necessarily a clash of worldviews. It is a clash between human reasoning and the knowledge of God, a clash between an autonomous worldview where reasoning is ultimate and the Christocentric worldview where God's word is ultimate. Both sides are not neutral. The unbeliever's mind is hostile toward the knowledge of God (Rom. 1:18; 8:7; Eph. 4:17-18; Col. 1:21).

Paul uses military metaphors to illustrate this conflict. We will elucidate the text in the following order: *Metaphors of Warfare, Rules of Engagement, Spiritual Weapons, Military Strategy* and *Prisoners of War*.

METAPHORS OF WARFARE

There are seven different metaphors of warfare used in vv. 3-5. In v. 3, the verb "war" (στρατεύομαι) means "to fight" and "to engage in battle." It can also refer to the service of a soldier. The present tense of the verb indicates continual fighting.

In v. 4, the terms "weapons," "war," and "stronghold" are used. "Weapons" (ὅπλον) denotes instruments of warfare, i.e., armament. The noun "war" (στρατεία) signifies a military campaign. Our English word *strategy* derives from this term. The noun "stronghold" (ὀχύρωμα) designates a fortress, such as a castle.

In v. 5, the terms "casting down," "high thing," and "bringing into captivity" are employed. The term "casting down" (καθαιρέω) means to throw down and demolish, such as destroying a fortress. It is a present participle indicating continual destruction. The noun "high thing" (ὕψωμα) denotes a tower, referring to the fortress. The verb "bringing into captivity" (αἰχμαλωτίζω) expresses the taking of prisoners of war. All of the above metaphors paint a very vivid picture of the work of apologetics.

RULES OF ENGAGEMENT

There are *rules of engagement* in every military battle. Paul tells us what the Christian's rules of engagement are, "Now I Paul myself beseech you by the meekness and gentleness of Christ." Paul's rule for conducting this military campaign is humility. Paul would imitate the behavior of his Lord – the very character of Christ was meekness and gentleness. "Meekness" (πραΰτητος)[20] has to do with inward virtue and is a condition of the heart and mind. "Gentleness" (ἐπιεικείας) is the outward expression of meekness, depicting one's conduct. In the Grk there is a single definite article that combines these two nouns

---

[20] πραΰτητος is the same Grk word used in 1 Pet. 3:15. See page 12.

together as a unit.[21] This character, *meekness* and *gentleness*, marks the rules of apologetic engagement for the Christian. The Christian is to be humble.

Paul's opponents did not use the same rules of engagement. They conducted a smear campaign. They maligned and misrepresented Paul's humble behavior. They accused him of being a weakling and a coward. Further, they accused him of "walking after the flesh," and tried to discredit his authority as an apostle. The world looks upon humility, kindness and graciousness as weaknesses. These virtues are vulnerable traits that are often manipulated and taken advantage of. However to the Christian, such virtues are not weaknesses, but rather a display of spiritual strength and self-control. The spiritual marks of a mature Christian defending the faith are patience, long suffering, kindness and gentleness. This is what gives Christianity its beauty.

SPIRITUAL WEAPONS

The weapons the apostle refers to in v. 4 are spiritual weapons. Paul states negatively, "We do not war after the flesh, for the weapons of our warfare are not carnal." Christians do not depend upon human weapons. Paul did not rely upon human reasoning, his power of argumentation, or *enticing words of man's wisdom*. Paul did not rely upon the worldly philosophies of empiricism, naturalism or the scientific method. On the contrary, Paul's weapons were "mighty through God" (δυνατὰ τῷ θεῷ). His confidence was in the supernatural power of God. Paul would pull down the intellectual strongholds through God's power.

We must realize that the conflict is a spiritual war between the kingdom of God and the kingdom of Satan. *For we wrestle not against flesh and blood, but against principalities, against powers, against the rulers of the darkness of this world, against spiritual wickedness in high places* (Eph. 6:12). The Christian apologist must arm himself by putting on the full armor

---

[21] Granville Sharp's rule.

of God as described in Eph. 6:13-17. "The sword of the Spirit" is the only offensive weapon mentioned as part of the panoply of armor in Eph. 6:17. The apologist must wield "the sword of the Spirit, which is the word of God" (Eph. 6:17).[22] In the phrase "the word of God," the Grk term used for "word" is ῥῆμα and designates the spoken or uttered word of God. Following the example of Christ, our battle cry must be "it is written" (Matt. 4:4, 7, 10). Further, spiritual warfare presupposes the utter necessity of prayer. In Eph. 6:18, Paul concludes his description of the panoply of armor with "Praying always with all prayer and supplication in the Spirit."

MILITARY STRATEGY

Let us consider the *military strategy*. What Paul describes as an offensive strategy alludes to different stages of a military campaign in ancient siege warfare. Three stages are mentioned with three dependent participles (vv. 5-6): destroying defensive fortifications, taking captives and punishing resistance when the city is brought into submission. Paul identifies the enemy's strongholds as "imaginations" and "every high thing" that opposes the knowledge of God. The Grk word for "imaginations" (λογισμούς) means logical arguments or reasonings. There is no definite article, which means that "imaginations" is not a specific kind of reasoning, but any and all human reasoning. Included are all the world's thought patterns, opinions and philosophies. The opponent's fortresses are the various intellectual arguments that humans construct to resist the truth of the gospel. It is a battle against the world's presuppositions and belief-systems. The Christian is called upon to dismantle and pull them down. Clearly, apologetics involves destroying arguments.

---

[22] The great example of wielding the sword of the Spirit is our Lord's utter defeat of Satan in his wilderness temptation (Matt. 4:1-11). Every temptation of Satan was answered with the words, "It is written." (γέγραπται). The perfect tense of this verb signifies that God's word stands written with undiminished authority.

"Every high thing" (ὕψωμα) is another military term alluding to high towers and the great height of the fortress. Here, it is used figuratively of man's pride and arrogance concerning human reasoning. Unregenerate man sets up his fortress of reason and thinks that it is impregnable. This is Satan's stronghold in the hearts of men – carnal reasoning and high thoughts exalting themselves against the knowledge of God. Paul speaks here of demolishing the fortresses of worldly reason. His war is against the world's system of thought, which is continually seeking to exalt itself against the knowledge of God.

The very nature of presuppositional apologetics is to argue the Christian's worldview against that of the unbeliever's. It is to challenge the unbeliever's system of thought. It is to strike at the heart of the unbeliever's belief system, i.e., the presuppositions that form the foundation of his worldview.

Apologetics is primarily a battle over authorities. The apostle Paul uses the term "reasonings" (λογισμούς) as a direct reference to his opponents' appeal to authority. Paul's opponents sought to discredit his apostolic authority and establish their own, but their authority was simply their own reasoning, opinions and ideas. Their authority did not go beyond themselves. All non-Christian worldviews can be characterized by exalting human reasoning as ultimate and man as autonomous, which is the world's empty notion of authority. Paul's opponents were resting on a false authority. Paul's strategy was to tear down and destroy their arguments by bringing them into submission to the totalitarian claims of Jesus Christ and his Word.[23] He would back them up to their own faith-commitments, and challenge them on what authority they based their arguments. As with Paul, every

---

[23] It is important to see how Paul asserts his authority as an apostle of the Lord Jesus Christ in 2 Cor. 10:1. The language is emphatic in the Grk. He says, "Myself, I, Paul" (Αὐτὸς δὲ ἐγὼ Παῦλος). Paul was a called apostle, given direct revelation by Christ, and commissioned by Christ. Although the Christian cannot claim the authority of an apostle, he does claim the absolute authority of the word of God.

Christian has the confidence that God's inscripturated Word is absolute in authority and the ultimate standard for all truth and reality. It is certain, infallible, inerrant and all-sufficient because God is its author. Therefore the Christian's military strategy is to challenge the unbeliever with the question, "What saith the Scripture?"

PRISONERS OF WAR

The fifth aspect of this battle concerns *prisoners of war*. Paul's siege demands that every thought be made captive to the obedience of Christ. The term "bringing into captivity" (αἰχμαλωτίζοντες) refers to prisoners of war. Paul does not just want to destroy his opponent's arguments; he is going to make them prisoners of war. Every thought is to be brought into submission to the totalitarian claims of Jesus Christ. Paul demands their allegiance to God's word. Their mind-set must be transformed and renewed. This implies regeneration, which can only be accomplished by the work of the Holy Spirit. The goal of apologetics is always the conversion of the opponent and the advancement of the kingdom of God is its triumph. Paul always looked to the sovereign grace of God for the salvation of his opponents. He not only trusted in the power of God to demolish worldly reasoning, but also to convert his opponents.

4. PAUL'S ADDRESS TO THE AREOPAGUS[24] (ACTS 17:16-31)

SETTING (vv. 16-21)

Acts 17:16-21 Now while Paul waited for them at Athens, his spirit was stirred in him, when he saw the city wholly given to idolatry. [17] Therefore disputed he in the synagogue with the Jews, and with the devout persons, and in the market daily with them that met with him. [18] Then certain philosophers of the Epicureans, and of the Stoicks, encountered him. And some said, What will this babbler say? other some, He seemeth to be a setter forth of strange gods: because he preached unto them Jesus, and the resurrection. [19] And they took him, and brought him unto Areopagus, saying, May we know what this new doctrine, whereof thou speakest, *is*? [20] For thou bringest certain strange things to our ears: we would know therefore what these things mean. [21] (For all the Athenians and strangers which were there spent their time in nothing else, but either to tell, or to hear some new thing.)

The apostle Paul's address to the Areopagus council on Mars Hill occurred in Athens during his second missionary journey. While traveling thorough Macedonia, Paul and his co-laborers were forced to flee Thessalonica because of Jewish opposition. The hostile opposition relentlessly followed them to Berea. It was at Berea that the brethren sent Paul away to Athens, leaving Silas and Timothy behind. Upon arrival, Paul sends the brethren back to Berea with the request for Silas and Timothy to join him in Athens as soon as possible.

---

[24] Primary sources are K. S. Oliphint, "Jerusalem Meets Athens" in *The Battle Belongs to the Lord* (Phillipsburg, NJ: P&R Publishing, 2003), pp. 143-173; G. Bahnsen, *Always Ready* (Atlanta, GA: American Vision, 1996), pp. 235-276; *The Risen Christ Conquers Mars Hill* (Birmingham, AL: Solid Ground Christian Books, 2013); C. Van Til, *Paul at Athens* (Phillipsburg, NJ: P&R Publishing); W. R. Downing's paper entitled "Paul at Athens: Presenting a Christian Theistic World-and-Life View."

Paul waits for them in Athens (vv. 16-19). Athens was the philosophical center of the world, a city famous for its intellectual tradition. As Paul walked around Athens, he became greatly distressed at the rampant idolatry he observed in the city. We are told that he "saw the city full of idols." The Grk verb for "saw" is θεωρέω and denotes "to view attentively" or "to carefully observe." This is reiterated when Paul addresses the Areopagus (v. 23), "For as I passed by, and *beheld* your devotions [objects of worship]." Here, the verb "beheld" (ἀναθεωρέω) is an intensified form of θεωρέω, indicating that he seriously contemplated the gross idolatry of the city. The city was "wholly given to idolatry." Athens was so "full of idols," it was said that there were more idols than people.[25] Paul's spirit was "stirred" (v. 16). In the Grk, "stirred" is a very strong verb (παροξύνω) giving the sense of being "infuriated." Paul was infuriated at the multitude of temples and idols he saw. Wherever he gazed, he saw the manifestations of polytheism: nature deified, humanity depicted as superhuman, and human virtues and vices exalted into divinities.[26] The imperfect tense of the verb "stirred" (παρωξύνετο) indicates that Paul was continually disturbed. Athens was steeped in idolatry and he was terribly provoked.

Although Paul's visit to Athens was supposed to be a time of rest as he waited for Silas and Timothy, he could not remain idle, being greatly disturbed by the gross idolatry of the city. Paul spent his time "disputing" the gospel in the Jewish synagogue[27] and in the agora (marketplace). In v. 17, the Grk verb translated as "disputed" (διαλέγομαι) conveys the ideas of discourse, discussion and debate.

---

[25] It has been estimated that Athens had over 30,000 idol statues or shrines. One historian remarked that the city itself was one whole altar, one entire sacrifice and offering to the gods. The most prominent idol was the gigantic gold and ivory statue of Athena in the Parthenon on the Acropolis.

[26] John Eadie, "Paul at Athens" in *The Risen Christ Conquers Mars Hill* (Birmingham, AL: Solid Ground Christian Books, 2013), p. 181.

[27] "The synagogue" (τῇ συναγωγῇ) is singular in the Grk. There was only one synagogue in Athens.

The use of the imperfect verb tense again denotes continual action. It refers to both his discourse in the synagogue and the marketplace.

Once a week, on the Sabbath, Paul would discourse with the Jews and Greek proselytes (τοῖς σεβομένοις) in the synagogue. Here, we would expect Paul to engage the Jews "as his custom was" described in Acts 17:1-3:

> **Acts 17:1-3** Now when they had passed through Amphipolis and Apollonia, they came to Thessalonica, where was a synagogue of the Jews: ² And Paul, as his manner was, went in unto them, and three sabbath days reasoned with them out of the scriptures, ³ Opening and alleging, that Christ must needs have suffered, and risen again from the dead; and that this Jesus, whom I preach unto you, is Christ.

During the week, Paul would debate the gospel in the market place (ἀγορά) with primarily a Gentile audience. The apostle did this on a daily basis (κατὰ πᾶσαν ἡμέραν), reasoning with those who were there, and urging them to turn from their idols to worship the true God. In particular, Paul discoursed with "certain philosophers of the Epicureans, and of the Stoics" (v. 18). We would expect Paul's method to be more declarative since the philosophers had no knowledge of or regard for the Scriptures. For weeks, Paul daily preached the gospel in the marketplace.

It was Paul's preaching of "Jesus and the resurrection"[28] that disturbed the philosophers. He excited such an interest among the philosophers that they called a special assembly of the council of the Areopagus on Mars Hill[29] to hear a full statement of the teaching Paul

---

[28] Paul preached a complete gospel message to the philosophers in the agora. "Jesus and the resurrection" is Luke's summary characterization of the gospel. See Acts 4:2 where preaching the gospel is equated to "proclaiming Jesus the resurrection from the dead."

[29] The Areopagus council was named after the location they originally convened at. Areopagus literally means "the hill of Ares." Ares was the Greek god of war, the Roman counterpart was Mars, thus Mars Hill. Geographically, Mars Hill is an adjacent hill located northwest of the Acropolis. Although it is very possible that Paul delivered his address on this hill, it is also possible that the Areopagus

brought into the city. They were curious of the "strange gods" Paul had discoursed.

The Areopagus was the governing council of Athens. It was a council of approximately thirty members consisting of ex-magistrates, influential philosophers and aristocrats. They had jurisdiction over all religion and morals, and hence over all public lectures and discourses in the agora. Representatives of the philosophical schools of the Epicureans and Stoics are specifically mentioned, who were the ones that called Paul a "babbler" (σπερμολόγος). This literally meant seed-picker, referring to a bird scavenging food. Metaphorically it denotes an intellectual scavenger, grabbing intellectual "scraps" from various places and throwing them out to the public. It was a derogatory term directed at the one who allegedly stirred up this controversy.

Paul was brought before the Areopagus council to give an account of the things he was teaching and discussing in the marketplace. The Grk verb used in v. 19 for "they took him" is ἐπιλαβόμενοί, which means to "lay hold of" and often takes the sense of "to arrest." It is uncertain whether the charges made against Paul were formal or informal. In all likelihood, this was an informal hearing.

Epicurean, Stoic and "other" philosophers that encountered Paul in the agora accused him of "setting forth strange Gods."[30] Paul's doctrine of Jesus and the resurrection was called into question. They had misconstrued what Paul said about Jesus and the resurrection as two different gods, male (τὸν Ἰησοῦν) and female (τὴν ἀνάστασιν), the

---

convened somewhere in the agora. "Paul stood in the midst of the Areopagus" (v. 22) has reference to the council and not the geographical hill.

[30] At seventy years of age, Socrates was judged and condemned for the same charge of "setting forth strange gods." He was found guilty of both corrupting the minds of the youth of Athens and of impiety ("not believing in the gods of the state"), and sentenced to death by drinking a mixture of hemlock.

gods of "health" and "restoration" respectively.[31] The resurrection especially challenged them. To the Athenians, these were strange deities and regarded as new teaching that needed to be examined. When Paul was brought before the Areopagus, they asked, "May we know what this new doctrine, whereof thou speakest, is? For thou bringest certain strange things to our ears: we would know therefore what these things mean" (vv. 19, 20).

Being brought before the Areopagus council, Paul begins his defense of the faith. In v. 22, we see Paul taking his stand (σταθείς)[32] as an orator in the midst of the council and skillfully addressing them, "Ye men of Athens." This was familiar Greek rhetoric, the same formula used by the famous orator, Demosthenes. What followed was nothing less than a masterpiece of apologetics. It is the prototype for all Christian apologetics. The following is an outline of Paul's apologetic method at Athens: *Asserting the Point-of-Contact* (v. 22), *Critique of the Unbeliever's Worldview* (v. 23), *Asserting Ultimate Authority* (v. 23), *Pushing the Antithesis of Different Worldviews* (vv. 24-26), *Revealing Spiritual Blindness and the Noetic Effects of Sin* (v. 27), *Illustrating the Point-of-Contact* (v. 28), *Applying the Point-of-Contact* (v. 29) and *Culpable Ignorance* (v. 29).

ASSERTING THE POINT-OF-CONTACT (V. 22)

Acts 17:22-23 ²²Then Paul stood in the midst of Mars' hill, and said, *Ye men of Athens, I perceive that in all things ye are too superstitious.* ²³For as I passed by, and beheld your devotions, I found an altar with this inscription, TO THE UNKNOWN GOD. Whom therefore ye ignorantly worship, him declare I unto you.

The apostle began his address by appealing to the religious nature of the Athenians, "... *I perceive that in all things ye are too superstitious*"

---

[31] Ἰησοῦν is masculine gender and ἀνάστασιν is feminine. They may have confused Ἰησοῦν with ἴασις, "healing" and Ιησω, the goddess of heath. F. F. Bruce, *Acts*, footnote 21, p. 351; G. Bahnsen, *Always Ready*, p. 247.

[32] Σταθείς (aor. participle) "having taken his stand," refers to assuming the posture of an orator. W. R. Downing, "Paul at Athens: Studies in the Greek Text," p. 6.

(δεισιδαιμονεστέρους, extremely religious – literally, fearers of supernatural spirits). The presence of a multitude of idols, temples, and altars throughout Athens proved Paul's point. Paul said, "in all things" or "in every respect" (κατὰ πάντα) you are very religious. The prepositional phrase "in all things – too superstitious" is emphatic, being placed first in word order.

Paul immediately draws on an obvious point-of-contact, the image of God in man and his innate sense of deity (*sensus divinitatus*). Man is inherently and inalienably a religious being. Every man possesses an inescapable sense of deity inscribed upon his heart, by virtue of being created in the image of God. This is the critical point-of-contact for the Christian apologist. Man was created a religious being; it is part of his natural constitution.

No man can escape knowing God. All men have a general knowledge of God (Rom. 1:18-32; 2:14-15). Indeed, God has revealed himself to all men through natural revelation. It is not a saving knowledge of God, for that can only be known through the special revelation of the gospel. However, all men do have knowledge of God; they understand his divine attributes, his moral character and judgment. Paul says, in Rom. 1:20, "these things are clearly seen." A sense of deity is present in every person.

Deep down in the heart of man, he knows that he is a creature of God and a culpable creature at that. He cannot escape the face of God. The problem with unregenerate man is that he is in a state of total depravity and his mind is permeated with the noetic effects of sin. Thus, he habitually suppresses his knowledge of God (Rom. 1:18). Although all men possess knowledge of God, they are wholly bent on perverting it. Man's intellectual problem is sin and its noetic effects. Natural man habitually and deliberately suppresses and perverts the truth of God he possesses.

> **Romans 1:18** For the wrath of God is revealed from heaven against all ungodliness and unrighteousness of men, who hold the truth in unrighteousness;

Romans 1:21 Because that, when they knew God, they glorified him not as God, neither were thankful; but became vain in their imaginations, and their foolish heart was darkened.

Ephesians 4:17-18 [17] This I say therefore, and testify in the Lord, that ye henceforth walk not as other Gentiles walk, in the vanity of their mind, [18] Having the understanding darkened, being alienated from the life of God through the ignorance that is in them, because of the blindness of their heart:

The inherent religious propensity of man's nature had lead the Athenians to seek after God, albeit ignorantly. Through self-deceit, they deliberately created a false reality and "exchanged the truth of God for a lie" (Rom. 1:25). The Athenians perverted the natural knowledge of God they possessed into a culture of idolatry. They were steeped in idolatry.

Romans 1:22-23 [22] Professing themselves to be wise, they became fools, [23] And changed the glory of the uncorruptible God into an image made like to corruptible man, and to birds, and fourfooted beasts, and creeping things.

What drives man to pervert his inherent knowledge of God? Man's inalienable self-consciousness of God must be suppressed at all cost to avoid the reality of being accountable to God for sin. Accordingly, the Athenians concocted a thousand idols, in an attempt to deny the true God, the Creator of heaven and earth, and the inescapable knowledge of God that was imbedded in their heart. As Paul says in Rom. 1:18, they suppressed the truth in unrighteousness. It was a deliberate and constant holding down of the truth.

Paul says, "I perceive that you are very religious." He appeals to that which is in man, but denied by every man. By employing this point-of-contact Paul was drawing them in. The term "religious" (δεισιδαιμονεστέρους) is somewhat ambiguous; it can be either complementary or critical.[33] If the Areopagus didn't know what he meant by using this word, they would surely want to know what he meant. Next, he will present a persuasive argument based upon man's

---

[33] K. S. Oliphint, *The Battle is the Lord's*, p. 154.

inherent religious nature, presupposing that all men have a sense of deity indelibly inscribed upon their heart because they are creatures created in the image of God.

From the word of God, we are assured that every man is in contact with the truth, and possesses a general knowledge of God. Although they may deny it, we know it to be true. Deep down inside, every man knows the Creator, the moral character of God, and that he is condemned under the judgment of God (Rom. 1:18-32; 2:14-15). The Christian must appeal to the truth the unbeliever seeks to suppress. This is our point-of-contact with the unbeliever. A sense of deity is indelibly inscribed upon the heart of every person because man was created in the image of God.

CRITIQUE OF THE UNBELIEVER'S WORLDVIEW (V. 23)

Paul critiques their religious worldview. He says, "For as I passed by, and beheld your devotions, I found an altar with this inscription, TO THE UNKNOWN GOD. Whom therefore ye ignorantly worship, him declare I unto you." The apostle points out the absurdity of worshiping an unknown God. He notes a contradiction; although they were ever conscious and aware of God, yet they were all the while ignorant of God. He exposes their ignorance and points out the underlying skepticism and irrationalism. An idol erected to an unknown god, revealed that they were aware of the inadequacy of their own polytheistic religion. There were gods who were being deprived of their rightful worship because they were unknown. Hence, they worshiped a god, not previously worshiped, one whom they had neglected and offended, and whose disfavor had to be appeased, and who, for all that, yet remained unknown.[34]

---

[34] Ned. B. Stonehouse, "The Areopagus Address" in *The Risen Christ Conquers Mars Hill* (Birmingham, AL: Solid Ground Christian Books, 2013), p. 306.

How can you worship something you don't know, which you even admit is unknown? It's irrational. Paul uses the Athenian's own words, "to the Unknown God" ('Αγνώστῳ θεῷ), an inscription on one of their own altars.[35] You are ignorant in your worship. You are incoherent in your concept of God; your knowledge of God is insufficient. This was quite bold to say to the Athenians, who prided themselves in coherent philosophical argumentation.

We note that Paul did not capitulate to some neutral ground between natural theology and Greek philosophy. Paul is very aware that their worldviews clash and are diametrically opposed. There is no neutral ground to Paul. Rather, he indicts the Athenians for the ignorance of their worship, an ignorance that they themselves admitted to. Their religious worldview and concept of deity was inadequate and defective. The apostle asserts, "You ignorantly worship."

This provided the starting point for Paul to present the true God in contrast to their polytheistic and pantheistic conceptions of God. Paul now introduces the antithesis between their ignorance and his God-given authority to declare the true God.

ASSERTING ULTIMATE AUTHORITY (V. 23)

In the synagogue, Paul used Scripture as the ultimate authority. With the philosophers, he asserted his authority as one having received the revelation of the true God. Paul in essence says, "I have knowledge of the true God, and I will declare him unto you." It is important to understand that Paul does not equate the unknown god with the true God. He refers to "what" (ὅ) they worshiped not "whom" they worshiped. The relative pronoun ὅ translated "whom"

---

[35] Ancient writers attest to altars erected to unknown gods in several Greek cities. One example of altars erected to unknown gods occurred in 550 B.C. when there was an outbreak of a plague. Epimenides counseled the Athenians to set white and black sheep loose on the Areopagus, and then construct altars wherever the sheep came to rest.

in the KJV is neuter in gender and is a general reference to deity; it is better translated "what." At any rate, Paul has created an opportunity from their ignorance of God to introduce the true God as Creator and Judge of the universe. Only Christianity possesses the true knowledge of God. Paul's purpose is to declare that God; the God who created heaven and earth is indeed knowable.

Paul speaks with divine authority, as one who knows the true God. When he says, "him [the true God] I declare unto you," he uses the emphatic pronoun "I" (ἐγὼ) to assert his divine authority. Paul is an apostle, commissioned and sent by God to authoritatively proclaim the truth of God. He is God's messenger. He speaks with such authority, that if they rejected his message, they rejected God himself. Paul asserts, "him [the true God] I declare to you." The verb "declare" (καταγγέλλω) denotes declaring with authority. The philosophers claimed there is an unknown God; the "seed-picker" announced he had knowledge of the true God, and declared that knowledge to them.

Paul employed his critique of their worldview as an opportunity to present the true God of Scripture. God is knowable, he is clearly revealed in nature, and everyone knows this because they are created in his image and have a sense of deity inescapably imbedded within them. Paul says, "I know the true God, and I declare him unto you with authority given to me by God himself." His opportunity to declare of the true God was precipitated by calling attention to the sense of deity the Athenians possessed as image bearers of God, and then critiquing their religious worldview as a perversion of this inescapable sense of deity. The God they were suppressing, the God that they wanted to escape from, the God they wanted extinguished from their minds – Paul proclaimed with authority, "Him I declare I unto you."

PUSHING THE ANTITHESIS OF DIFFERENT WORLDVIEWS
(vv. 24-26)

Acts 17:24-26 [24] God that made the world and all things therein, seeing that he is Lord of heaven and earth, dwelleth not in temples made with hands; [25]Neither is worshipped with men's hands, as though he needed any thing, seeing he giveth to all life, and breath, and all things; [26] And hath made of one blood all nations of men for to dwell on all the face of the earth, and hath determined the times before appointed, and the bounds of their habitation.

Having critiqued the Athenians' ignorance in worshiping God, Paul now declares in vv. 24-26 the true and living God. In doing so, he pushes the antithesis between two different worldviews. It is a clash between two different systems of thought, a collision between two different sets of presuppositions. The two are irreconcilable.

There is no neutrality between the two belief systems. The Athenians had their religious presuppositions, and they were antithetical to Paul's. The unbeliever suppresses the truth and exalts his reasoning against the knowledge of God. He is an enemy of God in his mind and his system of thought is according to the tradition of this world. The gods, idols, temples and philosophies that the Athenians had concocted were in rebellion against the truth of God seen in natural revelation. It was a suppression of the knowledge of God they already possessed. They were holding down the truth in unrighteousness (Rom. 1:18) and Paul brings this to the forefront by placing their pantheistic concepts of God in conflict with the Christian's worldview. In vv. 24, Paul begins to push the antithesis.

Acts 17:24 God that made the world and all things therein, seeing that he is Lord of heaven and earth, dwelleth not in temples made with hands;

The apostle presents God as the Creator, the Sovereign Lord and Ruler of heaven and earth. God as Creator is stated emphatically in the original language.[36] Thus, Paul immediately brings his audience into a Creator-creature relationship, which was completely contrary

---

[36] Restrictive attributive construction (ὁ θεὸς ὁ ποιήσας τὸν κόσμον).

to the Athenian conceptions of deity. They looked at God as immanent or inherent in nature, not transcendent to nature.

By declaring God the Creator, Paul makes them subject to "the Lord of heaven and earth." This was a declaration of the absolute sovereignty of God, which was diametrically opposed to the Athenians' worldview and concepts of God. Moreover, by declaring God to be Creator and Lord, Paul was affirming that God is a personal Being, not impersonal, as they believed. When Paul said, "He [God] dwelleth not in temples made with hands," he was also affirming that the true God cannot be confined or limited in any way. God is transcendent of his creation. God rules from on high; He is the all-mighty God.

It is God's transcendence as Creator that defines his relationship to his created universe. Yet, He is immanent in his creation, because of his divine attributes of omnipresence and immensity. Therefore, he is everywhere present in his creation in the fullness of his attributes. A God that was both transcendent and immanent was unimaginable to the Athenians.

Acts 17:25 Neither is worshipped with men's hands, as though he needed any thing, seeing he giveth to all life, and breath, and all things.

In v. 25, Paul declares, God is wholly independent of his creation. God created all things and needs absolutely nothing from his creatures. He is totally independent of the universe. He is absolute, and all of creation is wholly dependent upon him for its existence. The exact opposite is necessarily true for man; who is wholly dependent upon God for everything. We are his creatures. Paul says, "He himself gives life and breath and all things." "He himself" (αὐτὸς) is emphatic in the Grk text. This emphasizes the personal nature of God, again a concept utterly foreign to the Athenians. "Breath" is singled out as the very condition and means of life, breath that is given and governed by God. "All things" refer to God's bounty; God's bounty to all is overflowing. This defines our relationship to God. As his creatures, we are wholly dependent upon and subject to our Creator for our very existence and sustenance. God is the one universal and sovereign Benefactor to man. This is the God Paul declares unto the Athenians, the true and living God – the God who preserves our very being and existence.

> **Acts 17:26** And hath made of one blood all nations of men for to dwell on all the face of the earth, and hath determined the times before appointed, and the bounds of their habitation.

Further, as Creator, God is the Lord of heaven and earth, and according to his governance as sovereign Ruler of the universe, he has predestined all things. He has decreed and foreordained the rise and fall of all nations. Nothing happens by chance as the Epicureans believed. God "hath determined the times before appointed, and the bounds of their habitation." The Creator has determined the limits of a nation's territory and how far its dominion should extend. The Athenians did not control their own destiny; God commanded their destiny.

> **Psalm 75:7** But God *is* the judge: he putteth down one, and setteth up another.

> **Daniel 4:35** And all the inhabitants of the earth *are* reputed as nothing: and he doeth according to his will in the army of heaven, and *among* the inhabitants of the earth: and none can stay his hand, or say unto him, What doest thou?

In v. 26, Paul reminds his listeners who they are before this sovereign God. They were from "one blood."[37] The polytheism of Athens was bound up with the notion of distinct and different nations.[38] The Athenians thought themselves superior to others. They looked down upon the barbarians, for anyone not born in Greece was

---

[37] "Blood" (αἵματός) is omitted in some texts. Perhaps better translated "one man," i.e., Adam.

[38] J. Eadie, "Paul at Athens" in *The Risen Christ Conquers Mars Hill* (Birmingham, AL: Solid Ground Christian Books, 2013), p. 204. It was imagined that the various gods had separate and independent territories, beyond which their jurisdiction did not go, and which they were often obliged to defend against invasion.

a barbarian. Paul declared a common Creator who made all men equal – *of one blood*. He spoke of the created unity of the human race. God made all men from one common ancestor (Adam) and he is the Lord of history.

Thus, by declaring the true God, a clash of belief systems was brought to the forefront. Let's explore the clash of worldviews a little further. In v. 18, we see the two philosophical schools that brought charges against Paul as "setting forth strange gods." They were the Epicureans and the Stoics. The Epicureans and Stoics were two of the four major schools of philosophy in Athens. The other two were the Academy (founded ca. 287 B.C.) of Plato and the Lyceum (335 B.C.) of Aristotle.

Epicureanism was an atomistic/materialistic philosophy named after the philosopher Epicurus (341-270 B.C.). They believed that the universe consisted of eternal atoms of matter, which were ever changing by chance in various combinations and configurations. They believed the universe was the product of an evolutionary process (Yes, the predecessor of naturalistic evolution was Epicureanism). They maintained that all knowledge was obtained from sensual perception, and believed that all events could be given a naturalistic explanation. Since they denied immortality and the afterlife, pleasure became the goal of human life. Their view of deity identified nature with God, as does modern day science and naturalism. It was pantheistic.

A student of Socrates named Zeno founded the philosophy of Stoicism about 300 B.C. The Stoics viewed man as integrated with nature. They deified reason, and believed reason governed matter. They believed in a rational principle called the *Logos* that permeated all things, and determined all that happened. Reason was the immanent principle in nature that determined history (cyclic) and governed fate. Anything outside of reason such as pleasure, pain and even death was viewed as indifferent. The philosophy gave rise to a serious attitude, resignation to suffering and individualism. Both poets Paul quoted in v. 28 were Stoic philosophers.

Epicureanism and Stoicism were inherently pantheistic philosophies. They had their own theories about the universe and used those theories to suppress what they already knew about God. Just like today, evolutionists use their theory to suppress the knowledge of God. When Paul asserted God as Creator, who made the world and all things therein, it was in direct contradiction to their pantheistic worldviews. To them, God was identical to nature, bound in nature, and could never be outside of nature. In no way did they view God as Creator, transcendent and independent of his creation, determining all things, and governing all things. Nor did they view the universe (and man) existing in total dependence upon him. This created a clash of worldviews. It put everything in its proper context.

REVEALING SPIRITUAL BLINDNESS AND THE NOETIC EFFECTS OF SIN (V. 27)

Acts 17:27 That they should seek the Lord, if haply they might feel after him, and find him, though he be not far from every one of us.

Paul says in v. 27, "If perhaps they might feel after him and find him." "To feel after" (ψηλαφήσειαν) denotes the motions of a blind man groping along in the dark, trying to find something. The Athenians were under the noetic effects of sin, and their search for the knowledge of God and reality was like a blind man groping in the dark. In their alleged search for God, they were suppressing and denying the natural knowledge of God they already possessed as image bearers of God. There is a general knowledge of God that all men possess, which the heavens declare and clearly reveal to all mankind (Ps. 19:1-6; Rom. 1:18-21). "If haply they might feel after him, and find him" is a fourth class condition sentence denoting possibility. They were groping around in darkness, deliberately misinterpreting natural revelation, if *possibly* they should find God.

This is a description of self-deception. The noetic effects of sin had blinded them.

Paul states, "though he be not far from every one of us." Again, Paul makes an appeal to the image of God in man. The knowledge of God was within their reach, and they didn't have to look too far. The Grk verb translated "to be" is ὑπάρχω and means "to be there" or "to be at hand," i.e., God existing in his fullness. Their groping was not due to any deficiency in God or his revelation.[39] It was their hatred of the true God that blinded them. They did not want to be accountable to a holy, just and righteous God. The apostle John writes, "And this is the condemnation, that light is come into the world, and men loved darkness rather than light, because their deeds were evil. For every one that doeth evil hateth the light, neither cometh to the light, lest his deeds should be reproved" (John 3:19-20). The Athenian philosophers were culpable for their ignorance; they deliberately suppressed the knowledge of God, even though it cried out to them from heaven, and was clearly seen in creation (Ps. 19:1-6; Rom. 1:19-20). They became vain in their imaginations, and their foolish heart was darkened (Rom. 1:21).

The Athenian reaction to the clear revelation of God (natural revelation) was to concoct numerous gods, idols and vain philosophies, suppressing the truth in unrighteousness. (Rom. 1:18). They worshipped creation rather than the Creator (Rom. 1:25). They exchanged the truth of God for a lie. However, Paul appeals to the image of God in man and says, "God is not far from every one of us," and you know it. In the phrase "he is not far from us," Paul uses the negative particle οὐ rather than μη, making the statement emphatic. God is NOT far from each and every one of us. Referring back to the inscription to the unknown god, the apostle proclaims that God is not someone who is beyond reach or unknowable. The Creator-creature distinction cannot be hid and it is quite disingenuous to deny it.

---

[39] G. Bahnsen, *Always Ready*, p. 259.

Therefore, following Paul's example, the enterprise of apologetics must take into account the noetic effects of sin and the unbeliever's deliberate suppression of the truth. Although men do not acknowledge it, they are aware of their relation and accountability to the living and true God who created them.[40]

ILLUSTRATING THE POINT-OF-CONTACT (V. 28)

Acts 17:28 [28] For in him we live, and move, and have our being; as certain also of your own poets have said, For we are also his offspring.

In v. 28, Paul offers an illustration to clarify what he meant by God being not far from each one of us, though we grope around in the darkness. He quotes verbatim from two Greek philosopher-poets. "For in him we live and move and have our being," is a quotation from Epimenides' *Cretica*,[41] who was a philosopher-poet from the island of Crete in about 600 B.C.[42] The second quotation at the end of v. 28, "for we are also his offspring," was taken from a Cilician Stoic-philosopher-poet named Aratus, who lived about 315-240 B.C.[43] The two quotations are parallel and portray well-known philosophical concepts. In Aratus' poem, "we are his offspring" refers to a personification of Zeus and a pantheistic view of humanity

---

[40] Ibid.

[41] *They fashioned a tomb for you, holy and high one,*
Cretans, always liars, evil beasts, idle bellies.
But you are not dead: you lives and abides forever,
For in you we live and move and have our being.

[42] This is also the same philosopher Paul quotes when he writes to Titus, "*The Cretians are always liars, evil beasts, slow bellies.*"

[43] Paul quotes the fifth line of Aratus' *Phaenomena (below)*. Aratus may have been quoting from Cleanthes and perhaps explains the reference to "your poets."
Let us begin with Zeus, whom we mortals never leave unspoken.
For every street, every market-place is full of Zeus.
Even the sea and the harbour are full of this deity.
Everywhere everyone is indebted to Zeus.
For we are indeed his offspring ...

sharing the divine nature. In fact both quotations have reference to their chief god, Zeus, and sharing his divine nature.

Although these two quotations, "in him we live and move and have our being" and "we are his offspring" were made in reference to Zeus (the chief of the gods), it does not in any way mean that Paul agrees with their pagan context, but rather is using it to illustrate their innate sense of deity. The reality of an innate sense of deity is so plain that even their own poets recognized it. "We are his offspring" has reference to man being made in the image of God and possessing his paternal likeness. [44] As image bearers of God, man possesses an innate sense of deity. However, the Athenians deliberately perverted it into idolatry, which was ignorance they were fully culpable for.

When Epimenides and Aratus wrote these words, their propositions were utterly false. The "him" to whom they both referred to was not the triune God, but rather the false god of Zeus, which was an idol. Beyond any doubt, Paul is in no way trying to harmonize pagan philosophy with Christianity.

When Paul quoted the two pantheistic philosophers, there was no question what he meant when he said, "*In him* (ἐν αὐτῷ) we live and move and have our being" and "we are *his* offspring (τοῦ γένος)." He was referring to the true God, not Zeus the pagan god. The apostle was referring to the transcendent Creator-God he had just declared in vv. 24-27: the triune God "that made the world and everything in it," the God who is "Lord of heaven and earth," "who does not live in temples made with hands," who is not served by human "hands, as though he needed anything," who "gives to all life and breath and everything," who "made from one man every nation of mankind to live on all the face of the earth" and who "determined their appointed seasons, and the bounds of their habitation." There is no question to whom Paul is referring!

---

[44] "Offspring" is not to be construed in a redemptive context as "the redeemed children of God."

48

Immediately after declaring the true God, Paul quotes the philosophers to strengthen his point-of-contact, the *sensus divinitatus*. Paul had just clearly articulated an antithesis of belief systems. There was no neutrality in their worldviews. He was not committing the logical fallacy of equivocation by using pantheistically conceived premises to support a Christian theistic conclusion. He used pagan expressions to demonstrate that pagan thought had not eradicated the idea of God, albeit suppressed and perverted as it was.

Although the quoted philosophical statements reflected a religious nature and sense of deity, it was utterly perverted. Paul is correcting their false conceptions of God and "re-contextualizing" a familiar concept that was well known among the philosophers.[45] This re-contextualization was the necessary result of the clash of religious worldviews he set forth in vv. 24-27. By doing this, Paul was persuading them that they were accountable to God for their ignorance. Their deliberate refusal to acknowledge the true Creator-God was not an innocent matter. Paul quotes the philosophers to manifest their guilt. Because man was made in the image of God, he possesses a sense of deity indelibly inscribed upon the heart. Rather than suppress and wickedly pervert their natural knowledge of God, they should have glorified the true God (Rom. 1:21). They are guilty and without excuse before God (Rom. 1:20). Man cannot escape responsibility for his knowledge of God.

APPLYING THE POINT-OF-CONTACT (V. 29)

Acts 17:29 Forasmuch then as we are the offspring of God, we ought not to think that the Godhead is like unto gold, or silver, or stone, graven by art and man's device.

Verse 29 is a counter argument to the Athenian idolatry. The use of the particle οὖν (forasmuch) indicates Paul is drawing a conclusion from the poets he quoted in v. 28. "Forasmuch as we are the offspring

---

[45] K. S. Oliphint, *Reasons for Faith*, pp. 29-31.

of God." This refers to the image of God in man, the point-of-contact on which Paul has built his entire address. By applying writings from their own poets and placing them in their proper theological context, Paul now reveals an inconsistency in their idolatrous practices. If we resemble God and are his offspring, why do you think God resembles an inanimate object you can make with your hands? How can man depict the infinitude of God, his omnipotence, his omniscience, his goodness or truth with a man-made image? If you think God is something you can make, then doesn't that make God *your* offspring? Isn't it an obvious contradiction to say that God is like something you have made, while believing we are something he has made? "We ought not to think that the Godhead is like unto gold, or silver, or stone, graven by art and man's device."

Man alone is the image bearer of God. Man's reason, soul, conscience, genius, and immortality cannot be represented by an image. All of man's art and handiwork cannot reproduce the likeness of a living soul. If man cannot image himself, then how can he image the infinite God who created him – the Original? Man, as the image bearer and offspring of God, is a living argument against idolatry and polytheism.

CULPABLE IGNORANCE (VV. 30-31)

Acts 17:30-31 [30] And the times of this ignorance God winked at; but now commandeth all men every where to repent: [31] Because he hath appointed a day, in the which he will judge the world in righteousness by *that* man whom he hath ordained; *whereof* he hath given assurance unto all *men*, in that he hath raised him from the dead.

Verses 30-31 constitute the culmination of Paul's address to the Areopagus council on Mars Hill. Paul asserted that the Athenians were in a state of culpable ignorance. They were responsible to God for their willful and deliberate ignorance. They had sufficient knowledge of God to have kept them from atheism, polytheism and idolatry. Before the gospel dispensation, God had "overlooked" (ὑπεριδὼν) their ignorance. But "now" (νῦν) the time of God's forbearance has expired. Therefore, the apostle concludes his address with a call to repentance (v. 30) and to believe in the resurrected Jesus Christ (v. 31).[46]

Paul stated that all men must repent of their willful ignorance, "...but now commandeth all men every where to repent." "Commandeth" is a present imperative verb (παραγγέλλει) denoting a continual and perpetual command. The verb to repent (μετανοέω) in the Grk literally means "to change one's mind." It means to turn away from their sin (idolatry) and turn unto the true God.[47] The Athenians were accountable for their ignorance. A day of judgment was coming. Paul made it clear to the Areopagus that the same Jesus, who was discoursed in the market place, whom they mocked and called Paul into question about, shall be their judge. Jesus rose from the dead to judge the world in righteousness. The criteria for judgment will be "righteousness," according to the absolute moral character of God.[48] All must repent; no person is exempt.

After being charged with setting forth strange Gods, the apostle Paul answered the inquiry of the Areopagus council by asserting Jesus and the resurrection. He did not seek to prove the resurrection through evidence; rather he declared it by the authority given to him by God. The philosophers, locked in their pantheistic and polytheistic worldviews, first understood "the resurrection" as simply another god, the female god of restoration (τὴν ἀνάστασιν). This evaded any ethical or moral responsibility. But Paul places the resurrection in its proper context – the judgment to come. By doing so, he declares all men are held accountable before God.

---

[46] C. B. McManis, *Biblical Apologetics*. Bloomington, IN: Xlibris Corporation, 2012, p. 153.

[47] Repentance and faith are inseparable. They are two sides of one coin. A saving response to the gospel consists of both turning away from one's sin (repentance) and turning to God in faith. Both are necessary for salvation.

[48] All men have a natural knowledge of the moral character of God. It is written upon their hearts (Rom. 1:32; 2:14-15).

It was necessary that Paul first establish the doctrines of creation and final judgment in order to introduce Jesus and the resurrection. The facts of Jesus and the resurrection are what they are only in the framework of the doctrines of creation, providence, and the consummation of history in the final judgment.[49] The resurrection of Jesus Christ from the dead guarantees the final judgment of all men. It was Jesus the Son of God who had made the world and who will come to judge all men at the end of the world. Natural revelation revealed their guilt (Rom. 1:20) and the certain judgment of God (Rom 1:32). The special revelation asserted by the apostle Paul revealed that the Judge would be the resurrected Jesus.

> **John 5:22** [22] For the Father judgeth no man, but hath committed all judgment unto the Son:
>
> **John 5:26-27** [26] For as the Father hath life in himself; so hath he given to the Son to have life in himself; [27] And hath given him authority to execute judgment also, because he is the Son of man.

No one can be confronted with the fact of Christ and his resurrection and fail to have his own conscience tell him that he is face-to-face with his Judge.[50] *He [God] will judge the world in righteousness by that man [the resurrected Jesus] whom he hath ordained* (v. 31).

The philosophers on Mars Hill had no regard for or knowledge of the Old Testament scriptures. They were pagans. Paul understood this. The message of grace, the message of salvation through the risen Jesus, would have no meaning at all if Paul had not declared God to be the Creator and the Judge of sin. Paul did not present the resurrection of Christ as an isolated fact, but as part of a theistic worldview comprised of a coherent body of doctrine.

---

[49] C. Van Til, *Paul at Athens*, p. 5.

[50] Ibid, p. 3.

SUMMARY

The apostle Paul presented a biblical theistic worldview to the Areopagus counsel on Mars Hill. He defended the faith by critiquing the fallacy of the Athenians' worldview and exposing their ignorance. He then advanced a biblical worldview regarding creation, providence and final judgment. He concluded by declaring the resurrected Christ as Judge. The apostle held them accountable for their ignorance and idolatrous worship, and called them to repentance. At every point, he set his biblical position antithetical to their philosophical beliefs. The result was the salvation of some including one counsel member of the Areopagus.

Paul's entire address was built upon the absolute authority of God's revelation. Although he never quoted scripture, it was filled with references to the O.T.[51] His declaration of the true God was a summary of biblical theology – a succinct statement of biblical truth. Every statement was thoroughly scriptural and based upon his previous ministry in the agora.[52] Engaging the philosophers in the marketplace laid the biblical groundwork for his address on Mars Hill. Paul preached and discoursed Jesus and the resurrection daily in the marketplace (vv. 17-18). Furthermore, being Christ's called apostle, he spoke with divine authority. Indeed, the words of Paul that Luke recorded were the inspired word of God. It would be far from the truth to accuse Paul of neglecting the word of God in his address.

Paul's address on Mars Hill was thoroughly presuppositional. It consisted of all the basic tenets of presuppositional apologetics: the absolute authority of God's revelation, employing the *sensus divinitatus* as the point-of-contact, asserting the Creator-creature relationship,

---

[51] Bahnsen in *Always Ready* notes that *Nestle's Greek New Testament* lists 22 O.T. allusions in the margin.

[52] W. R. Downing, *Paul at Athens: The Great Scriptural Example of Presenting Christianity as a World-and-Life View*, p. 3.

pushing the antithesis of different worldviews and revealing the noetic effects of sin due to man's sinful depravity.

It has been argued that Paul "failed egregiously" in his address to the Areopagus.[53] There was no mention of the Lord Jesus Christ, no mention of the redemptive purpose, and no mention of grace or saving faith. This charge has no foundation and one questions the motive of such opinions. First of all, Paul was daily in the marketplace preaching the gospel and discoursing the person and work of the Lord Jesus Christ. This went on for weeks. Those that encountered Paul heard the name of Jesus (v. 18). It was one of the reasons Paul was brought before the Areopagus. Secondly, you cannot speak of the resurrection apart from a redemptive context. The redemptive meaning of Christ's death, burial and resurrection was unquestionably articulated in the marketplace. Although only repentance is commanded in Paul's address, faith cannot be separated from true repentance. In fact, repentance is sometimes used synonymously in scripture with saving faith. Paul's entire address challenged the Areopagus to believe the absolute revelation of God he asserted with divine authority as an apostle of the Lord Jesus Christ. Further, the divine attribute of God's grace is clearly described in v. 25, "He himself giveth to all life and breath and all things." In the context of a sovereign Creator (vv. 24-26), "all things" received are gifts of God for which man is wholly dependent upon. But most importantly, numerous people were saved! We read in v. 34, "certain men clave unto him, and believed [in Jesus]: among which was Dionysius the Areopagite, a woman named Damaris, and others with them." It was no small thing for a member of the Areopagus to believe in Jesus! No sermon that saves sinners can be a failure. It is reasonable to assume

---

[53] J. Eadie, *The Risen Christ Conquers Mars Hill*, p. 235.

that these individuals were baptized and became the founding members of a local church in Athens.[54]

---

[54] The ancient historian Eusebius records that Dionysius the Areopagite was the first bishop of the church at Athens according to the records of the pastor of the church in Corinth (*Ecclesiastical History*, 3.4.11).

5. APOLOGETICS FROM ROMANS 1:18-21

Romans 1:18-21 [18] For the wrath of God is revealed from heaven against all ungodliness and unrighteousness of men, who hold the truth in unrighteousness; [19] Because that which may be known of God is manifest in them; for God hath shewed *it* unto them. [20] For the invisible things of him from the creation of the world are clearly seen, being understood by the things that are made, *even* his eternal power and Godhead; so that they are without excuse: [21] Because that, when they knew God, they glorified *him* not as God, neither were thankful; but became vain in their imaginations, and their foolish heart was darkened.

INTRODUCTION

The epistle to the Romans was written by Paul in the Spring of A.D. 58 while at Corinth on his third missionary journey. Paul had not yet visited Rome. It was written 6-7 years after his address on Mars Hill in Athens (Acts 17:22-31). In regards to apologetics, Rom. 1:18-32 is very similar in content to Paul's address to the Areopagus. No doubt, the apostle had this address in mind when he wrote Romans chapter one.

Rom. 1:18-32 is a classic passage dealing with the natural revelation of God. What is natural revelation? It is God's revelation of himself in nature. God reveals to us who he is through his creation. All of created reality is revelational of God's nature; it is the universal revelation to all men. However, we must note that it is a general revelation of God which does not disclose the special revelation of the gospel.[55] Although natural revelation is not salvific, it exposes the need

---

[55] God has revealed himself to man in two forms of revelation: general (natural) and special (supernatural). God communicates special revelation to man in a supernatural manner, either directly to man, through a prophet or a messenger. Scripture is the special revelation of God. The two forms of revelation do not stand

of special revelation, because it is a sufficient revelation of God to condemn man, and render him without excuse before God.

Romans 1:18-32 is a pivotal passage for understanding the doctrine of natural revelation because it explains the unbeliever's certain knowledge of God acquired and apprehended through the witness of creation. It is arguably the most important passage of Scripture for establishing a biblical approach to apologetics. The purpose of this chapter is to exegete and expound the text, and to draw out some basic apologetic principles.

NATURAL REVELATION

1. God's Wrath Revealed

Romans 1:18 [18] For the wrath of God is revealed from heaven against all ungodliness and unrighteousness of men, who hold the truth in unrighteousness;

Roman 1:18 begins with "for the wrath of God is revealed from heaven." It is a revelation of God's wrath, not of his grace. In the Grk, the verb "revealed" (ἀποκαλύπτεται) is placed first in word order for emphasis. It means to cause something to be fully known.[56] Paul emphatically asserts that God's wrath is disclosed to all men.

What is God's wrath? It is the expression of his holiness toward sin. It expresses his moral character, his anger and judgment against sin. In our text, God's wrath is directed "against all ungodliness and unrighteousness of men."

---

next to each other as two separate means of revelation. For God that reveals himself in Scripture is the same God that reveals himself in nature. The two forms of revelation are complementary. They presuppose and supplement each other. However, there is no knowledge of grace in natural revelation. Only Scripture reveals the grace of God through the knowledge of his Son in the gospel. Natural revelation was never meant to function by itself. The light of Scripture is the superior light that lightens every other light. Scripture is the final authority for interpreting the light of nature.

[56] BDAG.

One may ask, "How can God's ethical character be revealed through a purely physical and material world? How can man observe the physical universe, and acquire such certain knowledge as to the moral character of God?" Yet, it is emphatically stated that God's wrath and judgment against all ungodliness and unrighteousness of men is revealed to all men. Further, "revealed" is a present tense verb in the original language ('αποκαλύπτεται), indicating that "God's wrath" is continually being revealed to all men. It is a universal revelation. Also significant is the passive voice used for the verb "revealed," which denotes that God himself does the revealing; man is the recipient. This knowledge is not because of any effort man has made to know God or see him. God is the one acting here.

In the latter part of v. 18, Paul describes man's reaction to the revelation of God's wrath. He says, "Who hold the truth in unrighteousness." The Grk verb translated "hold" (κατεχόντων) literally means "to hold down" (from κατα – down, and εχω – to hold). It denotes a deliberate act of suppressing the truth of God. This is done, not neutrally or innocently, but wickedly and deliberately. The unbeliever, in his unrighteousness, suppresses the truth. The present tense of this verb denotes continual action. The unregenerate are continually suppressing the truth about the existence of God, his nature and moral character. They are suppressing "the truth" (τὴν ἀλήθειαν) that has been clearly revealed to them in creation. Truth is out in the open, but men, so to speak, put it in a box and sit on the lid, and "hold it down in unrighteousness."[57]

In light of this reality, when we are engaged in apologetics, are we to assume that man doesn't know God's moral character, his hatred and judgment of sin? Is man somehow innocently ignorant of it? No, on the contrary, we are to assume that man does know God, but is habitually suppressing it. Therefore, we can expect him to deny it. We can expect him to lie about it because it is a terrible reality for the

---

[57] A.T. Roberson, *Word Pictures*, Rom. 1:18.

unregenerate to face, i.e., being made accountable for his sin. He must suppress it at all cost. He would rather live his life in an intellectually drunken stupor of self-deceit. Yet, despite all the denials, God continues to clearly reveal his righteous moral character to man. It is inescapable.

2. The Internal Revelation of God Introduced (v. 19)

Romans 1:19 [19] Because that which may be known of God is manifest in them (ἐν αὐτοῖς); for God hath shewed *it* unto them.

There are two aspects of natural revelation. They are distinguished by the terms *external* and *internal*. The *external* aspect of natural revelation is the acquisition of a general knowledge of God through the external works of creation. The *internal* aspect of natural revelation is the apprehension of this general knowledge of God by the very constitution of man's nature, due to the fact that man was created in the image of God, an image that has been defaced but not eradicated. Because of this two-fold natural revelation, every man possesses an inescapable knowledge of God, and as we shall see, it is this knowledge of God that renders every man guilty and without excuse.

Rom. 1:19 deals with the internal aspect of natural revelation. In v. 18, we noted the passive voice of "revealed," which means God himself is doing the revealing. Here, we find that God not only reveals himself *to* man but *in* man. Paul says, the knowledge of God is manifest "in them" (ἐν αὐτοῖς), i.e., in their hearts and minds, within the very constitution of their nature.[58] In the Grk, the phrase "of

---

[58] C. Hodge, *Romans* (Grand Rapids, MI: Wm. B. Eerdmans Publishing, 1950); L. Morris, *The Epistle to the Romans* (Grand Rapids, MI: Wm. B. Eerdmans Publishing, 1988); W. Sanday, and A. Headlam, *Romans* (Edinburgh: T&T Clark, 1992); M. Vincent, *Word Studies in the NT* (Peabody, MA: Hendrickson Publishers); A. T. Robertson, *Word Pictures* (Grand Rapids, MI: Baker Book House, 1931); P. E. Hughes, "Critical Biblical Passages for Christian Apologetics" in *Jerusalem and Athens* (Phillipsburg, NJ: P&R Publishing, 1980), p. 134; R. C. Lenski, *Romans* (Peabody, MA: Hendrickson Publishers, 1998).

God" is an objective genitive, meaning God is the object of our knowledge. It is not a nebulous and hazy knowledge, it is clear and manifest *in* all men. Man cannot charge God with hiding himself from them.[59]

Man possesses a general knowledge of God by virtue of being created in the image of God; this knowledge is innate and intuitive within man. A sense of deity (*sensus divinitatus*) has been implanted within the human mind of all men. It is stamped on man's innermost being. Therefore, because man was made a morally rational creature as God's image bearer, he *morally* apprehends the manifestations of God in his works of creation and providence. He understands the moral character and judgment of God against sin. This is not an acquired knowledge of God; it is something that he is born with. It is part of his very being. It is impossible for man to separate himself from the reality of his own constitution. We will come back to this inward revelation of God later on.

3. The Creator-creature Distinction

Romans 1:20 [20] For the invisible things of him from the creation of the world are clearly seen, being understood by the things that are made, *even* his eternal power and Godhead; so that they are without excuse.

I want to draw your attention to the phrase "from the creation of the world" in v. 20 where Paul takes us back to creation. God's general revelation is embedded in creation itself. When the apostle Paul states, "For the invisible things of him from the creation of the world are clearly seen, being understood by the things that are made," he is asserting the absolute reality of the Creator. "From the creation of the world" presupposes the eternality of God, existing prior to creation. It presupposes the self-existence of God and the absolute independence of God. Hence, all other being and existence is wholly

---

[59] R. C. Lenski, *Romans*.

dependent upon God the Creator. Paul asserted this very thing, when he engaged the Areopagus council in Acts 17.

> **Acts 17:24-25** [24] God that made the world and all things therein, seeing that he is Lord of heaven and earth, dwelleth not in temples made with hands; [25] Neither is worshipped with men's hands, as though he needed any thing, seeing he giveth to all life, and breath, and all things;

In Rom. 1:20, the apostle establishes a crucial relationship between God and man, a relationship that distinguishes between the Creator and the creature. God owns everything in creation; all things were created to serve him and his purposes (especially man). This is the ultimate reality of man's existence. If the world is to be known, we must consult its Creator. [60] The Creator-creature distinction is absolutely essential for a truly Christian worldview.[61] Any worldview that excludes the Creator-creature relationship necessarily becomes incoherent and departs from reality. Only through this critical distinction can the three basic worldview elements of *metaphysics*, *epistemology* and *ethics* be unified.[62]

Interestingly, the noun "world" (κόσμος) relates to the whole of God's creative order. It denotes an orderly arrangement, a harmonious arrangement. In the context, it speaks of the entire creative order of the universe.

Why do scientists become so intolerant when they hear the term intelligent design? Because it necessarily assumes the Creator-creature distinction and the absolute order of creation. This term infuriates the scientific world. Careers are destroyed, tenures taken away, and scientists are blackballed for using this term. Why? They must suppress the truth about God the Creator.

---

[60] G. Bahnsen, *Presuppositional Apologetics*. Powder Springs, GA: American Vision Press, 2008, p. 278.

[61] A *worldview* can be defined as the sum of one's presuppositions, which provide the framework to view and interpret the world and all reality.

[62] For discussion on the three basic worldview elements see Chapter 10, *The Necessity of the Creator-creature Relationship for a Coherent Worldview*.

4. The External Revelation of God

Consider the phrase "the invisible things of him" in v. 20. What are the "invisible things of him" that the apostle Paul says the unbeliever knows about God? Paul tells us they are "his eternal power and Godhead." The term "Godhead" in the Grk (θειότης) is a collective term for all the divine perfections, i.e., the attributes of God. The apostle makes special note of God's "eternal power" (τε ἀΐδιος αὐτοῦ δύναμις) revealed in his works of creation. Both terms are joined together as an expressive unit in the original language.[63] We see that natural revelation does not just reveal the existence of God, but his divinity as well, i.e., his nature and moral character. Man apprehends this knowledge "by the things that are made." For all of creation is a revelation of God, an imprint of the divine mind and will.

Paul says that "the invisible things of him" are "clearly seen." This is a paradox that needs some explanation. The Grk verb "clearly seen" (καθορᾶται) has reference to looking down from above and means to see thoroughly. It denotes full comprehension. Our English expression "bird's eye view" accurately portrays the meaning. Man clearly sees the invisible things of God: his existence, his divine perfections, his attributes and his eternal power. All men possess this knowledge.

Furthermore, the phrase "being understood by the things that are made" explains how the invisible things of God are clearly seen. The Grk participle "being understood" (νοούμενα)[64] is very interesting and gives the sense of being intellectually apprehended (different than the process of reasoning). Here, if we were empiricists (or evidentialists), we might expect the use of the verb γινώσκω, which means to know by experience; a knowledge acquired by the senses. The Grk word

---

[63] Granville-Sharp rule.

[64] BDAG, to grasp or comprehend something on the basis of careful thought, *perceive, apprehend, understand, gain an insight into*. Νοούμενα is the present passive participle of νοεω. Νοεω briefly defined is the use of νοός (the mind).

νοούμενα denotes a perceived understanding. [65] It depicts an immediate and intuitive comprehension, something that is instinctive and innate. Hence, there is an inseparable correlation between the *external* and *internal* aspects of natural revelation.

By using the term νοούμενα, the apostle Paul is reinforcing the *sensus divinitatus* he has just introduced in v. 19, i.e., the knowledge of God manifested "in them" (ἐν αὐτοῖς). Paul removes the paradox between "invisible" and "clearly seen" by the use of this term (νοούμενα).[66] Man clearly sees the unseen. There is an apprehension of the Creator that is innate in the very nature and constitution of man. Denney rightly observes, "There is that within man which so catches the meaning of all that is without as to issue in an instinctive knowledge of God."[67] Moreover, both verb (καθορᾶται, "clearly seen") and participle (νοούμενα, "being understood") are in the present tense denoting that man is in continual possession of this general knowledge of God. The intention of the apostle is not to infer God's being from the world, but to uncover the being of the world from God's revelation.[68]

5. God's Moral Character Revealed

From Rom. 1:19-20 we see that both *external* and *internal* aspects of natural revelation are correlative. There is a mutual relationship of both external and internal aspects functioning together, which assures us that every man possesses a clear understanding of the nature of God.

---

[65] TDNT, 4:950-951.

[66] Ibid, p. 950.

[67] James Denney, "Romans" in *The Expositor's Greek Testament*, Vol. 2, p. 592.

[68] Bornkamm, "Revelation of God's Wrath in Experience," p. 59 taken from James D. G. Dunn, referenced in the World Biblical Commentary on Romans, Vol. 1.

Natural revelation clearly discloses the ethical nature of God, his moral character and consistency. This is very critical to our understanding; through natural revelation God's moral attributes and standards are clearly understood. When the unbeliever looks into the heavens, he understands God is declaring his wrath against sin (Rom. 1:18). Rom. 1:32 teaches that every man knows the righteous judgment of God and his condemnation is "worthy of death," i.e., eternal death. Remarkably, Paul speaks of the unbeliever in v. 32 as "knowing the judgment of God." He uses an intensified form of the participle "knowing" (ἐπιγνόντες), which means to fully know. The unbeliever has a full comprehension of the righteous character and justice of God. He knows the holiness of God, which God's justice expresses. In Rom. 2:14-15, Paul argues how the work of the law of God, being the very expression of God's moral character, is written in the heart of the Gentiles; every unbeliever's conscience bears witness to the moral law of God. Indeed, every human being has a sense of deity by which he understands the judgment of God, knows he is under the wrath of God and is worthy of eternal death.

No person can escape this witness of God; it is indelibly inscribed upon the heart. Every man knows God by virtue of being created in the image of God. God has revealed himself to each and every person with unmistakable clarity. Therefore, natural revelation gives a sufficient knowledge to render every man inexcusable.[69] Because this knowledge is inescapable, Paul asserts that the unbeliever is "without excuse" (ἀναπολογήτους) before God (Rom. 1:20). The unbeliever has no defense and is without an apologetic. He knows that he is guilty and accountable to God. This is the certain knowledge of every person.

---

[69] This does not mean that everything that can be known about God has been revealed to the unbeliever. For example, the gospel of Jesus Christ is only revealed through the special revelation of Scripture.

6. Man's Knowledge of God Asserted

Romans 1:21 [21] Because that, when they knew God, they glorified *him* not as God, neither were thankful; but became vain in their imaginations, and their foolish heart was darkened.

Look at the statement "when they knew God" in v. 21. It explicitly states that natural man knows God. All people have a general knowledge of God – it is inescapable. This reality is the apologist's point-of-contact, but more on that later. Here is a definite statement of man's certain knowledge of God comprehended through natural revelation as described in the previous verses (vv. 18-20). The apostle Paul asserts "they knew God" (γνόντες). All people have enough knowledge of God to render them guilty without excuse. Whether they admit it or not doesn't change anything. All people know God, if they didn't, then they would have an excuse. But Rom. 1:20 says all men are without an excuse (ἀναπολογήτους).

7. The Unbeliever's Reaction to the Knowledge of God

Romans 1:22-26 [22] Professing themselves to be wise, they became fools, [23] And changed the glory of the uncorruptible God into an image made like to corruptible man, and to birds, and fourfooted beasts, and creeping things. [24] Wherefore God also gave them up to uncleanness through the lusts of their own hearts, to dishonour their own bodies between themselves: [25] Who changed the truth of God into a lie, and worshipped and served the creature more than the Creator, who is blessed for ever. Amen.

When we approach an unbeliever in the work of apologetics, we are not trying to prove something he already knows. Do you think man will respond any differently to scientific evidences, since he already "clearly sees" the unmistakable evidence of God every day? The real issue is *why* does man so vehemently deny the knowledge of God he already possess. It is because of man's sinful nature. All men know the truth about the existence of the Creator, but in their unrighteousness they continually seek to suppress it and hold it down (Rom. 1:18).

The natural knowledge of God that every man possesses must be carefully distinguished from the reaction that man expresses toward this revelation. Unregenerate man rebels against the knowledge of God because it brings him face-to-face with his Creator and condemns him. He knows he is guilty before God and hates it. He loves darkness and hates the light, because his deeds are evil (John 3:19-20).

> **John 3:19-20** [19] And this is the condemnation, that light is come into the world, and men loved darkness rather than light, because their deeds were evil. [20] For every one that doeth evil hateth the light, neither cometh to the light, lest his deeds should be reproved (ἐλεγχθῇ, exposed).

Paul says in Rom. 1:21, "Because that, when they knew God, they glorified him not as God, neither were thankful; but became vain in their imaginations, and their foolish heart was darkened." This describes the utter ingratitude of all men in their natural and unregenerate state. Unregenerate man refuses to acknowledge God; he refuses to show any kind of gratitude or thankfulness to God. He will not recognize God as his Creator, neither give glory to him as God. Rather, man rebelliously engages in futile reasoning to do away with God in his thoughts. The apostle says they "became vain in their imaginations." "Vain in their imaginations" denotes futile speculation and worthless reasoning. It is the result of an inherent bias and hostility against God. The unbeliever obstinately exalts his reasoning against the knowledge of God (2 Cor. 10:5). His very intellect is constantly devising schemes by which he thinks he may overthrow God. Scripture everywhere teaches that natural man is hostile to the knowledge of God he possesses.[70]

The remainder of Romans 1 (vv. 22-32) goes on to show how unregenerate man constantly suppresses the knowledge of God. It describes how man reacts to the clear revelation of God in nature.

---

[70] P. H. Hughes, "Critical Biblical Passages for Christian Apologetics" in *Jerusalem and Athens*. Phillipsburg, NJ: P&R Publishing, 1980, p. 134.

(1) In Rom. 1:23, we find fallen man changing the glory of God revealed in creation into idols. Man invents false religion. Paul writes, "And changed the glory of the uncorruptible God into an image made like to corruptible man, and to birds, and fourfooted beasts, and creeping things." Suppressing the truth about the Creator will inevitably result in some form of idolatry. The religious propensity of man's corrupt nature leads him to seek after false gods, and grossly pervert the knowledge of God he possesses by natural revelation. Unregenerate man invents false religion in the form of idolatry because of his inherent religious nature.

(2) Natural man changes the truth of God for the lie (v. 25). The Grk word for "changed" (μεταλλάσσω) actually means to exchange, i.e., to exchange one thing for another. The unbeliever exchanges the natural revelation of God for a lie. The noun "lie" possesses a definite article, and should be translated "the lie." To deny the Creator is to believe "the lie." It is the lie of Satan since he is the father of lies. It was "the lie" that plunged the human race into sin. Also noteworthy to comment on is the preposition used in the phrase "more than the Creator." The preposition παρά means "beside" in the sense of location. Here, it denotes sidestepping the Creator, in order to believe the lie. The result is to worship creation rather than the Creator.

The worship of *creation* (κτίσις, better rendered creation rather than creature) mentioned in v. 25 is a reference to the pantheistic tendencies of man to ascribe the attributes of God to nature. The prime example today is secular science and the philosophy of evolution. Secular science ascribes divine attributes to nature such as the eternality of matter and the immutability of natural law. It is a religious philosophy that changes the truth of God into a lie.[71] It is nothing more than a form of pantheism.

---

[71] Science is legitimate only if it assumes the absolute authority of Scripture for the interpretation of all created facts.

(3) In suppressing the truth, man pursues immorality, "Wherefore God also gave them up to uncleanness through the lusts of their own hearts, to dishonour their own bodies between themselves" (v. 24). Immorality is an expression of rebellion and hatred against the clear revelation of God. When man rejects God, he gives them over to immorality (v. 28). The immorality described in vv. 26-28, is the consequence of suppressing the truth in unrighteousness (v. 18)

> **Romans 1:26-28** [26] For this cause God gave them up unto vile affections: for even their women did change the natural use into that which is against nature: [27] And likewise also the men, leaving the natural use of the woman, burned in their lust one toward another; men with men working that which is unseemly, and receiving in themselves that recompence of their error which was meet. [28] And even as they did not like to retain God in their knowledge, God gave them over to a reprobate mind, to do those things which are not convenient;

(4) The natural revelation of God is obnoxious to the unbeliever. In Rom. 1:28 Paul states, "they did not like to retain God in their knowledge." Again, the Grk term ἐπίγνωσις is used for knowledge, which means full and sufficient knowledge. The Grk term for "retain" (ἔχω) means "to have" or "to hold." Unregenerate man cannot handle the truth. It is appalling to recognize the truth already revealed in natural revelation. They must reject it.

(5) Finally, in vv. 29-32 Paul gives us a dark catalog of sins that describes our society. This is the result of man's effort to suppress the knowledge of God:

> **Romans 1:29–32** [29] Being filled with all unrighteousness, fornication, wickedness, covetousness, maliciousness; full of envy, murder, debate, deceit, malignity; whisperers, [30] Backbiters, haters of God, despiteful, proud, boasters, inventors of evil things, disobedient to parents, [31] Without understanding, covenantbreakers, without natural affection, implacable, unmerciful: [32] Who knowing the judgment of God, that they which commit such things are worthy of death, not only do the same, but have pleasure in them that do them.

In summary, the reaction of natural man to the certain knowledge of God revealed in creation is rebellion. Sinful man actively, constantly and deliberately suppresses the truth of God. At all cost he will exchange the truth of God for the lie. He seeks to define and re-interpret reality apart from God. He is buried in self-deception; but try as he may, it is impossible for man to escape the knowledge of God. The *sensus divinitatus* is indelibly inscribed upon his heart.

APOLOGETIC PRINCIPLES

The Noetic Effects of Sin

The noetic effects of sin refer to the effects the Fall had upon the mind. In Rom. 1:21, Paul describes the noetic effects of sin in natural man, "But became vain in their imaginations." This is what happened to man's reasoning capacity. By using the strong adversative conjunction "but" (ἀλλ'), the apostle penetrates deep into the inner condition of man. Men are "vain in their imaginations." The Grk verb for "became vain" (ἐματαιώθησαν) denotes having no intrinsic value, i.e., futile and empty. "Imaginations" (διαλογισμοῖς) in the Grk properly means thoughts or reasonings with the implication of evil. The phrase denotes a state of vain delirium characterized by evil rationalization. Unbelieving thought is nothing but futile reasoning.

"And their foolish heart was darkened." The Grk word for "foolish" (ἀσύνετος) literally means "unable to put together." It expresses the notion that natural man is unintelligent and destitute of understanding due to an inherent depravity. He deliberately will not put together the manifest evidence about God as disclosed in natural revelation. Paul states that their foolish "heart" (καρδία) was "darkened" (ἐσκοτίσθη). The darkness of sin does not reside in any one faculty but has its seat in the heart (καρδία). The verb "darkened" (ἐσκοτίσθη) is placed forward for emphasis. Its passive mood gives the sense of being covered with darkness.

The apostle is speaking of a pervasive depravity that has corrupted man's entire heart – not only the mind, but the will and

70

affections as well. It is an inherent corruption that extends to every part of man's nature, to all the faculties and powers of the soul. The foolish heart of the unbeliever, being covered in darkness, manifests itself in evil reasoning.

Both verbs used for "became vain" (ἐματαιώθησαν) and "darkened" (ἐσκοτίσθη) are aorist passive, pointing back to the Fall and the subsequent judgment of sin upon the human race. The Fall of man had a drastic effect on man's reasoning capacity and his ability to understand reality. Man will not accept God as the ultimate authority for all knowledge and truth; he must remain autonomous.

As a result, man concocts a false theory of knowledge. He exchanges the truth of God for "the lie" (v. 25) and lives in a world of self-deception. He is noetically blind and spiritually insane. He doesn't live in the real world and deliberately misinterprets it in his own way.

The term "noetic effects of sin" refers to the doctrine of total depravity and that aspect which emphasizes the intellectual corruption of man. In addition to references we have already considered in Romans 1:18-21, the Bible characterizes natural man's depraved mind as having his understanding darkened (Eph. 4:18), groping around in darkness (Acts 17:27), walking in the vanity of his mind (Eph. 4:17), hostile to God in his mind (Rom. 8:7), being blinded by the god of this world (2 Cor. 4:4), an enemy of God in his mind (Col. 1:21) and his thoughts overcome by moral corruption (Gen. 6:5). In short, because of the Fall, man's reasoning ability has become totally depraved. He has become destitute of the truth because of his hatred of God.

The reality of original sin and its consequent noetic effects correlates directly to the unbeliever's inability to truly know anything because he is constantly suppressing the truth in unrighteousness. Consequently, one's apologetic method must take into account the total depravity of man's intellectual faculty.

No Neutrality

The necessary correlary to the noetic effects of sin is natural man's incapacity to reason objectively without bias against God. Intellectual neutrality is impossible because of the depravity of his mind.

However, the unbeliever will claim intellectual autonomy in order to interpret the universe without reference to God. He will say, "Let us be neutral in interpreting the evidence, let us be objective and scientific." All the while he hates God, suppresses the truth of God and is an enemy of God. He has his own worldview to interpret the facts, and it is hostile to God. Sinful man adheres to a fallacious epistemology that would do away with God in every respect and determine for himself what is true and what is false. Sinful man naturally will make himself ultimate in determining truth and reality; he will be the judge of what is true. This is the expression of a depraved nature and there is nothing neutral about it. Neutrality is a myth.

A Conflict of Worldviews

Understanding the antithesis between the regenerate and the unregenerate worldviews is fundamental to presuppositional apologetics. Because of the Fall and the consequent noetic effects of sin, the unbeliever invents a worldview [72] that facilitates the suppression of both the truth of God revealed in creation (v. 18) and a conscience that renders him guilty before God (v. 20). The unbeliever's system of thought is hostile to God. It is a worldview characterized by futile reasoning (v. 21) that exalts itself against the knowledge of God (2 Cor. 10:5). Unregenerate man deliberately abandons the Creator-creature relationship in his presuppositions and makes himself autonomous. His presuppositions justify "exchanging

---

[72] A worldview is defined as the sum of one's presuppositions, which provide the framework to view and interpret the world and all reality.

the truth of God for the lie, and worshiping and serving the creature rather than the Creator" (v. 25). He would deny any need for divine revelation to understand the world he lives in. He is wholly against God and will not be brought under the authority of Christ. His worldview is antithetical to Christian theism.

The two belief systems are irreconcilable because their basic assumptions differ. One submits to the authority of God's word as a presuppositional commitment, and the other doesn't. It is a clash between two completely different sets of presuppositions. Therefore, this debate will eventually work its way down to the level of one's ultimate authority.[73] The essence of the unregenerate worldview is that man is assumed to be autonomous. Since the Fall, man has sought in principle to be a law unto himself. Fallen man will be subject to none but himself. He seeks to interpret the universe without reference to God. He is epistemologically in rebellion against God. He has no need of revelation. He thinks of himself as the absolute reference point in all predication and his mind is the final court of appeal for all interpretation of facts.

Thus, there is an antithesis between all non-Christian philosophies and the Christian theistic worldview. It is fundamentally a clash between ultimate presuppositional commitments and assumptions, which are contrary to each other. The two worldviews are in collision; one submits to the authority of God's word as a matter of presuppositional commitment, and the other to the autonomy of man. Both are totalitarian in nature. The Christian apologist must realize the utter epistemological futility of the unbeliever's reasoning and seek to expose it. The argument must be on the presuppositional level. In the final analysis, the unbeliever must renounce his system of thought; his presuppositions must be altered.

---

[73] G. Bahnsen, *Always Ready*. Texarkan, TX: Covenant Media Foundation, 1996, p. 68.

His mindset and worldview must be brought into captivity to the obedience of Christ (2 Cor. 10:5).

Only by the regenerating work of the Holy Spirit can unregenerate man be restored to true knowledge. By the sovereign grace of God and through the operation of the Spirit, man's mind is renewed and is able to come to the true knowledge of God and reality (Eph. 4:23-24). The blindness and darkness of man's mind is removed in the work of regeneration; the eyes are opened to see the knowledge of God as it is in Jesus Christ. The hatred and bias against God is definitively broken. Hence, Christ is realized as the fountain "in whom are hid all the treasures of wisdom and knowledge" (Col. 2:3). This is why apologetics is necessarily evangelistic and must never be separated from the context of the gospel.

Point-of-Contact

Where can we find a point-of-contact or common ground for our apologetic endeavor? Is there some area in which believers and unbelievers can agree? Is there some area, which is known by both believer and unbeliever that we can start from, some common ground? How is this possible if there is no neutral ground? What we have spoken of thus far seems to drive us away from any point-of-contact with the unbeliever whatsoever.

The answer is yes; there is a point-of-contact! Our point-of-contact is the *sensus divinitatus*. There is a sense of deity present in every human. This sense of deity is inscribed upon the heart of every man; it is to this sense of deity that the Christian apologist must appeal.

As we have seen, the apostle Paul speaks of natural man as actually possessing the knowledge of God.[74] No man can escape knowing God. Man was created as the image bearer of God and thus

---

[74] C. Van Til, (Ed. William Edgar), *Christian Apologetics*, 2nd Ed., Phillipsburg, NJ: Presbyterian & Reformed Publishing, 2003, p. 117.

he cannot escape the face of God. Deep down in the heart of man, he knows that he is a creature of God and a culpable creature at that. Man cannot open his eyes without being compelled to see God.[75]

The word of God assures us that every man is in contact with the truth. This is our point-of-contact with the unbelievers. A sense of deity is indelibly inscribed in the heart of man, because he is created in the image of God. Below are some pertinent quotes from R. C. Lenski and John Calvin:

> This fact of the wrath from heaven constantly breaks through the clouds of human perversions, false reasonings and philosophies, blatant denials and lies, beneath which men seek to hide in helpless efforts to escape. Man's moral mind cannot avoid connecting flagrant sin and crime with its due punishment.[76]

> Men of sound judgment will always be sure that a sense of divinity which can never be effaced is engraved upon men's minds. Indeed the perversity of the impious, who though they struggle furiously are unable to extricate themselves from the fear of God, is abundant testimony that this conviction, namely, that there is some God, is naturally inborn in all and is fixed deep within, as it were in the very marrow... I only say that though the stupid hardness in their minds, which the impious eagerly conjure up to reject God, wastes away, yet the sense of divinity, which they greatly wished to have extinguished, thrives and presently burgeons. From this we conclude that it is not a doctrine that must first be learned in school, but one of which each of us is master from his mother's womb and which nature itself permits no one to forget, although many strive with every nerve to this end.[77]

Closely related to the point-of-contact is common ground. Man is a creature made in God's image and living in God's created world. All men, believers and non-believers alike, have in common the world created by God, governed by God and revealed by God. Therefore, the common ground is all of God's creation.

---

[75] J. Calvin, *Institutes of the Christian Religion*, ed. John T. McNeil, trans. Ford Lewis Battles, Library of Christian Classics (London: SCM, 1960), 1.5.1.

[76] R. C . Lenski, *Romans*.

[77] J. Calvin, *Institutes*, 1.3.3.

So, although there is no neutral ground, there is indeed an ever-present common ground between the believer and the unbeliever, but this common ground is God's ground. As Creator, God has defined the meaning of all things. He is the ultimate interpreter of all things. Therefore, we as creatures are to think God's thoughts after him. Any fact or observation can be used as a point-of-contact. For all facts are created facts and not brute facts. This is our common ground with the unbeliever – all of God's creation.

CLOSING OBSERVATIONS

Observation 1. All people know God. There are no true atheists. Atheism is simply the suppression of the knowledge of God. Man may say there is no God and deny his very existence, but in his heart, he has a clear knowledge of God, which he must "hold down" at all cost. Unbelievers are in a relationship with God; it is not a saving relationship, but one of condemnation and judgment. The unbeliever understands this relationship.

When we are defending the faith, we are speaking to people who are not ignorant of God. However, we must expect them not to acknowledge that they know God. This is what Paul has told us in Romans 1. Our defense of the faith is to reveal what they already know to be true and point to the gospel, which is man's remedy for the wrath and judgment of God.

Observation 2. In Rom. 1:18-21, Paul is telling us about evidences. He is saying that everything in creation is evidence for God's existence. The evidence for God's existence is abundant. God's created order screams at man day and night. Everything in God's created universe proves God. There is no lack of evidence for God's existence.

Psalm 19:1-4 The heavens declare the glory of God; and the firmament sheweth his handywork. ² Day unto day uttereth speech, and night unto night sheweth knowledge. ³ There is no speech nor language, where their voice is not heard. ⁴ Their line is gone out through all the earth, and their words to the end of the world. In them hath he set a tabernacle for the sun.

What good does evidentialism do, if man is confronted with the clear revelation of God every day? Evidentialism seeks to prove something that man already knows. Do you think an apologist can present better evidence than God does? Evidence is not the issue. The issue is man's wicked heart, which continually will suppress the truth of God. The whole gist of the unbeliever's life is to suppress what is clearly revealed by God.

6. DID GOD HIDE HIMSELF?[78]
(ROM. 1:18-32; 2:14-16)

INTRODUCTION

The atheistic philosopher Bertrand Russell was asked, "What would happen if you die and immediately find yourself before God? What will you say?" He responded, "I would say to him, not enough evidence! Not enough evidence!"[79] More recently renowned atheist Richard Dawkins (ring leader of the new atheism) was interviewed by Ben Stein in the movie "Expelled" and asked, "What if after you died, and ran into God, and he asked you, 'What have you been doing Richard?'" He answered in similar fashion to Bertrand Russell, "Sir, why did you take such pain to hide yourself?" Are the arguments from these men valid? Will God accept their excuse? Did God hide himself?

I want to answer these questions by looking at Romans 1:18-32 (and 2:14-15) and consider the natural revelation of God.[80]

> **Romans 1:18-32** [18] For the wrath of God is revealed from heaven against all ungodliness and unrighteousness of men, who hold the truth in unrighteousness; [19] Because that which may be known of God is manifest in them; for God hath shewed *it* unto them. [20] For the invisible things of him from the creation of the world are clearly seen, being understood by the things that are made, *even* his eternal power and Godhead; so that they are without excuse: [21] Because that, when they knew God, they

---

[78] The reader will find this chapter similar to the previous one. However, since the content of this article is different in perspective, it was selected for inclusion in the book.

[79] K. S. Oliphint, *The Battle Belongs to the Lord*. Phillipsburg, NJ: Presbyterian and Reformed Publishing Co., 2003, pp. 131-132.

[80] Natural revelation is the revelation of God in nature. It describes the fact that God is self-revealed in his work of creation. It is a general revelation of God and not salvific.

glorified *him* not as God, neither were thankful; but became vain in their imaginations, and their foolish heart was darkened. [22] Professing themselves to be wise, they became fools, [23] And changed the glory of the uncorruptible God into an image made like to corruptible man, and to birds, and fourfooted beasts, and creeping things. [24] Wherefore God also gave them up to uncleanness through the lusts of their own hearts, to dishonour their own bodies between themselves: [25] Who changed the truth of God into a lie, and worshipped and served the creature more than the Creator, who is blessed for ever. Amen. [26] For this cause God gave them up unto vile affections: for even their women did change the natural use into that which is against nature: [27] And likewise also the men, leaving the natural use of the woman, burned in their lust one toward another; men with men working that which is unseemly, and receiving in themselves that recompence of their error which was meet. [28] And even as they did not like to retain God in *their* knowledge, God gave them over to a reprobate mind, to do those things which are not convenient; [29] Being filled with all unrighteousness, fornication, wickedness, covetousness, maliciousness; full of envy, murder, debate, deceit, malignity; whisperers, [30] Backbiters, haters of God, despiteful, proud, boasters, inventors of evil things, disobedient to parents, [31] Without understanding, covenantbreakers, without natural affection, implacable, unmerciful: [32] Who knowing the judgment of God, that they which commit such things are worthy of death, not only do the same, but have pleasure in them that do them.

Romans 2:14-15 [14] For when the Gentiles, which have not the law, do by nature the things contained in the law, these, having not the law, are a law unto themselves: [15] Which shew the work of the law written in their hearts, their conscience also bearing witness, and *their* thoughts the mean while accusing or else excusing one another.

GOD'S MORAL NATURE REVEALED

First, natural revelation clearly discloses the ethical nature of God, i.e., his moral character and consistency. Rom. 1:18, 32 and 2:14-15 describe man as knowing the wrath of God against all ungodliness and unrighteousness, the judgment of God against sin, and God's moral law respectively.

God's Wrath Revealed

Romans 1:18 For the wrath of God is revealed from heaven against all ungodliness and unrighteousness of men, who hold the truth in unrighteousness.

Rom. 1:18 begins with "For the wrath of God is revealed from heaven." It is a revelation of God's wrath, not of his grace. In the Grk, the verb "revealed" is placed first in word order for emphasis. Revealed and disclosed beyond any question is God's wrath, i.e., his anger and judgment against sin. It is a universal revelation given to all people. The verb "revealed" occurs in the present tense ('αποκαλύπτεται), indicating that "God's wrath" is continually being revealed to all men. Further, the passive voice denotes that God himself does this revealing. Man is the recipient; God is the one acting.

The last clause of v. 18 describes man's reaction to the revelation of God's wrath. The apostle Paul says "Who hold the truth in unrighteousness." The Grk verb for "hold" is κατεχόντων and literally means to "hold down" (from κατα – down, and εχω – to hold). It is a deliberate act of suppressing the truth of God; it is done "in unrighteousness." Man is not neutral or innocent in the matter, he wickedly and intentionally suppresses this revelation. The present tense of the verb "to hold down" denotes continual action. The unregenerate are habitually suppressing "the truth" (τὴν ἀλήθειαν) about the existence of God, his nature and his moral character – the truth that has been clearly revealed to them in creation. What follows in vv. 19-32 is but an explanation of this.

Why does man continually suppress the truth creation reveals about God? Because he cannot accept the terrible reality that he is accountable for his sin; so he must deny it at all cost. He must suppress it to justify the way he lives his life. Yet, despite all the denials, man remains accountable for the continual revelation of God's wrath.

God's Justice Revealed

Romans 1:32 Who knowing the judgment of God, that they which commit such things are worthy of death, not only do the same, but have pleasure in them that do them.

Rom. 1:32 tells us through natural revelation all men know the judgment of God. It is not a vague knowledge, but a fully sufficient knowledge. In the clause, "Who knowing the judgment of God," the apostle Paul uses an intensified form of the participle "knowing" (ἐπιγνόντες), which means to fully know.[81] The phrase, "the judgment of God" refers to the judicial verdict of God and denotes what God has ordained as just. It is further explained by the clause, "That they which commit such things are worthy of death."

Every man has a sense of deity by which he comprehends the punitive judgment of God and the consequence of his sin. All unbelievers know they are condemned before the bar of God's justice and deserve the sentence of death. Paul states that the unregenerate understand "they which commit such things are worthy of death." Man understands he is guilty before God and deserves to be punished with death. The context of v. 32 requires us to view death in its fullest sense, i.e., eternal death. "Such things" refers to the dark catalog of sins listed in vv. 29-31:

> **Romans 1:29-31** Being filled with all unrighteousness, fornication, wickedness, covetousness, maliciousness; full of envy, murder, debate, deceit, malignity; whisperers, [30] Backbiters, haters of God, despiteful, proud, boasters, inventors of evil things, disobedient to parents, [31] Without understanding, covenant breakers, without natural affection, implacable, unmerciful:

Knowledge of the judgment of God is ineradicably embedded in the human conscience.[82] The most depraved and degenerate of men are not destitute of understanding the righteous judgments of God. Man's sins are not committed in ignorance. Here, we are clearly taught that man is morally responsible for his sin, because he has a sufficient comprehension of the punitive justice of God.

---

[81] John Murray, *Epistle to the Romans*. Grand Rapids, MI: Eerdmans Publishing Co., Reprinted 1977, pp. 50-53.

[82] R. C. Lenski, *Romans*. Hendrickson Publishers, 1998, p. 124. Commentary on the New Testament.

God's Moral Law Revealed

Natural revelation also reveals God's moral law to every person. The apostle Paul affirms in Rom. 2:14-15, "the works of the law are written in their heart." Every person's conscience bears witness to the moral character of God.

> **Romans 2:14-15** [14] For when the Gentiles, which have not the law, do by nature the things contained in the law, these, having not the law, are a law unto themselves: [15] Which shew the work of the law written in their hearts, their conscience also bearing witness, and *their* thoughts the mean while accusing or else excusing one another.

In the above text, Paul observes that the Gentiles, who did not have the written law, "by nature" did the things contained in the law. "By nature" is a description of the natural constitution of man. The law is engraved on man's natural constitution. Although unregenerate man is a fallen creature and totally depraved, he is still a morally responsible creature because the law of God is embedded in his heart. Natural man is not devoid of God's moral law. This is the basis of morality in a fallen and sinful world.

The expression "a law unto themselves" is somewhat misleading in today's vernacular. Today "a law unto themselves" denotes autonomy, not being subject to any authority. However, in Rom. 2:14, it means exactly the opposite. Man, by virtue of what is implanted in his nature, is continually confronted with the law of God. Man himself is the revealer of the moral character of God to himself. The fact that man "does the things contained in the law" and is "a law unto himself," demonstrates that the work of the law is written in his heart.

When Paul says, "The work of the law is written in their hearts," he is alluding to the Ten Commandments, which were written in stone. The Ten Commandments are the codification of the moral law of God, the very transcript of God's moral character. No man can escape the witness of God's moral character; it is indelibly inscribed upon his heart as the image bearer of God. Every man's conscience bears witness to the moral law of God.

We also note that the law operates in the heart of man through the conscience. Conscience is a function of the heart that discriminates between right and wrong. God's law is the standard by which man discerns what is right and wrong. Human morality is not something that evolved, or based upon social consensus; it is indelibly inscribed upon the heart. The conscience is the evidence of man's indestructible moral nature and proof of the fact that God bears witness to himself in our hearts.[83] Man has an inborn moral nature. If the work of the law was not written in the heart, then no conscience would exist, and man would be devoid of morality.

THE INTERNAL REVELATION OF GOD

Romans 1:19 [19] Because that which may be known of God is manifest in them; for God hath shewed *it* unto them.

Rom. 1:19 deals with the internal aspect of natural revelation. Here, we find that God not only reveals himself *to* man but *in* man. Paul says, this knowledge of God is manifest "in them" (ἐν αὐτοῖς), i.e., in their hearts and minds, within the very constitution of their nature.[84] It is not a nebulous and hazy knowledge, it is clear and "manifest" in them. Man cannot charge God with hiding himself from them.[85]

---

[83] J. Murray, p. 75.

[84] C. Hodge, *Romans* (Grand Rapids, MI: Wm. B. Eerdmans Publishing, 1950); L. Morris, *The Epistle to the Romans* (Grand Rapids, MI: Wm. B. Eerdmans Publishing, 1988); W. Sanday, and A. Headlam, *Romans* (Edinburgh: T&T Clark, 1992); M. Vincent, *Word Studies in the NT* (Peabody, MA: Hendrickson Publishers); A. T. Robertson, *Word Pictures* (Grand Rapids, MI: Baker Book House, 1931); P. E. Hughes, "Critical Biblical Passages for Christian Apologetics" in *Jerusalem and Athens* (Phillipsburg, NJ: P&R Publishing, 1980), p. 134; R. C. Lenski, *Romans (*Peabody, MA: Hendrickson Publishers, 1998).

[85] R.C. Lenski, *Romans*.

Man possesses a general knowledge of God by virtue of being created in the image of God; it is a knowledge that is innate and intuitive within him. A sense of deity (*sensus divinitatus*) has been implanted within the human mind of all men. It is stamped on man's innermost being. Therefore, because man was made a morally rational creature as God's image bearer, he morally apprehends the manifestations of God in his works of creation and providence. He understands the moral character and judgment of God against sin. This is not an acquired knowledge of God; it is something that is inborn. It is part of man's very being.

THE CREATOR-CREATURE DISTINCTION REVEALED

Romans 1:20 [20] For the invisible things of him from the creation of the world are clearly seen, being understood by the things that are made, *even* his eternal power and Godhead; so that they are without excuse.

Consider the phrase "from the creation of the world" in Rom. 1:20. Paul takes us back to the creation of the world. When the apostle Paul states, "For the invisible things of him from the creation of the world are clearly seen, being understood by the things that are made," he is asserting the absolute reality of the Creator. God's general revelation is embedded in creation itself. "From the creation of the world" presupposes the eternality of God as existing prior to creation. It presupposes the self-existence of God. It presupposes God's transcendence and absolute independence of his creation. Hence, all other being and existence is wholly dependent upon God the Creator.

The apostle Paul proclaimed the Creator-creature relationship in his address to the Areopagus on Mars Hill:

Acts 17:24-26 God that made the world and all things therein, seeing that he is Lord of heaven and earth, dwelleth not in temples made with hands; [25] Neither is worshipped with men's hands, as though he needed any thing, seeing he giveth to all life, and breath, and all things; [26] And hath made of one blood all nations of men for to dwell on all the face of the earth, and hath determined the times before appointed, and the bounds of their habitation.

To Paul, the Creator-creature relationship between God and man was crucial to the work of apologetics. God owns everything in creation; all things were created to serve him and his purposes (especially man). This is the ultimate reality of man's existence. *We live and move and have our being in him* (Act 17:28).

THE EXTERNAL REVELATION OF GOD

What are the "invisible things of him" (v. 20) that the apostle Paul says the unbeliever knows about God? The apostle tells us they are "his eternal power and Godhead." The term "Godhead" in the Grk (θειότης) is a collective term for all the divine perfections, i.e., the attributes of God. Paul makes special note of God's "eternal power" (τε ἀΐδιος αὐτοῦ δύναμις) revealed in his works of creation. Both terms are joined together as an expressive unit in the original language.[86] Natural revelation does not just reveal the existence of God; it reveals God's divinity – his nature and character. Man apprehends this knowledge "by the things that are made." For all of creation is a revelation of God.

Paul says "the invisible things of him [God]" are "clearly seen." The Grk verb "clearly seen" (καθορᾶται) has reference to looking down from above and it means to see thoroughly, i.e., to have a full comprehension. Man clearly sees the invisible things of God: his existence, his divine perfections, his attributes and his eternal power. All men have this knowledge.

In addition, the phrase "being understood by the things that are made" explains how the invisible things of God are clearly seen. The Grk participle "being understood" (νοούμενα)[87] is very interesting and gives the sense of being intellectually apprehended (different than the

---

[86] Granville-Sharp rule.

[87] BDAG, to grasp or comprehend something on the basis of careful thought, *perceive, apprehend, understand, gain an insight into*. Nοούμενα is the present passive participle of νοεω. Noεω briefly defined is the use of νοός (the mind).

process of reasoning). It is a perceived understanding.[88] It depicts an immediate and intuitive comprehension, something that is instinctive. Thus, by using the term νοούμενα, the apostle Paul is reinforcing the *sensus divinitatus* he introduced in v. 19, i.e., the knowledge of God manifested *in them* (ἐν αὐτοῖς). There is an apprehension of the Creator that is innate in the very nature and constitution of man. Man clearly sees the unseen. Moreover, both verb (καθορᾶται, clearly seen) and participle (νοούμενα, being understood) are in the present tense denoting that man is in continual possession of this general knowledge of God.

SUPPRESSION PRESUPPOSES POSSESSION OF KNOWLEDGE

Man's deliberate suppression of the knowledge of God (Rom. 1:18, 23-25, 28) presupposes possession of knowledge. You cannot suppress knowledge without first possessing it. The unbeliever's reaction to the clear revelation of God is to constantly suppress it. This again proves that natural man has a sufficient comprehension of God.

Unregenerate man rebels against the knowledge of God because it brings him face-to-face with his Creator and condemns him. He knows he is guilty before God and hates it. He loves darkness and hates the light because his deeds are evil (John 3:19-20). Rom 1:18-32 explicitly teaches that natural man is hostile to the knowledge of God. Consider the following:

1. The unbeliever is so opposed to the truth of God he actively and deliberately suppresses it. It is the epitome of his rebellion against God. Rom. 1:18 asserts that all unbelievers "hold [suppress] the truth in unrighteousness." It is an intentional act of quashing and repressing the truth of God. It is not done ignorantly, but "in unrighteousness."

---

[88] TDNT, 4:950-951.

2. In Rom. 1:21, we find unregenerate man refusing to acknowledge God. He refuses to exhibit any kind of gratitude or thankfulness to God. Paul says, "They glorified him not as God, neither were thankful." Rather, they rebelliously engaged in futile reasoning to do away with God in their thoughts. They "became vain in their imaginations," which denotes futile speculation and worthless reasoning. The unbeliever obstinately exalts his reasoning against the knowledge of God (2 Cor. 10:5). His very intellect is constantly devising schemes by which he thinks he may overthrow God. He lives in a stupor of self-deception.

3. In Rom. 1:23, we see fallen man changing the glory of God revealed in creation into idols. Paul writes, "And changed the glory of the uncorruptible God into an image made like to corruptible man, and to birds, and fourfooted beasts, and creeping things." God originally created man to worship Him. He created man as a religious being, but fallen man has perverted his religious nature into the worship of idols. Although man has a general knowledge of the true God, he is wholly bent on perverting it.

When Paul addressed the Areopagus on Mars Hill, he began by stating, "I perceive that in all things ye are too superstitious" (Acts 17:22). The Grk term for "superstitious" (δεισιδαιμονεστέρους) means to be extremely religious (literally, fearers of supernatural spirits). He was alluding to the very constitution of man; man by nature is religious. Man possesses an innate sense of deity (*sensus divinitatus*). Athens was a city steeped in idolatry, a plethora of polytheistic gods and pantheistic conceptions of God. The presence of such a multitude of idols, temples and altars in Athens proved Paul's point – all men are religious. Paul says, "in all things" or "in every respect" you are very religious. The religious propensity of man's corrupt nature had lead them to seek after false gods, and grossly pervert the knowledge of God they possessed by natural revelation. Paul points out the absurdity of worshiping "the unknown God." They were ignorantly worshiping false gods. It was a deliberate suppression of the truth of

God. "They changed the glory of the uncorruptible God into an image made like to corruptible man, and to birds, and fourfooted beasts, and creeping things." Unregenerate man invents false religion in the form of idolatry because of his inherent religious nature.

4. In Rom. 1:25, Paul observes how unregenerate man changes the truth of God for a lie. The Grk word for "changed" (μεταλλάσσω) actually means to exchange, i.e., to exchange one thing for another. The unbeliever exchanges the natural revelation of God for a lie ("the lie" – definite article in the Grk). The result is to worship creation rather than the Creator. Verse 25 is a reference to the pantheistic tendencies of man to ascribe the attributes of God to nature. The prime example today is secular science and the philosophy of evolution. Secular science ascribes divine attributes to nature such as the eternality of matter and the immutability of natural law. It is a religious philosophy that changes the truth of God into a lie.[89] It is nothing more than a form of pantheism.

5. The natural revelation of God is obnoxious to the unbeliever. In Rom. 1:28 Paul states, "they did not like to retain God in their knowledge." The Grk term ἐπίγνωσις is used for "knowledge," which means full and sufficient knowledge. The Grk term for "retain" (ἔχω) means "to have" or "to hold." Unregenerate man cannot handle the truth. It is appalling to recognize the truth already revealed in natural revelation. They must reject it.

6. Ultimately, man's revolt against the knowledge of God is his pursuit of immorality. Immorality is an expression of rebellion and hatred against the clear revelation of God. In suppressing the truth, natural man actively pursues immorality. When man rejects God, God gives them over to immorality (v. 28). In Rom. 1:28-31, Paul gives us a dark catalog of sins that describe the result of man's deliberate effort to suppress the knowledge of God.

---

[89] Science is legitimate only if it assumes the absolute authority of Scripture for the interpretation of all created facts.

Romans 1:28-31 [28] And even as they did not like to retain God in their knowledge, God gave them over to a reprobate mind, to do those things which are not convenient; [29] Being filled with all unrighteousness, fornication, wickedness, covetousness, maliciousness; full of envy, murder, debate, deceit, malignity; whisperers, [30] Backbiters, haters of God, despiteful, proud, boasters, inventors of evil things, disobedient to parents, [31] Without understanding, covenantbreakers, without natural affection, implacable, unmerciful.

In summary, the reaction of natural man to the certain knowledge of God revealed in creation is rebellion. Sinful man actively, constantly and deliberately suppresses the truth of God. He seeks to re-define and interpret reality apart from God. He is buried in self-deception. But try as he may, it is impossible for man to escape the knowledge of God. The *sensus divinitatus* is indelibly inscribed upon his heart.

THE REALITY OF MAN'S KNOWLEDGE OF GOD ASSERTED

Rom. 1:21 is a definitive statement of man's certain knowledge of God comprehended through natural revelation. The apostle Paul asserts "they knew God" (γνόντες). Indeed, all people have a general knowledge of God.[90] All people not only know God exists, but know his divine attributes and character (1:20). All people know God as their Creator (1:20). All people know the moral character of God: his law (2:14-15), his justice (1:32), his wrath (1:18), their condemnation (1:32; 2:15) and a judgment day to come (2:16). Hence, all people possess sufficient knowledge of God to render them guilty without excuse. Whether they admit it or not doesn't change a thing.

CONCLUSION

God has sufficiently revealed himself to man. Consequently, all people know God. If they didn't, they would have a valid excuse for their unbelief. But Rom. 1:20 declares all men are "without an

---

[90] This does not refer to the salvific knowledge of God. The gospel of Jesus Christ is revealed to man only through special revelation.

90

excuse." The Grk word for "excuse" (ἀναπολογήτους) literally means without a defense. Before the tribunal of God, fallen man can never use the excuse that God did not reveal himself. God will hold all men accountable.

The hypothetical questions directed at God from atheists Bertrand Russell (Why didn't you give us more evidence?) and Richard Dawkins (Why did you take such pains to hide yourself?) attempt to make God culpable for not revealing himself. Nothing could be farther from the truth. Both questions betray a deliberate effort to suppress the clear revelation of God – to "hold down" the truth in unrighteousness. Every person possesses a sufficient knowledge of God. This reality is inescapable, and thus man is inexcusable. God did not hide himself!

All people know God. There are no true atheists. Atheism is simply the suppression of the true knowledge of God. Man may say there is no God and deny God's existence, but in his heart, he has a clear knowledge of God, which he must 'hold down" at all cost. Unbelievers are in a relationship with God, and it is not a saving relationship, but one of condemnation and judgment. Deep down inside, the unbeliever understands this relationship.

MAIN TENETS

OF

PRESUPPOSITIONAL APOLOGETICS

7. AN INTRODUCTION TO PRESUPPOSITIONAL APOLOGETICS

2 Cor 10: 4-5 (For the weapons of our warfare are not carnal, but mighty through God to the pulling down of strong holds;) [5] Casting down imaginations, and every high thing that exalteth itself against the knowledge of God, and bringing into captivity every thought to the obedience of Christ.

INTRODUCTION

Back in the 1980's, when I was working as a research scientist in the analysis and chemical synthesis of DNA, I came across a brief critique of the Creation Research Institute in *Science* magazine. It was a short editorial letter and the gist of it was this, "Why do the scientists at the Creation Research Institute act like deists when they profess to be theists?" The critic was exactly right. At that point, I knew something was terribly wrong with my evidential approach to apologetics.

A deist doesn't believe in the inscripturated word of God. The word of God has no authority to him. Man's ability to reason is ultimate to the deist, and he must interpret facts and observations from his rationalistic point of view. He would not dare use Scripture as an authority to interpret any fact or observation because he doesn't believe in the revelation of God. This opened my eyes to the inconsistency of evidential apologetics in defending the faith.

I began to understand that to reason apart from God's word was anti-biblical and anti-Christian. I am a Christian theist and I ought to act like one! I must take God's word as ultimate in authority and the absolute standard of truth. Anything less is sin and compromises the Christian faith. Defending the faith is not arguing about isolated facts and historical data, rather it is the defense of Christian theism as a whole.

DEFINITION OF PRESUPPOSITIONAL APOLOGETICS

Cornelius Van Til defines apologetics as "the vindication of the Christian philosophy of life against the various forms of non-Christian philosophy of life."[91] His abbreviated definition is "the vindication of Christian theism."

Van Til did not look at apologetics as trying to defend isolated historical facts such as the resurrection. To him, it was useless to vindicate Christianity by only a discussion of facts. For to interpret a fact of history (such as the resurrection) requires a philosophy of history, and a philosophy of history is based upon one's presuppositions and belief system. Presuppositional apologetics defends the Christian's worldview, the entire system of truth as revealed in the Holy Scriptures. Christian theism is to be defended as a unit, as a belief-system. The defense of our faith must never compromise the content of our faith. It is not a defense against details but of principle, an exposition and vindication of the Christian's worldview.[92]

The very nature of presuppositional apologetics is to argue the Christian's worldview against that of the unbeliever's worldview. It is to strike at the heart of the unbeliever's belief system, i.e., the presuppositions that form the foundation of his worldview. It is to challenge the unbeliever's system of thought; to show that the unbeliever cannot make sense out of anything in this world without using the Christian's worldview.

---

[91] C. Van Til, C. (Ed. William Edgar), *Christian Apologetics*, 2nd Ed., Phillipsburg, NJ: Presbyterian & Reformed Publishing, 2003, p. 17.

[92] James Orr, *The Christian View of God and The World*, Grand Rapids, MI: Kregel Publications, 1989, p. 4.

John Frame's definition of presuppositional apologetics has merit as well; "Apologetics is the application of Scripture to unbelief." Frame emphasizes the Christian's basic presupposition that forms his worldview; Scripture is the absolute and ultimate authority for all truth and knowledge. It is the absolute authority for determining the meaning of anything and the absolute reference point for the interpretation of all facts. The right understanding of all reality must be based solely on God's revelation. K. Scott Oliphint's definition is essentially identical to Frame's, "The application of biblical truth to unbelief."[93]

THE MEANING OF PRESUPPOSITION

We speak of presuppositional apologetics, but what exactly do we mean by the term *presupposition*? A presupposition is an assumption in one's reasoning. It is a pre-condition for knowledge. It is not something that you prove, but rather it is where one begins his reasoning. Therefore, presuppositions are a matter of faith. Accordingly, our worldview is made up of the sum total of our presuppositions. A worldview is necessarily a faith commitment.

Augustine's motto (which Anselm later adopted) was *credo ut intelligam*, "I believe in order that I may understand." His motto gives us insight into presuppositionalism. Belief precedes understanding. Faith in God and the revelation of his inspired and infallible Word precedes the understanding of everything else. The writer to the Hebrews shows this in Heb. 11:3, "Through faith we understand that the worlds were framed by the word of God, so that things which are seen were not made of things which do appear."

Man is by nature a presuppositionalist; he thinks and acts from his presuppositions.[94] Presuppositions form the basis of one's

---

[93] K. S. Oliphint, *Covenantal Apologetics*. Wheaton, IL: Crossway, 2013, p. 29.

[94] W. R. Downing, *An Introduction to Biblical Epistemology*. Morgan Hill, CA: PIRS Publications, 1998, p. 59.

knowledge and understanding of what is true; they form the basis of all reality to us. They comprise the very foundation by which man interprets and evaluates the world he lives in and everything contained in it

In short, the presuppositions that we espouse form our worldview, which is an all-inclusive view of reality. The meaning of the universe cannot be interpreted without a coherent worldview. Therefore, the defense of the faith is unavoidably a presuppositional matter. In presuppositional apologetics, the triune God and his revelation to man are presupposed to be absolute and ultimate. This is the first and overshadowing presupposition for a truly biblical approach to apologetics. The preeminent presupposition of unregenerate thought is the ultimacy of man's reasoning.

MAIN TENETS OF PRESUPPOSITIONAL APOLOGETICS

Creator-creature Distinction

Fundamental to a Christian's theory of reality (metaphysics) is the Creator-creature distinction.[95] When God revealed himself to Moses at the burning bush, he revealed himself as the self-existent God, "I am that I am" (Ex. 3:14). He is the self-existent and self-sufficient Being who is absolutely independent of his creation. He is wholly independent in his council, mind and will. He is infinite, eternal and unchangeable. God alone is absolute, self-contained and dependent upon nothing. He is the transcendent God. There is no criterion above or next to God whereby he can be measured or judged.[96]

God owns everything in creation, and everything in creation serves him and his purposes. All creatures, willingly or unwillingly,

---

[95] R. L. Reymond, *The Justification of Knowledge*. Nutley, NJ: Presbyterian & Reformed Publishing Co., 1976, p. 29.

[96] H. Hoeksema, *Reformed Dogmatics*. Grand Rapids, MI: Reformed Free Publishing Association, 1985, p. 69.

add to his glory.[97] He sovereignly rules over all unto the uttermost parts of the universe. He upholds "All things by the word of his power" (Heb. 1:3). There is not a square inch of the universe, not a microsecond of time and not a spin of an electron that is not dependent upon, controlled by and subservient to God.[98] All his creatures and all of creation are wholly dependent upon the Creator for their existence and being.

Accordingly, by virtue of creature-hood, man is entirely dependent upon God for all knowledge and truth. This reality forms the basis of a Christian's epistemology.[99] We live in a God-created and God-defined universe. Every fact is a created fact that has been defined by God. As creatures we are to give the same meaning to everything that God has given to it, i.e., we are to think God's thoughts after him; that is our moral obligation. To think autonomously, i.e., to assume man's ability to reason as ultimate, is immoral and sinful. It is an attempt to redefine meaning apart from God and his infallible word.

God's being is absolute and independent, and created being is necessarily derivative and dependent.[100] Therefore, there are two levels of knowledge. One is absolute and original in God, and the other is derivative and subordinate in created man. Man's knowledge is necessarily derivative of God.

As Creator, God is self-revealing and we can only know him as he has revealed himself to us. Therefore, Scripture is to be the basis of all knowledge and truth. The word of God is the final and ultimate court

---

[97] C. Van Til, *Christian Apologetics*, p. 28.

[98] G. Bahnsen, *Always Ready*. Texarkan, TX: Covenant Media Foundation, 1996, p. 42.

[99] Theory of knowledge, the justification of what we know to be true.

[100] C. Van Til, *The Defense of the Faith*. Phillipsburg, NJ: Presbyterian & Reformed Publishing Co., 1967, p. 46.

of appeal in every area of human existence.[101] The Creator's voice is the voice of absolute, unquestionable authority, and his word must be the standard by which we judge all things and the very starting point of all our thinking.[102]

Within the Creator-creature relationship, God's revelation is the basis for all meaning. All of Adam's knowledge was derived from God. Adam's knowledge was subordinate to and dependent upon God's revelation. God never intended Adam to be independent in his knowledge, because no fact in the universe existed independently of God. Every fact in the universe has its meaning by virtue of its relationship to God. To Adam, before the Fall, every single fact revealed God as its Creator. Adam had true knowledge because his interpretation was in line with the prior divine interpretation. Adam knew the true meaning of a fact because God had previously interpreted it and revealed it to him. God's revelation was Adam's ultimate *pou sto*,[103] the ultimate reference point from which he was to know God, and interpret the world he was created in.

Therefore, when it comes to thinking and reasoning, we must take into account the Creator-creature distinction. Man's thinking is derivative and must replicate God's thinking in order to know reality. He must re-interpret what God has pre-interpreted.[104] In other words, he must *think God's thoughts after him.*

---

[101] R. Reymond, *The Justification of Knowledge*, p. 31.

[102] G. Bahnsen, *Always Ready*, p. 25.

[103] The Grk mathematician Archimedes once boasted, "Give me a place where I may stand on and I will move the earth." Archimedes discovered the laws of the lever and it was to this mechanical device that he was referring to. From this saying came the Grk term *pou sto* which means *"to stand on"* referring to a basis of operation. Epistemologically, *pou sto* denotes a final point of reference for all human predication. The *pou sto*, the Archimedean point of reference, is one's ultimate authority, which he reasons from.

[104] C. Van Til, *An Introduction to Systematic Theology.* Phillipsburg, NJ: Presbyterian and Reformed Publishing Co., 1974, p. 171.

The Noetic Effects of Sin

The noetic effects of sin were introduced into the human race as a consequence of Adam's original sin and his rebellion against the Creator. The Bible characterizes man's depraved mind as groping around in darkness (Acts 17:27), having his understanding darkened (Eph. 4:18), his mind at emnity against God (Rom. 8:7), suppressing the truth in unrighteousness (Rom. 1:18), changing the truth of God into *the lie* (Rom. 1:25), walking in the vanity of his mind (Eph. 4:17), vain in his imaginations (Rom. 1:21), an enemy of God in his mind (Col. 1:21), having vain deceit (Col. 2:8), having vain thoughts (1 Cor. 3:20) and ignorant (Eph. 4:18); yet all the while seeking to exalt himself against the knowledge of God (2 Cor. 10:5). See Scripture references below.

> **Acts 17:27.** That they should seek the Lord, if haply they might feel after him, and find him, though he be not far from every one of us:

> **Eph. 4:17-18.** This I say therefore, and testify in the Lord, that ye henceforth walk not as other Gentiles walk, in the vanity of their mind, 18 Having the understanding darkened, being alienated from the life of God through the ignorance that is in them, because of the blindness of their heart:

> **Rom. 8:7.** Because the carnal mind is enmity against God: for it is not subject to the law of God, neither indeed can be.

> **Rom. 1:18.** For the wrath of God is revealed from heaven against all ungodliness and unrighteousness of men, who hold the truth in unrighteousness;

> **Rom. 1:21.** Because that, when they knew God, they glorified him not as God, neither were thankful; but became vain in their imaginations, and their foolish heart was darkened.

> **Rom. 1:25.** Who changed the truth of God into a lie, and worshipped and served the creature more than the Creator, who is blessed for ever. Amen.

> **Col. 1:21.** And you, that were sometime alienated and enemies in your mind by wicked works, yet now hath he reconciled.

> **Col. 2:8.** Beware lest any man spoil you through philosophy and vain deceit, after the tradition of men, after the rudiments of the world, and not after Christ.

2 Cor 10:5. Casting down imaginations, and every high thing that exalteth itself against the knowledge of God, and bringing into captivity every thought to the obedience of Christ;

1 Cor. 2:14. But the natural man receiveth not the things of the Spirit of God: for they are foolishness unto him: neither can he know them, because they are spiritually discerned.

Sadly, all men come into this world under the noetic effects of sin. Such is the state of sin and misery for the natural man. It is only by the grace of God that the unregenerate mind is renewed in the work of regeneration (Eph. 4:23-24) and enabled to come to the true knowledge of God. It is only through the Holy Spirit, applying the work of redemption, that the sinner's mind is illuminated (1 Cor. 2:14) to understand spiritual things.

Total depravity is a theological term that designates the pervasive character of man's inherited pollution of sin. It is an inherent corruption that extends to every part of man's nature, to all the faculties and powers of both soul and body. There is no spiritual good (in respect to God) in the sinner at all, but only perversion.[105] Sin involves every aspect of man's personality, including his rational faculties.

When we speak of the noetic effects of sin, we are simply speaking of the biblical doctrine of *total depravity* with emphasis on the intellectual inability of man. You cannot omit the fact of sin from your epistemology, or theory of knowledge. Abraham Kuyper said every theory of knowledge must accept the hard reality of the fact of sin. A defective view of sin will result in a defective apologetic.

When dealing with the noetic effects of sin, it is important to understand that man's intellectual faculties cannot be separated from his will and affections. Sin does not reside in any one faculty but has its seat in the heart. From the heart, the influence and operations of sin spread to the intellect, the will, the affections, in short, the entire

---

[105] L. Berkhof, *Systematic Theology*. Grand Rapids, MI: Eerdmans Publishing Co., 1988, pp. 246-247.

man.[106] The soul is corrupted with all its faculties. If the heart is corrupt, then the whole soul in all its powers and faculties are corrupt. Therefore, the intellect of man and his rational faculties are biased against God. Man's intellect is not neutral; it is in rebellion to God and is wholly set against God. It is impossible to separate man's intellect from his will and affections. All three are involved in the ethical depravity of man's heart.

Let us consider Adam and original sin. While knowing God, Adam rebelled against God by suppressing what God had revealed to him. He denied the absolute and ultimate authority of God's revelation. Adam sought after knowledge and meaning independently of God. He set aside the law of his Creator and became a law unto himself. Adam wanted to be autonomous. He sought to interpret the universe without reference to God. He wanted to be his own authority and determine for himself what was true and what was false, what was right and what was wrong. Adam wanted to be as God, to judge good and evil, and to be the standard of truth. When man fell, it was his attempt to do away with God in every respect. It was an attempt to preclude God with his autonomous interpretation of the universe.

The consequent noetic effects due to original sin are far reaching. The perverted epistemology of our first parents has been inherited by all their posterity. Unregenerate man daily changes the truth of God into a lie. He daily worships and serves the creature more than the Creator (Rom. 1:25). He daily holds the truth in unrighteousness (Rom 1:18). He is spiritually dead (Eph. 2:1). Since the Fall of Adam, "there is none that understandeth" (Rom. 3:11). All are noetically blind. None can come to a true knowledge of God. Only by the regenerating work of the Holy Spirit, can man be restored to true knowledge.

---

[106] Ibid, p. 233.

The Fall of man has *drastically* effected man's ability to reason. Man's reasoning ability has become totally depraved. The entire creation became subject to vanity (Rom. 8:20) and is in confusion and skeptical despair. Moral corruption has overcome man's thoughts (Gen. 6:5). Man continually uses his mind for evil. Unregenerate man suppresses the truth in unrighteousness to embrace *the lie* (Rom. 1:18-25). He suppresses the truth to distort it into a naturalistic scheme, thus precluding God's interpretation – the very One who created, defined and gave meaning to all things.

The crucial issue in apologetics is the noetic effects of sin. The extent of man's noetic corruption determines his ability to understand reality and have true knowledge. From the Scripture references previously listed, we understand that the natural man's epistemology, i.e., his theory of knowledge is necessarily biased against God. He is unable to come to true knowledge by himself. The unregenerate's worldview is utterly perverted and antithetical to the Christian's worldview. In contrast, the believer's epistemology and worldview are determined by presupposing the ultimacy and authority of Scripture. The two worldviews are unavoidably in conflict.

In the context of the noetic effects of sin, it should be apparent that one's apologetic method is determined by his view of the Fall of Adam. The extent and degree of Adam's fall correlates directly to man's ability to know truth and reality. If one truly adheres to the biblical doctrine of total depravity, then presuppositionalism is the only consistent apologetic method. There is no alternative method. All other worldviews deny the depravity of the mind and allow for intellectual neutrality where the unbeliever remains the ultimate authority for determining truth.

Antithesis – Conflict of Worldviews

In light of natural man's sinful nature and depravity, he stands in an absolute ethical antithesis to God. Fundamental to presuppositional apologetics is the irreconcilable antithesis between the regenerate and the unregenerate mind-sets. It is a clash between two completely different worldviews; two different sets of presuppositions and two different systems of thought are in collision with each other. One submits to the authority of God's word as a presuppositional commitment and the other doesn't. The unbeliever's system of thought is according to the philosophy of this world and he is an enemy of God in his mind. He suppresses the truth and exalts his reasoning against the knowledge of God. He walks in the vanity of his mind and his understanding is darkened; he's blind. The unbeliever is wholly against God and he will not be brought under the authority of Christ. This, indeed, is the presuppositional root that the apologist must aim to expose and eradicate. The apologetical debate will develop into a question of ultimate authority. Every worldview has its unquestioned assumptions about truth and reality.

Unregenerate man believes that his autonomous reasoning is ultimate. This is the fundamental presupposition that determines his worldview. Fallen man will be subject to none but himself; he seeks in principle to be a law unto himself. The unbeliever will not subject himself to the absolute authority of God. He will seek to interpret the universe without reference to God and believes he can obtain unto genuine knowledge independent of God's revelation. He thinks of himself as the absolute reference point in all predication, the final court of appeal for all interpretation of knowledge. He has no need of revelation. He is hostile to God, he hates God and his presuppositions allow him to suppress the knowledge of God. The non-Christian is epistemologically in rebellion against God; he believes he is autonomous[107] and is his own *pou sto*.

Thus, as a consequence of the Fall and its accompanying noetic effects, fallen man possesses a *pou sto* antithetical to that of the Christian. The two systems differ because of the fact that their basic

---

[107] Ibid, p. 46.

assumptions or presuppositions differ.[108] The difference between the two systems of thought, believer and unbeliever, is fundamentally a clash between two worldviews – between ultimate presuppositional commitments and assumptions, which are contrary to each other. Van Til refers to this as two opposing principles of interpretation.[109] The Christian principle of interpretation is based upon the assumption of God as the final and self-contained reference point. The unbeliever's principle of interpretation presupposes man as self-contained and the final reference point, i.e., that he is autonomous.

Thus, there is a simple and all comprehensive *antithesis* between the knowledge concept of all non-Christian philosophies and the Christian view.[110] The two worldviews are in collision; one submits to the authority of God's word as a matter of presuppositional commitment, and the other to the autonomy of man.[111] Both are totalitarian in nature. The apologist must bring the conflict to the forefront and seek to expose the utter epistemological futility of the unbeliever's reasoning. The unbeliever must renounce his system of thought – his presuppositions must be altered.

A Revelational Epistemology

Epistemology is the theory of knowledge. It determines how we know something to be true. A revelational epistemology holds God's revealed truth as absolutely necessary and foundational for all understanding and knowledge.

To the Christian, God is the *pou sto* for all knowledge, the final reference point for all human predication. [112] His revelation in

---

[108] C. Van Til, *A Christian Theory of Knowledge*. Phillipsburg, NJ: Presbyterian & Reformed Publishing Co., 1969, p. 15.

[109] Ibid, p. 44.

[110] C. Van Til, *Defense of the Faith*, p. 47.

[111] G. Bahnsen, *Always Ready*, p. 68.

[112] R. Reymond, *Justification of Knowledge*, p. 66.

Scripture is the absolute standard for all knowledge. It is the presuppositional starting point for all thinking. By faith, the Christian presupposes the word of God as the ultimate standard for truth. The believer must renounce all intellectual self-sufficiency, all human autonomy, that claims neutrality in thought and does not recognize a complete dependence upon God the Creator for true knowledge and understanding. God's word is the final criterion of truth. This is the Christian's epistemology and it is revelational in nature.

There are two major apologetical methods in defending the faith; *evidential* and *presuppositional* apologetics. The difference in these two methods is the place they give to Scripture in the enterprise of apologetics. The evidentialist must first credential the Bible through evidences such as archaeological discoveries, historical records, etc., before it can be used authoritatively. In other words, he must first prove the reliability of the Bible before it can be used as a standard for true knowledge. Necessarily, he must start from alleged neutrality outside of Scripture, accepting the world's apostate epistemology. The Bible does not appeal to human reason as ultimate in order to justify what it says. It comes to the human being with absolute authority.[113]

On the other hand, the presuppositionalist takes the position that the Bible is self-attesting and therefore does not need to be validated. It has its authority because God is its author. God himself has validated it; it does not need to be proven nor credentialed by man. Scripture is the absolute, infallible and authoritative word of God, the only ultimate standard of truth. Therefore, the presuppositionalist begins by presupposing Scripture as the absolute authority for all human reasoning and knowledge.

Consequently, God's word cannot be challenged by some higher criterion – there is none. God's word is ultimate. Man does not have the prerogative to call God's word into question. This is the

---

[113] C. Van Til, *A Christian Theory of Knowledge*, p. 15.

fundamental presupposition of Christianity, which is diametrically opposed to the unbeliever's epistemology. In fact, the unbeliever is by nature hostile to the Christian worldview. He views human reasoning as autonomous and ultimate, where the believer, standing in faith, knows Gods word to be true.

Point-of-Contact

1. *No Neutrality*. In light of what we have said about the noetic effects of sin, and the conflict of worldviews between the believer and unbeliever, it should be obvious that there is no neutrality. There are no neutral facts (evidences). For all facts are created facts, defined and interpreted by God. We cannot assume that unregenerate man will be intellectually unbiased in his reasoning. Quite the contrary, he will be biased against God in the interpretation of evidences, for he is an enemy of God, enslaved to the noetic effects of sin and is spiritually dead.

The apologist cannot begin with some neutral ground outside of Scripture and reason *to* Scripture. That would be adopting the world's epistemology. No, the Christian is called upon and commanded to reason *from* Scripture as his ultimate authority. Christians must refuse to think or reason according the mind-set of the world. The Christian is completely different from the world, and he cannot reason from neutrality because there is no such thing. It would be immoral to do so. We are to bring every thought into captivity to the obedience of Christ (2 Cor. 10:5).

To assume neutrality in the interpretation of any fact or data would be to give up the ultimate and absolute standard for all truth and reality. Yielding to neutrality is a suppression of the truth (Rom. 1:18). To be neutral is to deny the antithesis of worldviews between believers and unbelievers. It forces the Christian to use the world's apostate epistemology and submit to the unregenerate's mind-set. For all men have their presuppositions, none are neutral. Neutrality is nothing short of immorality.[114]

The Christian must begin with Scripture and reason *from* Scripture. That is our moral obligation. To assume some neutrality and then reason without Scripture would effectively make us deists. A deist believes in the existence of God purely on rationalistic grounds without any reliance on the authority of revelation. A theist believes in the authority of God's self-attesting revelation. To take a neutral approach is to follow after vain deceit and endorse presuppositions that are hostile to the Christian faith. It would be following after the traditions of this world. We do not have the right to set apart God's word in any of our thinking.

2. *Point-of-Contact.* Without neutrality and in light of the conflict of worldviews between the believer and the unbeliever, and given the Christian's revelational epistemology, where can we find a point-of-contact or common ground for our apologetic endeavor? Is there anything that believers and unbelievers can agree on? Is there some area, which is known by both believer and unbeliever that we can start from, some common ground? How is this possible if there is no neutral ground? The things we have considered seem to drive us away from any point-of-contact with the believer whatsoever.

The answer is yes, there is a point-of-contact because there is a sense of deity present in every man. The Christian apologist must appeal to the sense of deity inscribed upon the heart.

> **Rom. 1:18-21.** For the wrath of God is revealed from heaven against all ungodliness and unrighteousness of men, who hold the truth in unrighteousness; 19 Because that which may be known of God is manifest in them; for God hath shewed it unto them. 20 For the invisible things of him from the creation of the world are clearly seen, being understood by the things that are made, even his eternal power and Godhead; so that they are without excuse: 21 Because that, when they

---

[114] G. Bahnsen, *Always Ready*, p. 9.

knew God, they glorified him not as God, neither were thankful; but became vain in their imaginations, and their foolish heart was darkened.

Rom. 1:32. Who knowing the judgment of God, that they which commit such things are worthy of death, not only do the same, but have pleasure in them that do them.

Rom. 2:14. For when the Gentiles, which have not the law, do by nature the things contained in the law, these, having not the law, are a law unto themselves:

In the above texts, the apostle Paul speaks of natural man as actually possessing a general knowledge of God.[115] No man can escape knowing God. Man was created as the image bearer of God and thus he cannot escape the face of God. Deep down in the heart of man, he knows that he is a creature of God and a culpable creature at that.

Rom. 2:14 tells us that the law of God is written on the heart and manifests itself in the conscience of man. Because man was made in God's image, he is impressed with the law of God, which is inscribed upon his conscience.

Rom. 1:32 tells us that natural man knows the judgment of God and that he is guilty before his Creator. He knows that he is worthy of death; all men are without excuse. No man can claim ignorance of his Creator, for God has made himself known to every man.

From the word of God, we are assured that every man is in contact with the truth. This is our point-of-contact with the unbeliever. A sense of deity is indelibly inscribed in the heart of man because he was created in the image of God.

However, we must note, the innate knowledge of God that every man possesses must be carefully distinguished from the reaction that sinful man makes to this revelation.[116] Unregenerate man rebels against this knowledge. Although inwardly he has a general knowledge of God; outwardly he adamantly and vehemently denies

---

[115] Van Til, *Christian Apologetics*, p. 117.
[116] Ibid. p. 109.

the truth of God. Unregenerate man will deny the Creator even though he cannot escape the knowledge of him. Every unbeliever, every sinner, seeks to suppress this knowledge.

> **Rom. 1:18.** For the wrath of God is revealed from heaven against all ungodliness and unrighteousness of men, who hold the truth in unrighteousness;

> **Rom. 1:25.** Who changed the truth of God into a lie, and worshipped and served the creature more than the Creator, who is blessed for ever. Amen.

As his creatures, all men know God, but as sinners all men refuse to acknowledge their Creator and live by his revelation.[117] Ironically, the very thing the unbeliever denies provides the only foundation for him to make sense of anything.

3. *Common Ground.* Closely related to the point-of-contact is common ground. Man is a creature made in God's image and living in God's created world. All men, believers and non-believers alike, have in common the world created by God, governed by God and revealed by God. Therefore, the common ground is all of God's creation.

Although there is no neutral ground, there is indeed an ever-present common ground between the believer and the unbeliever. This common ground is God's ground. As Creator, God has defined the meaning of all things. He is the ultimate interpreter of all things. Therefore, any area of life and any fact or observation can be used as a point-of-contact. For all facts are created facts, not brut facts, but created facts defined by God and given meaning by God. This is the Christian apologist's common ground with the unbeliever – all of God's creation.

METHOD

The presuppositional apologetic method is to argue *the impossibility of the contrary*. It is to demonstrate to the opponent that his worldview

---

[117] G. Bahnsen, *Always Ready*, p. 38.

111

(his presuppositions) would destroy meaning and any possibility of knowledge. Only the Christian worldview provides the framework for true knowledge. The apologist must contend that the true starting point of thought cannot be anything other than God and his revealed word, for no reasoning is possible apart from that ultimate authority.[118]

The method or procedure for presuppositional apologetics can be broken down into two basic steps. 1) A critique of the unbeliever's thought demonstrating that his system of thought is a foolish destruction of knowledge. The purpose is to expose the futility of autonomous reasoning apart from Scripture. 2) An invitation into the Christian's worldview and a revelational epistemology. It articulates a biblical worldview, the impossibility of the contrary, and how the unregenerate thought must borrow from the Christian worldview to make sense out of anything.

1. First, a critique of the unbeliever's thought. The Christian is to place himself in the unbeliever's worldview in order to show how it results in the destruction of knowledge. We must prove how unbelieving thought is futile. All argumentation will terminate on some logical starting point, a presupposition held as unquestionable. The apologist is to back the unbeliever up to his ultimate starting points or presuppositions and expose them for what they are.

Let me give an example. I used to work for a prominent biotech corporation in the Bay Area. Every year they would send their research scientists to a retreat at some fancy resort. Big name scientists from academia were invited as consultants, and for three days we would brain storm new technologies and new trends in science in order to come up with new product ideas. On one of these occasions, I was eating dinner with nine other scientists at a round table; all were Ph.Ds., some of them very well published, and some of them big

---

[118] Ibid, p. 73.

names from prominent universities. They engaged in a conversation about evolution that waxed deeper and deeper. All of them, of course, assumed evolution to be true. Many at the table knew that I believed in creation. I waited quietly for the opportune time to challenge them on absolute truth.

I asked them, "What one thing about evolution do you know to be absolutely true?" There was dead silence. Just a few moments ago they were quite arrogant about "the fact" of evolution, and now they couldn't tell me one sure thing about evolution. Finally, a German scientist spoke out and said, "We don't know anything absolutely, but we do know it is highly probable." So I said, "The best you can say is that evolution or any alleged fact of evolution is only probable." The conversation then developed into discussing probabilities, randomness and chance, and how they were the driving forces in evolution. They, in essence, made chance ultimate.

Next, I attempted to challenge their presupposition of chance and randomness. I said, "If this world and the universe is based upon chance and randomness, then how do you explain uniformity in nature? The whole concept of science and the scientific method is based upon the laws of nature, i.e., uniformity in nature. But you just told me that everything is a result of chance and randomness, the very opposite of natural law and uniformity." At this point, the marketing folks got up from their tables and stood around the scientist's table. We became the entertainment for the night.

To make a long story short, I told them, "You have to borrow from my worldview to make sense out of this – that there is a Creator who created this uniformity, and He controls and governs it. You can't make sense of this world, or use the scientific method without it." I was trying to prove to them *the impossibility of the opposite.* Science is impossible without the Christian worldview.

Well, the president of the company, attempting to rescue me, came over to the table and put his hands on my shoulders and said,

"You have to understand that Paul is very religious." I turned around, and said to him in front of everyone, "I'm not the one having the problem in this conversation." That evening was a great victory for the Lord.

2. The second part of the methodology for presuppositional apologetics is to invite the subject into the Christian's worldview and a revelational epistemology. It is to demonstrate that the only workable foundation for true knowledge is the self-attesting word of God. The apologist must contend that the true starting point of thought cannot be anything other than God and his revealed word, for no reasoning is possible apart from that ultimate authority. We must point the unbeliever to the word of God, our absolute authority for truth, and to the Lord Jesus Christ to whom all our thinking must bow down.

CLOSING REMARK

We must always remember, that presuppositional apologetics rests ultimately in the regenerating grace of God to open the minds and hearts of the unconverted individuals that they might savingly believe the truth and close with Christ in faith.[119] The work of the apologist is necessarily evangelistic. Any intellectual argument will not convince nor convert the non-Christian. Those who do not presuppose the truth of God's word need to be renewed in their minds; this takes the regeneration power of the Holy Spirit. The apologetical reasoning of the Christian is the means by which the Holy Spirit penetrates into the mind and hearts of unregenerate men. Only God can open the eyes of the blind. God must grant faith and repentance for true knowledge to be obtained. Therefore, the Christian must humbly and prayerfully approach the task of apologetics.

---

[119] W. R. Downing, *An Introduction to Biblical Epistemology*. Morgan Hill, CA: PIRS Publications, 1998, p. 87.

8. APOLOGETICS AND THE IMAGE OF GOD

INTRODUCTION

The Bible distinctly defines man as the image bearer of God. Since apologetics is an appeal to man as man, the apologist must be faithful to the biblical view of man. The doctrine of the image of God has a direct bearing on defending the faith; it provides the foundation for biblical apologetics. To error here is to engage in defective apologetics.

This chapter sets forth the doctrine of the image of God in man. It will show the necessity of a two-fold image interpretation (moral and ontological) and relate each to some of the main tenets of presuppositional apologetics.

WHAT IS MAN?

In Psalm 8:4, David asks the question, "What is man?" No doubt, David wrote this Psalm remembering his former days as a shepherd when he would camp out under the stars at night and meditate on the creation of God and the significance of man. David wrote in v. 3, "When I consider thy heavens, the work of thy fingers, the moon and the stars, which thou hast ordained," and then asked the question, "What is man?" David was not the first to ask this question and obviously not the last.

"What is man?" is an age-old question that has confronted every generation. To ask this question is to introduce a host of inherent problems concerning the origin of man, the future of man, his soul, his body, his freedom, his responsibility and his relationship to his fellow man. There are an astonishing variety of views regarding the nature of man. Philosophers, scientists, psychologists, sociologists and humanists all have their own views. Our universities are filled with rival anthropological theories. They are all products of an unbeliever's worldview.

The most common theory today is materialistic (naturalistic) anthropology. It teaches that man is composed of material elements; his mental, emotional and spiritual aspects are simply byproducts of his material structure. Many forms of anthropology flow from this. Evolution, for example, defines man as evolving from the material cosmos being a product of chance. The philosophy of evolution dominates as "the" theory to explain the physical, social and psychological development of man. Man is simply an animal, a primate that evolved out of primordial soup, as did every living thing. Sigmund Freud thought the nature of man to be nothing but an evolutionary animal governed by irrational urges. B. F. Skinner believed man was but a product of stimulus and response. Like any other organism, man is simply a complex machine devoid of a will and consequently not responsible for what he does. Skinner asserted that all human behavior is a function of environmental variables. To Karl Marx, the nature of man was a "species-being." He looked at humanity as parts of the whole, i.e., a species, and human nature as the totality of society. Man was not important as an individual. Today, behavioral genetics has taken the forefront alleging that man's nature and behavior is the result of what is programed in his DNA.

Over the years, a multitude of theories have emerged attempting to define the nature of man. All such theories conceive of man as isolated from any dependency on or responsibility to God the Creator. Accordingly, secular anthropologists are guilty of idolatry because they worship aspects of creation in place of God. Of whom the apostle Paul writes, "Who changed the truth of God into a lie, and worshipped and served the creature more than the Creator, who is blessed for ever. Amen." (Rom. 1:25). These theories are futile attempts of man to exalt himself against the knowledge of God.

However, man's relationship to God is essential to his being. He is inescapably related to God. Man can never be viewed as isolated but always in relation to God, and this relationship defines the whole being of man. Any anthropology that separates man from his relationship to God can never penetrate the mystery of man, nor answer the question, "What is man?"

It is in the light of Scripture that the mystery of man is made clear. Since the Christian possesses God's revelation, the absolute and ultimate standard of truth, he can truly answer the question, "What is man?" We are creatures of God made in his image. The created image of God in man is what defines man. It distinguishes man from the animals and from every other creature. It gives man a distinct identity. Man and man alone is made in the image of God. This is the biblical definition of human nature; it defines man in an inescapable relationship to God. It is a Creator-creature relationship.

When David asked the question, "What is man?," it was a rhetorical question. He was expressing his astonishment at the grace of God. David was saying that man is a creature made by God to exercise dominion over the earth. Man was created to be God's steward of the earth, to serve and glorify God. He occupies a unique position within God's creation, for God crowned him with glory and honor. Man stands supreme as head of the entire creation. David defined who man was; distinctly created as the image bearer of God and called to express that image through dominion over the earth.

Psalm 8:5-6 [5] For thou hast made him a little lower than the angels, and hast crowned him with glory and honour. [6] Thou madest him to have dominion over the works of thy hands; thou hast put all *things* under his feet:

MAN DEFINED AS THE IMAGE BEARER OF GOD

Genesis 1:26 [26] And God said, Let us make man in our image, after our likeness: and let them have dominion over the fish of the sea, and over the fowl of the air, and over the cattle, and over all the earth, and over every creeping thing that creepeth upon the earth.

God created man in his own image. In Gen. 1:20-25, we read that the creatures were created "after its kind."[120] However with man's creation, it is distinctly stated that God created man "in our image and after our likeness." The difference in terminology identifies man as unique in the order of creation. Man is the image of his Creator, the very reflection and analogue of God himself. It is the image of God that distinguishes man from all other creatures. Man stands supreme as head and crown of the entire creation.

All previous creative acts were spoken into existence by the impersonal words, "Let there be."[121] In the first five days, God simply commanded his creation into existence by his fiat decree. But on the sixth day, when almighty God forms the most excellent of his creation, man, God enters into consultation between the three Persons of the Godhead. He says, "Let *us* make man in *our* image and after *our* likeness." This speaks to the great honor and dignity God conferred upon man, setting him apart in superior glory from the rest of his creatures.

In Genesis 1:26, there are two Hebrew words that describe man as being constituted the image bearer of God: "image" and "likeness."[122] The Hebrew word for *image* (tselem, צֶלֶם) literally means shadow, an outline or a sketch of something. The word for *likeness* (demuwth, דְּמוּת) means a copy, portrait or model of something. It can denote a statue. The basic sense of both words, image and likeness, is resemblance.

It is not possible to discover any well-defined distinction between the ordinary uses of the two words. They are used essentially in the

---

[120] Better translated "according to its kind."

[121] The Hebrew verb *to let be*, or *to become* (יְהִי) always appears in the singular.

[122] The Greek words translated in the LXX for the Hebrew of *image* and *likeness* are εἰκών (likeness, image, representation, form, appearance, statue) and ὁμοίωσις (likeness, resemblance, state of being, similar) respectively.

same way and are interchangeable. When the two terms are combined, they add intensity to the thought; it is common in the Hebrew language to repeat the same thing with different words.[123] Hence, the second term, "after our likeness," is added to heighten the meaning of image. It explains the term "in our image."

These two terms, the figure of a shadow and the figure of a portrait, are combined together to describe man's resemblance to God. Man was created as the analog of God, a resemblance of God that constituted him unique from the rest of creation and with a status far superior to any other creature. Man was created to be the image bearer of God.

Although Gen. 1:26-27 tells us man was created in the image of God, it does not describe what the content of the image of God is. We see that being made in God's image definitely implies more than it says.[124] However, we do see three essential aspects of the image of God in vv. 27-29: the Creator–creature relationship, man's dominion over the earth and the institution of marriage. This is only a partial description of the image of God. Thus, to define the content of the image of God one must collate all the passages of Scripture relevant to this important subject.

BROAD AND NARROW DEFINITIONS OF THE IMAGE OF GOD

When all the scriptural teaching regarding the image of God in man is collated, two senses of the image emerge. There is a broad and more comprehensive sense of the image of God. It is referred to as the *ontological image*. In this sense, the image of God remains in man even after the Fall. It constitutes the very essence and nature of man. It makes man unique and separate from all of creation. This aspect of

---

[123] J. Calvin, "Genesis" in *Calvin's Commentaries*.

[124] G. Clark, *The Biblical Doctrine of Man*. Jefferson, Maryland: The Trinity Foundation, 1984.

the image of God in man is indestructible and inseparable from man. Without it man would cease to be man.

The other sense of the image of God consists in the *original righteousness* God endowed man with in creation. Man was created in a sinless state of moral perfection before the Fall. This is the narrow sense of the image of God and is referred to as the *moral image*. Man completely lost the narrow image of God in the Fall. The moral image can only be restored in man through the sovereign work of God in regeneration, sanctification and glorification. It is the restoration of the moral qualities of knowledge, righteousness and holiness (Eph. 4:24; Col. 3:10).

In the following, each aspect (broad and narrow) of the image of God in man will be dealt with separately along with corresponding apologetical implications. It is important for the reader to understand that the doctrine of the image of God in man is the foundation of the main tenets of presuppositional apologetics.

THE BROAD VIEW: THE ONTOLOGICAL IMAGE OF GOD

What is the meaning of ontological? Ontology is derived from the Greek word οντος, which means *being*. Ontology is the study of *being*. In philosophy, it deals with the larger issue of absolute reality. In anthropology (the study of man), it deals with the essence and nature of man's being.

When we say the image of God is ontological in a broad sense, we mean that it is part of the very being of man. It constitutes man's very nature and without it man would cease to be man. It is the very essence of man. Herman Bavinck said, "Man is the image of God precisely because he is man. And he is man precisely because he is the image of God." This aspect of the image of God in man is indestructible, inseparable and inalienable.

The Bible speaks of man still retaining the image of God after the Fall. When man fell in the garden, he did not loose his nature. For after the Fall, man was still man. We must make a distinction between what was *lost* and what was *left* of the image of God after the Fall. The whole image was horribly defaced by sin; the spiritual and moral qualities of the soul (original righteousness) were completely lost. However, it is biblically unwarranted to say that the image of God in man has been totally eradicated by the Fall. We cannot restrict our concept of the image of God to the original righteousness that was entirely lost by the fall (true knowledge, righteousness and holiness of the truth), but must also consider all elements which belong to the natural constitution of man.

There are ontological elements of the image of God that belong to man as man, such as his personality, rationality and moral responsibility. The faculties of his soul: his mind, his will, his affections and his conscience still remain after the fall, though terribly defaced and totally depraved. The law of God has not been erased from his conscience (Rom. 2:14-15). He still retains a sense of deity in his heart. These are resemblances of the communicable attributes[125] of God that still reside in man after the Fall. All this is delineated in Romans 1-2 where Paul asserts the condemnation of fallen man. The ontological image is why man is guilty of his sin and without excuse before God. So in the wider sense, the ontological sense, the image of God includes those elements that are natural and essential to the constitution of man.

It is true that man completely lost his original righteousness in the Fall; the moral rectitude in which he was originally endowed became totally depraved with an evil corruption that permeated his entire being and all the faculties of his soul (his intellect, his will and affections). However, man still remains man and therefore possesses a

---

[125] The incommunicable attributes of God are attributes that only God possesses; communicable attributes of God are attributes that humans possess to a degree. Communicable attributes are properties in man that bear analogy to God.

remnant of the image of God; a sense of deity is still inscribed upon his heart, and he cannot escape it.

Let us now look at some biblical texts where man is still considered as having the image of God even after the Fall.

Old Testament Texts

Genesis 5:1-3

Genesis 5:1-3 This *is* the book of the generations of Adam. In the day that God created man, in the likeness of God made he him; [2] Male and female created he them; and blessed them, and called their name Adam, in the day when they were created. [3] And Adam lived an hundred and thirty years, and begat *a son* in his own likeness, after his image; and called his name Seth.

This text is a reminder that God made man in his likeness and is a statement of how the image of God passed to Adam's offspring. The Hebrew word for "likeness" is *demuwth* (דמות), which is the same term used in Gen. 1:26. The omission of the word *image* (צֶלֶם, tselem) is not significant, for these terms are used interchangeably in regards to the image of God and is sufficient by itself.[126]

This statement, occurring after the Fall, still speaks of Adam as someone who was made in the likeness of God. It would make no sense if Adam had completely lost the image of God. Further in v. 3, we are told that Adam begat his son, Seth, in his own likeness and after his image. It is implied that the image of God is now passed to Adam's posterity. Seth was made in the image of Adam, his father,

---

[126] In Gen. 5:3, there is a transposition of the order of the two terms, *image* and *likeness,* when compared to Gen. 1:26. The prepositions in the two phrases, "in" our image and "after" our likeness, are equally interchangeable. Some try to derive different meanings from the prepositions. But the two prepositions; "in" (ב) our image, and "after" (כ) our likeness are equally interchangeable as well.

while Adam was still the image bearer of God. The implication is that Seth is also the image bearer of God.[127]

Adam, who God created in his image and likeness, begat offspring in his own likeness and image. The propagation of the human race continues with man retaining the ontological image of God.

Genesis 9:5-6

Genesis 9:5-6 [5] And surely your blood of your lives will I require; at the hand of every beast will I require it, and at the hand of man; at the hand of every man's brother will I require the life of man. [6] Whoso sheddeth man's blood, by man shall his blood be shed: for in the image (צֶלֶם tselem) of God made he man.

The shedding of blood (murder) is forbidden because man is made in the image of God. The killing of man is the destruction of the image of God. This could not be said unless the divine image remained in the very nature of man. There is an inherent value in a man's life because he is made in the image of God. In this text, the sanctity of human life is underscored. The reason why murder is such a heinous crime and must be punished by death is because the image of God has been murdered. It is, therefore, a heinous offence against God. To kill the image of God is to do violence to God himself. The punishment is commensurate with the weight of the crime.[128] This teaches that man has a unique value, a value not attributed to any other of God's creatures. The justification for the extremity of capital punishment is due to the value of the victim, who is the image bearer of God.

---

[127] We can argue the same way for the transmission of Adam's sinful and corrupt nature being passed to Seth.

[128] Kenneth A. Matthews, *Genesis*, p. 404.

James 3:9

James 3:9 ⁹ Therewith bless we God, even the Father; and therewith curse we men, which are made after the similitude of God.

The context of Js. 3:9 is a discussion of the sins of the tongue. James is pointing out an inconsistency between praising God and cursing men; he is condemning the duplicity of the tongue. Praising God with one side of your mouth and cursing your neighbor with the other side. We bless God with praise, thanksgiving and worship, but we curse his image.

To curse men made in the likeness of God, is to curse God. To curse means to utter curses against someone; it is to show detest, abhorrence and contempt. It is evil because it is directed against a human being made in the *similitude of God*. The word translated "similitude" (ὁμοίωσις) means "likeness" and is the counter part of *demuwth* (דְּמוּת) in the Hebrew. James is teaching that the image of God is still present in man and is to be respected. To slander someone is to slander God himself. To attack our fellow man, curse or violate him in some way is an attack against God, who made man in his image and likeness.

The Grk participle *"made"* is γίνομαι, which means "to become." It is in the perfect tense denoting past action with an abiding result. Man is described as being made in the likeness of God at some point in time (creation) and continues to bear that likeness. Again, this passage would make no sense unless fallen man still bears the image of God. What ever the Fall has done to man, it has not totally obliterated the image of God, for the image constitutes his very being.

1 Corinthians 11:7-9 ⁷ For a man indeed ought not to cover *his* head, forasmuch as he is the image and glory of God: but the woman is the glory of the man. ⁸ For the man is not of the woman; but the woman of the man. ⁹ Neither was the man created for the woman; but the woman for the man.

We need to start at v. 3 to get the context of vv. 7-9. Here, we find the order of relationships. "Head" is used as the figurative expression of authority.

1 Corinthians 11:3 ³ But I would have you know, that the head of every man is Christ; and the head of the woman *is* the man; and the head of Christ *is* God.

Christ has authority over man, man over woman, and God over Christ. From this proposition, practical consequences are deduced in the following verses. Just as Christ is the head of every man and of the church, the husband is the head of the wife. Also, as Christ submits to God the Father, so the wife submits to her husband. This is based upon the created order of being made in God's image, "male and female, made he them."

In vv. 7-9, Paul is teaching on the order of the church and worship. He takes us back to the opening chapters of Genesis to establish the unchanging basis of this order; the fact that man was created in the image and glory of God.[129] Although the image of God is only mentioned in v. 7, the entire argument of this passage (vv. 3-11) is based upon the created image of God in man, and in particular, the creation mandate given to man in the marriage relationship to have dominion over the earth (Gen. 1:26-28).

The apostle Paul reprehends the church for the manner in which the women prayed and prophesied in the assembly without a head covering. He also reproves men for praying with their head covered. This was a reversal of the created order of God. By this behavior, the

---

[129] The Grk word for "image" is εἰκών, which is the LXX translation of the Hebrew *tselem* in Gen. 1:26-27.

women were taking a position of headship, and the men were taking a position of submission. Paul rebukes them by arguing from the Genesis account where man was created in the image of God, the ontological image that still remains in man.

When God created man in his image, he created man in the marriage relationship. We read in Gen. 1:27, "So God created man in his own image, in the image of God created he him; male and female created he them." The cultural mandate to have dominion over the earth was given in the context of the marriage relationship. We read in Gen. 1:28, "And God blessed them, and God said unto them, Be fruitful, and multiply, and replenish the earth, and subdue it: and have dominion over the fish of the sea, and over the fowl of the air, and over every living thing that moveth upon the earth." Here, God addresses them as a couple and speaks to them in the context of the marriage relationship. The five dominion imperatives of Gen. 1:28 begin with, "And God blessed *them*, and God said unto *them*."

Man's dominion over the earth was to reflect God's sovereignty. God appointed man to represent his authority on earth. Man was to exercise dominion over the earth in the context of the marriage relationship, and within the marriage relationship, man was specifically to have dominion over the woman (Gen. 3:16). The man was the representative of God in dominion. He was the glory of God, and the woman, as the apostle Paul tells us, was the glory of man (1 Cor. 11:7).

Dominion over the earth was the manifestation of the image of God in man. This is the biblical basis for the priority of the male over the female in the marriage relationship, and as Paul teaches in the text, it is the basis for the order of the church as well. It is God's creative order. Obviously, it was never intended to be a tyrannical or despotic rule, treating the woman as a slave. It was an order designed to glorify God.

The four texts discussed above (Gen. 5:1-3; 9:5-6; Js. 3:9; 1Cor. 11:7-9) are sufficient proof that the image of God has not been completely eradicated by the Fall. The ontological image of God still remains in man, which constitutes his very nature and essence. This is the broad view of the image of God in man.

Apologetical Implications of the Broad View

Sensus divinitatus

Sensus divinitatus is Latin for "sense of deity." Every man possesses an inescapable sense of deity inscribed upon his heart, by virtue of being created in the image of God. Man possesses a general knowledge of God that is innate and intuitive within him (Rom 1:18-21). A sense of deity has been implanted within the human mind of all men. It is stamped on man's innermost being and inscribed upon his heart. Because man was created a morally rational creature as God's image bearer, he morally apprehends the manifestations of God in his works of creation and providence. He understands the moral character and judgment of God against sin. This is not an acquired knowledge of God; it is something man is born with and is part of his very being. It is impossible for man to separate himself from the reality of his own constitution. No man can escape knowing God. Apologetics is an appeal to the knowledge of God that natural man already possesses but habitually denies (Rom. 1:18).

Natural Revelation

Natural revelation is God's revelation of himself in nature. All of created reality is revelational of the nature of God. It is the universal revelation to all men. However, we must note it is a general revelation of God in the sense that it cannot save man (for that takes the special revelation of the gospel, which is revealed in Scripture).[130] Yet, it is a

---

[130] God has revealed himself to man in two forms of revelation: general (natural) and special (supernatural). Special revelation is that communicated to man

sufficient revelation of God to render all men without excuse before God.

Romans 1:18-32 is a pivotal passage for understanding the doctrine of natural revelation because it explains the unbeliever's certain knowledge of God acquired and apprehended through the witness of creation. God has revealed himself to all men through natural revelation (Rom. 1:18-32). Indeed, all men have a general knowledge of God. Scripture teaches that all men understand God's divine attributes, his moral character and judgment. Paul says in Rom. 1:20, "these things are clearly seen." All people have enough knowledge of God to render them guilty without excuse. Whether they admit it or not doesn't change anything. All people know God, if they didn't, they would have an excuse, but Rom. 1:20 teaches that all men are without an excuse.

There are two aspects of natural revelation: *external* and *internal.* The *external* aspect of natural revelation is the acquisition of a general knowledge of God through the external works of creation. The *internal* aspect of natural revelation is the apprehension of this general knowledge of God by the very constitution of man's nature as the image bearer of God, an image that has been defaced but not eradicated.

Romans 1:19 Because that which may be known of God is manifest in them; for God hath shewed *it* unto them.

---

by God in a supernatural manner, either directly to man, through a prophet or messenger. Scripture is the special revelation of God. The two forms of revelation do not stand next to each other as two separate means of revelation. For the God that reveals himself in Scripture is the same God that reveals himself in nature. The two forms of revelation are complementary. They presuppose and supplement each other. However, there is no knowledge of grace in natural revelation. Only Scripture reveals the grace of God through the knowledge of his Son in the gospel. Natural revelation was never meant to function by itself. The light of Scripture is the superior light that lightens every other light. Scripture is the final authority for interpreting the light of nature.

In Rom. 1:19, Paul says the knowledge of God is manifest "in them" (ἐν αὐτοῖς), i.e., in the hearts and minds of all men, within the very constitution of their nature. In the Grk, the phrase "of God" (τοῦ θεοῦ) is an objective genitive, meaning God is the object of our knowledge. It is not a nebulous and hazy knowledge, it is clear and manifest *in* them. Rom. 2:14-15 teaches that all men are endowed with a moral character by virtue of being created in the image of God. The work of God's law is written on the heart. It is the basis of man's moral character and bears witness to his conscience. Man cannot charge God with hiding himself. Presuppositional apologetics assumes that all men have an inherent knowledge of God instilled through natural revelation.

Point of contact

The point of contact in apologetics is the common ground the believer shares with the unbeliever. Natural revelation and the *sensus divinitatus* assure us that every man is in contact with the truth of God. The apologist must appeal to man's innate sense of deity (Rom. 1:18-21, 32; 2:14-15). Man was created as the image bearer of God and thus he cannot escape the face of God. Deep down in the heart of man, he knows that he is a creature of God and a culpable creature at that. This is precisely what the apostle Paul appealed to in his address to the Areopagus (Acts 17:22-31). He employed an obvious point-of-contact; the image of God in man and his innate sense of deity. Man is inherently and inalienably a religious being.

Man is a creature made in God's image and living in God's created world. All men, believers and non-believers alike, have in common the world created, governed and revealed by God. Therefore, the common ground is all of God's creation. There is an ever-present common ground between the believer and the unbeliever. This common ground is God's ground. As Creator, God has defined the meaning of all things. He is the ultimate interpreter of all things. Therefore, as creatures made in the image of God, we are to think God's thoughts after him. Any fact or observation can be used as a point-of-contact. For all facts are created facts, not brute facts, but created facts, defined by God and given meaning by God. This is our common ground with the unbeliever.

Creator-creature Relationship

As the image bearer of God, man was created in a relationship to God. He lives in an inescapable Creator-creature relationship. This relationship defines man's reality and existence. The reality of this relationship is indelibly inscribed upon his heart.

The Creator-creature relationship is the absolute basis for all reality. It is the basis for all knowledge and determinative of all morality. Presuppositional apologetics makes this distinction; evidentialism does not.

The Creator-creature relationship establishes the absolute coherency of the Christian's worldview.[131] There are three essential elements that comprise a worldview: metaphysics, epistemology and ethics. A worldview is only valid when all three elements are coherent. Christian theism is the only coherent worldview; all others are incoherent and contradictory. The essence of the unregenerate's worldview assumes man to be autonomous and epistemologically a law unto himself. Natural man seeks to be his own ultimate reference point. He seeks to interpret the universe without reference to God, making himself the final authority for all knowledge and truth. The unbeliever lives in a world of false assumptions and false pretentions. His reasoning ends in futility because he will not admit to the Creator-creature distinction.

The method of presuppositional apologetics is to contrast the Christian worldview with the unbeliever's worldview in order to expose the irrationality of unbelieving thought. The antithesis of the

---

[131] See Chapter 10: *The Necessity of the Creator-creature Distinction for a Coherent Worldview*.

Creator-creature worldview must be pushed against the unregenerate's worldview. This was the method of the apostle Paul on Mar's Hill when he declared the true God to the Areopagus council and put man in an inescapable relationship to the Creator, "…Whom therefore ye ignorantly worship, him declare I unto you. God that made the world and all things therein, seeing that he is Lord of heaven and earth, dwelleth not in temples made with hands" (Act 17:23-24).

A worldview devoid of the Creator-creature relationship is a worldview of insanity. It is a fictitious worldview that has no grasp on reality. To deny the Creator-creature relationship is to deny reality all together.

Revelational Epistemology

By virtue of being created in the image of God, man is in an inescapable relationship to his Creator. As Creator, God is absolutely independent of his creation. He is the self-existent Being. As creature, man is wholly dependent on God for his existence and being. Accordingly, by virtue of creature-hood, man is entirely dependent upon God for all knowledge and truth. Man's knowledge is necessarily derivative of God and must replicate God's thinking in order to know reality. We live in a God-created and God-defined universe. Every fact is a created fact that has been defined by God. As creatures we are to give the same meaning to everything that God has given to it; we are to think God's thoughts after him. This is our moral obligation. To think autonomously, i.e., to assume man's ability to reason as ultimate, is immoral and sinful. It is an attempt to redefine meaning apart from God and his infallible word.

As Creator, God is self-revealing and we can only know him as he has revealed himself to us. Therefore, Scripture (God's revelation) is the basis for all knowledge and truth. Revelational epistemology holds God's revealed truth as absolutely necessary and foundational for any understanding or knowledge. The Christian apologist must presuppose the word of God as the ultimate standard for truth. The Creator's revelation to man is the voice of absolute, unquestionable authority, and his word must be the standard by which we judge all things and the very starting point of all our thinking.[132] The word of God is the final and ultimate court of appeal. Scripture is the absolute criterion of truth. We must renounce all intellectual self-sufficiency and all human autonomy that claims neutrality in thought and does not recognize the creature's dependence upon God the Creator for true knowledge and understanding.

THE NARROW VIEW: THE MORAL IMAGE OF GOD

Having first considered the broad sense (ontological) of the image of God in man, we now turn to the narrow sense, which is commonly referred to as the *moral image* of God. In man's original state, Adam was created righteous. Man, as he came from the Creator's hand, was not created in a state of moral neutrality or innocence, but was endowed with a positive righteousness.

Let us first consider Gen. 2:7, which is a more detailed account of Gen. 1:26-27:

> **Genesis 2:7** And the LORD God formed man *of* the dust of the ground, and breathed into his nostrils the breath of life; and man became a living soul.

In the above text, we note that the origin of Adam is distinct from Eve. God breathed "the breath of life" directly into the nostrils (face) of Adam, in a manner corresponding to the nature and character of God, and man became a living soul. Gesenius' Hebrew-Chaldee Lexicon defines "breath of life" (*neshamah*, נְשָׁמָה) as man's soul. By an omnipotent, creative act, God infused a living soul into Adam. Adam's soul was created *ex nihilo* (out of nothing) by a unique and immediate act of God.

---

[132] G. Bahnsen, *Always Ready*. Texarkana, AR: Covenant Media Foundation, 1996, p. 25.

From this we understand that the principle seat of the image of God in man is the human soul. With the same breath God breathed into Adam a living soul, he breathed into him a morally righteous soul. Adam was created with a sinless, moral rectitude that controlled all the faculties of his soul: his intellect, will, emotions and conscience. God made man morally righteous, possessing a righteousness that corresponded to the moral character of God. In Adam's original state, before the Fall, he enjoyed perfect communion with God and lived in blessed harmony with his Creator in sinless obedience. This original state of man, known as *original righteousness*, constituted the moral image of God in man.

The primary content of the image of God in man was the original righteousness that God endowed him with. Sadly, when man fell in the Garden, he totally lost the moral image of God and entered into a state of *original sin*. This state was a state of total depravity.

In this section, we will look at some of texts of Scripture relating original righteousness to the moral image of God in man. It is divided into three parts; original righteousness *created*, *lost* and *restored*.

Original Righteousness Created

Ecclesiastes 7:29

Ecclesiastes 7:29 Lo, this only have I found, that God hath made man upright; but they have sought out many inventions.

Lo, this only have I found. Solomon is quite certain about this and he wants us to contemplate it as a matter of great importance. Lo, behold, this have I found! This one thing I know for sure. He had been searching out the wickedness of man and this is the conclusion of his investigations.

God hath made man upright; but they have sought out many inventions. Here is a contrast between man's original created state and man's fallen state. It is contrast between the way man was created, and the way he is now, which is a state of total depravity and wickedness. It is a contrast between what God originally did, and what man subsequently did. Solomon traces back the source of man's inherent wickedness to the Fall and considers how man was originally made.

God hath made man upright. Man was originally created righteous. Of the various synonyms for "man" in the Hebrew language, the one used here is *'adam* (אָדָם); *it* refers here to our first parents, Adam and Eve, from which all mankind has descended. It refers to them before the Fall in their original state.

The Hebrew word for "upright" is *yashar* (יָשָׁר). The word means straight or level, but when used with regards to people it means righteous, i.e., morally straight and conforming to the will and law of God. In our text, it denotes the possession of a positive righteousness.

Being *upright* presupposes law, a moral standard to conform to. Adam was made in conformity to the law of God. His power and ability to conform to God's moral law was not supernatural, but rather was his natural created state. He delighted in the will of God; it was his joy and happiness. He walked with God, and communed with God in righteousness. The virtue and moral integrity of Adam was entirely agreeable to the holy, just, and good law of God. The moral virtue that regulated the faculties of his soul had no defects. Adam was created sinless with a positive righteousness.

When we speak of the law, we are not just speaking of the verbal prohibition to eat of the tree of the knowledge of good and evil, but there was an internal law written upon Adam and Eve's heart. This law would later be codified on Mt. Sinai with Moses.

In Rom 2:14-15, we are told that works of the law are written on man's heart:

> **Romans 2:14-15** [14] For when the Gentiles, which have not the law, do by nature the things contained in the law, these, having not the law, are a law unto themselves: [15] Which shew the work of the law written in their

hearts, their conscience also bearing witness, and *their* thoughts the mean while accusing or else excusing one another.

This is a description of man's state after the Fall. The Gentiles who did not have the written law of God as the Jews did, but had an internal witness of God's law in their heart. The conscience bears witness of being lawbreakers by convicting and condemning. Because of the Fall, living in obedience to the law of God is no longer man's natural state; man now lives in a state of continual conviction of sin, with a conscience that is disapproved of God. This is inescapable. Man cannot rid himself of the perpetual witness of the moral character of God written internally on his heart.

Not so with Adam's original state. If the work of the law is written in the heart of fallen man, then how much more was this internal witness to Adam before the Fall. As God's image bearer, perfect obedience to God's law was natural to Adam's originally created state. The virtue and moral rectitude of his soul was made in perfect harmony with the will of God; he was fully capable of doing the will of God, and to do God's will was his delight and happiness. Adam was made morally upright. This is what we call *original righteousness*.

God made man upright. The Hebrew verb for "made" is *'asah* (עָשָׂה); in the Qal perfect tense, it denotes completed action. Adam did not acquire his righteousness, nor was it an imputed righteousness; he was made righteous. God himself testified to the perfection of his work in Gen. 1:31. After God completed the sixth day of creation with his masterpiece, making man in his image, he surveyed and evaluated his work and said it was exceedingly good! In the Hebrew, it is expressed as an absolute superlative – Lo, behold, it was exceedingly good!

The second part of Eccl. 7:29 speaks about the fall of man and how he ruined himself. *But they sought out many inventions.* Man did not remain in the original state God made him, but sought out inventions, which morally ruined him. This refers to the terrible defacement of the image of God in man.

Original Righteousness Lost:
The Defacement of the image of God

In Gen. 2:16-17, God gave Adam a probationary command to test him. Here, Adam received his first lesson on the fundamental relationship between the Creator and the creature. It was one of obedience:

> **Genesis 2:16-17** [16] And the LORD God commanded the man, saying, Of every tree of the garden thou mayest freely eat: [17] But of the tree of the knowledge of good and evil, thou shalt not eat of it: for in the day that thou eatest thereof thou shalt surely die.

With this commandment, Adam became acutely aware of his moral obligation to obey his Creator. From the very beginning man was under God's authority and God's law. He was never autonomous.

The probationary commandment of Gen. 2:16-17 has two clauses: a permissive clause and a prohibitive clause. "Of the tree of the garden thou mayst freely eat" is the permissive clause. It articulates God's generous and bountiful provision for man. You may eat freely – an emphatic expression of God's generosity. It is an infinitive absolute (אָכֹל תֹּאכֵל); "Eating, you may eat!" The prohibitive clause is "But of the tree of the knowledge of good and evil thou shalt not eat." The prohibitive command was given to test man's moral relationship to his Creator. This commandment expresses the absolute right of the Creator over man.

The prohibition is stated to Adam in the strongest terms. It stands in stark contrast to God's gracious provision to freely eat of the garden. The normal Hebrew word order is verb-subject-object, but here the object "tree" is placed first in the word order making it emphatic. The preposition "from it" stresses the object, which is the tree. Tree!-from it!-thou shalt not eat. The prohibitive command is very emphatic.

The penalty threatened is emphatic as well. It is also an infinitive absolute construction (מוֹת תָּמוּת) – dying, you will die! The emphasis by repetition is very strong; it intensifies the consequence of disobedience and reinforces the certainty of it. *Thou shalt surely die!* Death will result in the day you eat of the tree of the knowledge of good and evil.

Death was threatened as the punishment for disobedience. And as we all know, Adam rebelled and disobeyed the explicit commandment not to eat of the tree of the knowledge of good and evil. Death was God's judgment upon the rebellion of Adam. Death in its fullest extent: *physical, spiritual,* and *eternal.* Death became the curse of the human race.

Romans 5:12 [12] Wherefore, as by one man sin entered into the world, and death by sin; and so death passed upon all men, for that all have sinned.[133]

Physical Death

Physical death was one of the consequences of the Fall. The day Adam sinned was the day his body received its death-wound, and became mortal. Although physical death did not occur on the very day Adam ate the forbidden fruit, his body began to decay and daily advanced towards physical death. Death overtook his body in sickness and aging, which ultimately resulted in physical death (Gen. 5:5).

Spiritual Death

When Adam ate of the forbidden fruit, he died spiritually. Immediately, he was alienated from God, and cut off from communion with God. He instantly lost his *original righteousness.* The moral rectitude that dominated his heart, and regulated all the faculties of his soul was lost. His love to God vanished. His original desire to serve and obey God vanished. All at once, Adam became dead in sin and wholly corrupt. He became spiritually dead. Although

---

[133] The verb for *sinned* is in the aorist tense (ἥμαρτον) and points back to the sin of Adam.

Adam did not die physically for 930 years after the Fall, he did die spiritually the very moment he sinned.

This corruption extended to all the faculties of Adam's soul. His entire nature became depraved. His conscience condemned him, becoming calloused and deceitful. His understanding was darkened, and the noetic effects of sin overtook his intellect. All his affections and emotions were alienated from God. The sinful desires of his body ruled over his mind. He became a bond slave to sin. Thus, spiritual death passed from Adam to all his descendants.

This horrible defacement of the image of God in man is commonly called *original sin*. It is *original* because it is derived from Adam, the original progenitor of the entire human race. Because of the sin of Adam, all his descendants have inherited a sinful nature and are born spiritually dead (Ps. 51:5; 58:3). This sinful state and condition has passed from Adam to all his posterity. *There is none that doeth good, no, not one* (Ps 14:3; 53:2; Rom. 3:12).

Original sin consists of two elements: *original guilt* and *original corruption*. They are also referred to as the *immediate* and *mediate* imputation of Adam's sin respectively. *Original guilt* or the *immediate* imputation of Adam's sin refers to the universal condemnation of man that resulted from the sin of Adam acting as our representative head. *Original corruption* or the *mediate* imputation of Adam's sin refers to Adam's corrupt nature that all men inherit. These two elements constitute the state man is born in, which is a state of spiritual death. They are the predominant parts of the defacement of the image of God in man.

Original Guilt

> **Romans 5:12-19** Wherefore, as by one man sin entered into the world, and death by sin; and so death passed upon all men, for that all have sinned: [13] (For until the law sin was in the world: but sin is not imputed when there is no law. [14] Nevertheless death reigned from Adam to Moses, even over them that had not sinned after the similitude of Adam's transgression, who is the figure of him that was to come. [15] But not as the

138

offence, so also *is* the free gift. For if through the offence of one many be dead, much more the grace of God, and the gift by grace, *which is* by one man, Jesus Christ, hath abounded unto many. [16] And not as *it was* by one that sinned, *so is* the gift: for the judgment *was* by one to condemnation, but the free gift *is* of many offences unto justification. [17] For if by one man's offence death reigned by one; much more they which receive abundance of grace and of the gift of righteousness shall reign in life by one, Jesus Christ.) [18] Therefore as by the offence of one *judgment came* upon all men to condemnation; even so by the righteousness of one *the free gift came* upon all men unto justification of life. [19] For as by one man's disobedience many were made sinners, so by the obedience of one shall many be made righteous.

Original guilt is the immediate imputation of Adam's sin that constitutes death for all men. Rom. 5:12-19 is a contrast between the federal headship of Adam and the federal headship of Christ. It is a contrast between man's condemnation by the imputation of Adam's sin, and justification by the imputation of Christ's righteousness. Death and condemnation were passed to all men by the sin of one. Justification and life are passed to "the many" by the righteousness of one. Both Adam and Christ acted as the federal representatives of man.

In v.12 Paul states, "Wherefore, as by one man sin entered into the world, and death by sin; and so death passed upon all men, for that all have sinned." Here, the apostle is referring to Adam and the Genesis account (Gen. 2:17 and 3:17-19). Clearly, there is a causal relationship between the one man, Adam, and the entrance of sin into the world. Adam was the cause of sin entering the world; sin invaded the human race through Adam. Man became guilty and condemned before God. Man's very nature became corrupt and depraved; he began to habitually commit sin. Hence, "death passed upon all men," i.e., death spread to all men. Because of one man's offence, death now reigns over the human race. As in Adam all sinned, so in Adam all die. Death is the result of Adam's sin that spread to all his posterity.

We note the phrase "For that all have sinned" (ἐφ᾽ ᾧ πάντες ἥμαρτον). The verb "sinned" is an aorist tense (ἥμαρτον·) referring

139

back to a specific point in time, a specific event in history (punctiliar action in time past). The very tense of the verb points to Adam's first transgression. When Adam sinned, we sinned. He acted as the federal head for the entire human race.

Furthermore, in the immediate context, Paul establishes beyond dispute that universal condemnation and death passed to all men by the one trespass of the one man Adam. Five more times in vv. 15-19 Paul asserts man's universal guilt and condemnation as grounded in and proceeding from the one trespass of the one man Adam. Death as the punishment of sin passed from Adam to all his descendants. Death and condemnation reign over all men because of the one sin of the one man Adam. Paul writes in 1 Cor. 15:22, "In Adam all die."

Therefore every person is born with original guilt by the immediate imputation of Adam's sin, who acted as the federal head for the entire human race.

Original Corruption

The second aspect of spiritual death, *original corruption*, is the inherent state of corruption that all human beings are born with. Eph. 2:1-5 describes the universal and natural state of man as spiritual death:

> **Ephesians 2:1-5** And you *hath he quickened*, who were dead in trespasses and sins; ² Wherein in time past ye walked according to the course of this world, according to the prince of the power of the air, the spirit that now worketh in the children of disobedience: ³ Among whom also we all had our conversation in times past in the lusts of our flesh, fulfilling the desires of the flesh and of the mind; and were by nature the children of wrath, even as others. ⁴ But God, who is rich in mercy, for his great love wherewith he loved us, ⁵ Even when we were dead in sins, hath quickened us together with Christ, (by grace ye are saved).

The above text describes man's natural state before conversion; it is a state of inherent corruption and death. In v. 1, Paul states that man is "dead in trespasses and sins." The adjective "dead" (νεκροὺς) describes man as a spiritual corpse. Two terms are used to vividly describe man's spiritual deadness: *trespasses* and *sins*. "Trespasses" (παραπτώμασιν) literally means "falling aside" and can refer to outward transgressions. "Sins" (ἁμαρτίαις) literally means "missing the mark" and is a more inclusive term denoting sin as an inherent principle in man. The two terms are used synonymously to give a full expression denoting a state of spiritual death. Spiritual death is the original corruption that passes to all mankind from the one sin of the one man Adam.

Paul asserts a real and present state of death. He is not talking about physical death, but spiritual death – the totality of man's soul is dead. In vv. 2-3, the apostle goes on to characterize the spiritually dead state of natural man. They "walked according to the course of this world." They walked in sin; they were surrounded by it and they were clothed in it. They lived wickedly in subjection to Satan, "according to the prince of the power of the air." All people are born in subjection to Satan and are held captive by his will (2 Tim. 2:26). The spiritually dead are further described as "the children of disobedience." Man's natural state is to live in disobedience to God; it is a life governed by "the lusts of the flesh, fulfilling the desires of the flesh." "They are by nature the children of wrath." They are enemies of God and the objects of his wrath. This describes the universal condition of natural man; it is an inherent depravity characterized by spiritual death.

Negatively, original corruption is the loss of original righteousness, the loss of the image of God in the narrow sense. As a consequence of the Fall, man lost the moral integrity that regulated all the faculties of his soul. *Positively*, original corruption is an inherent depravity, the total corruption of man's nature. Man is born with an inclination to evil, an inherent disposition to sin. This corruption has been passed to all men by natural generation, i.e., through natural procreation. A radical corruption of man's moral and spiritual nature has been transmitted to man from his mother's womb (Ps. 51:5). It is a fatal defect. Man is a slave to sin and entirely unable to deliver himself from its bondage and corruption. All, without any exception, are defiled from birth and infected with it.

Finally, there are two aspects of *original corruption* to consider: *total depravity* and *total inability*. Total depravity deals with the pervasive character of original sin. This inherent corruption extends to every part of man's nature, to all the faculties and powers of the soul. It is a morally corrupt state, a wholesale corruption of the heart (Mk. 7:21-23; Gen. 6:5; Job 14:4; Jer. 17:9; Jn. 5:42; Rom. 7:18-19; Eph.4:17-19; Tit. 1:15-16). The other aspect is total inability. As a result of the fall, every person is born into a state of spiritual inability, unable to do anything spiritually good. Natural man, unregenerate man, cannot do, say or think anything that meets God's approval. He is unable to love God, to live a life pleasing to God or do anything to merit his favor. He has absolutely no ability to turn to God in faith and repentance. Man's *will* is spiritually impotent; he possesses a fixed bias in his will against God (Jn. 5:40; 6:44). His *mind* is spiritually blind and completely unable to understand spiritual things (1 Cor. 2:14). After the Fall, the image of God in man was defaced to point that it left man spiritually dead and spiritually impotent.

Eternal Death

As a consequence of the Fall, man not only died physically and spiritually, but eternally as well. Eternal death is the culmination and completion of spiritual death.[134] It is the eternal punishment of sin. The eternal punishment of sin is due to the entire fallen race of Adam. All are under the sentence of condemnation and are liable to the fury of God's wrath. Only those who are covered in the blood of Christ, who are clothed in the righteousness of Christ and justified by faith, will escape eternal death.

---

[134] L. Berkhof, *Systematic Theology*, p. 261.

The justice of God is glorified in the execution of judgment. God is just, and therefore the punishment of sin must be exacted. All the demands of God's law must be fully satisfied.

Eternal death will occur at the end of world, at the return of Christ and the resurrection; there will be a Day of Judgment. There will be a resurrection of life and a resurrection of damnation. Christ will return as Judge, for all judgment has been given unto the Son (John 5:22). At the resurrection of damnation, the bodies of wicked men will come forth from their graves, reuniting with their souls in order to be destroyed in hell and punished with an everlasting destruction. Every person "shall give account thereof in the day of judgment" (Matt. 12:36). The wicked shall be cast into hell to be punished forever.

When we try to contemplate hell and eternal damnation we are very limited. Man cannot comprehend with his finite mind the magnitude and intensity in which the wicked will be punished. Hell is spoken of as a "furnace of fire" (Matt. 13:42), an "unquenchable fire" (Mk. 9:44), an "everlasting fire" (Matt. 18:8; 25:41) and a "lake of fire" (Rev. 20:14-15) into which the wicked are cast. This describes unspeakable torture of a magnitude that simply is incomprehensible.

In summary, the terrible defacement of the image God in man was the consequence of the Fall. Death was God's judgment upon the rebellion of Adam, which has passed to all his posterity. It is death in its fullest sense: physical, spiritual and eternal.

Original Righteousness Restored

The New Testament teaches the restoration of the image of God in man through God's sovereign work of salvation in Christ Jesus. The content of the moral image of God can be elucidated from specific passages that present salvation as God's restoration of man's nature from his fallen state in the work of regeneration, sanctification and glorification. If we examine these passages from the N.T., we will get a clearer understanding of what the original moral image of God was.

In the N.T., we find a contrast between the old man (unregenerate man) and the new man (regenerate man). The old man is crucified (Rom. 6:6),[135] and the believer is created anew in Christ Jesus as the new man. In the work of salvation, God restores, repairs and renews his image in fallen sinful man. Accordingly, it is logical to conclude that the image of God, which was lost by the fall, must be the same as that which is restored by the new creation. The N.T. passages that speak of the restoration of the image of God necessarily imply the original integrity Adam possessed as the image bearer of God. Calvin argues, "That which holds the first place in the renovation of man, must have held the first place in the first creation."[136]

The two pivotal texts in the N. T. to consider are Col. 3:9-10 and Eph. 4:22-24. These texts identify three aspects of the moral image of God that are restored to fallen man in the work of salvation: *knowledge, righteousness* and *holiness.*

Colossians 3:9-10

Colossians 3:9-10 Lie not one to another, seeing that ye have put off the old man with his deeds; [10]And have put on the new *man*, which is renewed in knowledge after the image of him that created him.

Regeneration involves the renewing of God's image in true knowledge. The participles *"putting off"* (ἀπεκδυσάμενοι) and *"putting on"* (ἐνδυσάμενοι) literally denote putting off an old garment and putting on a new garment. They are used metaphorically to describe regeneration as putting off the old man, and putting on the new man. In the context, the old man is the unregenerate man and the new man

---

[135] The Grk verb for "crucified" (συνεσταυρώθη) is aorist tense and denote past action referring to an event, i.e., the work of God in regeneration when the sinner was converted.

[136] *Institutes*, 1.15.3.

is the regenerate man. Both participles are aorist tense, punctiliar in action, indicating events that have already taken place. What this means is that the new man replaces the old man; the two do not co-exist together.

The new man that is put on is described with some emphasis in the Grk; there is an attributive clause that takes on a second definite article known as a restrictive attributive construction. Restructured to show the emphasis, it might read like this, "The new man, I mean that which is renewed in knowledge after the image of him that created him!" "Renewed" (ἀνακαινούμενον) is a compound word derived from ἀνα (again) and καινός (new). The passive voice indicates that God is the one that renews. Further, as a present tense participle, it denotes continual *renewing*, which is a progressive process (progressive sanctification). The phrase, "after the image of him that created him" is a clear allusion to Gen.1:26-27 and the image in which man was originally created.

"Knowledge" is what is renewed and restored in fallen man. The noun "knowledge" (ἐπίγνωσιν) is anarthrous (no definite article) indicating the quality of knowledge; it is intensified with the preposition ἐπι, meaning full and comprehensive knowledge. This knowledge is a genuine and true spiritual knowledge of God and created reality. It is a knowledge resulting from an intellect that is governed by a renewed moral rectitude, a moral integrity that rules man's mind and thinking process, bringing every thought into captivity to the obedience of Christ. It is the knowledge of a believer's mind.

This knowledge is said to be "after the image of him that created him." True knowledge presupposes the Creator-creature distinction. God has created all things, defined all things and given meaning to all things. True knowledge is to give the same meaning to creation as God has, to think God's thoughts after him. True knowledge derives from the Creator.

In regeneration, the Christian has been transformed by the renewing of his mind. Paul writes:

Romans 12:2 And be not conformed to this world: but be ye transformed (present imperative passive) by the renewing of your mind, that ye may prove what *is* that good, and acceptable, and perfect, will of God.

A transformed mind, a regenerate mind, is one that discerns the will of God: the good, acceptable and perfect will of God. This describes a full, living and practical knowledge of God. The spiritual nature of this knowledge regulates man's will and affections in order to walk with God in obedience to his law. The body is no longer controlled by sinful lusts and appetites, but by a regenerate mind-set. Christianity is not an emotional religion of feelings, but is an intelligent walk with God. True knowledge is the effect of moral renovation; it is the effect of being restored to the image of God.

In regards to moral image of God in man, we conclude that Adam was originally created with true knowledge of God and his will, and this understanding dominated the faculties of his soul. This knowledge has been and is being restored to the believer in the work of salvation (regeneration, sanctification and glorification)

Ephesians 4:22-24

Ephesians 4:22-24 [22] That ye put off concerning the former conversation the old man, which is corrupt according to the deceitful lusts; [23] And be renewed in the spirit of your mind; [24] And that ye put on the new man, which after God is created in righteousness and true holiness.

In Eph. 4:22-24, we find the same contrast between the old man (unregenerate man) and the new man (regenerate man). It is a very close parallel to Col. 3:9-10 and we should expect Eph. 4:22-24 to express the same thought. Again, "putting on the new man" is a description of regeneration. The parallel passages differ only in that one is more concise than the other. The "knowledge" mentioned in Col. 3:10, which is the effect of being restored to the image of God, is further elaborated in Eph. 4:24 to include righteousness and holiness.

The same verbs "to put on" and "to put off" (ἐνδύω and ἀποτίθημι) are used. However, in this passage, the verbs are aorist infinitives of result, which also denotes something that has already taken place. The two verbs are not imperatives as some translations have it, but rather express result.[137] The verb "to put on" (ἐνδύω), which is the same term used in Col. 3:10, has the meaning of clothing oneself, like putting on a garment. Likewise, the verb "to put off" (ἀποτίθημι) means to put off as one puts off clothing. In both texts, putting off the old man and putting on the new man are described as definitive acts. The Christian is a person who has irrevocably put off the old self and put on the new self (definitive sanctification).[138] Putting on the new man presupposes putting off the old man.

Consider v. 23, which is sandwiched in between putting off the old man and putting on the new man. *Be renewed in the spirit of your mind.* The verb "renewed" (ἀνανεοῦσθαι) is a present tense infinitive indicating continuous renewal of the mind. Likewise, in Col. 3:10, "which is renewed in knowledge after the image of him that created him," is a present tense participle denoting a continual *renewing*. When Paul speaks of the image of God being restored, he uses present tenses, which denote continual action. The new man is in a process of being continually restored to the image of God. Restoring the image of God is a progressive act; it speaks of progressive sanctification.

And here we make a very important distinction between definitive sanctification and progressive sanctification. When Paul writes about putting off the old man and putting on the new man, he is referring to definitive sanctification, i.e., the result of regeneration where the bondage of sin has been broken through a radical breach with sin (the old man has been put off). It is a definitive act of God.

---

[137] See John Murray's *Principles of Conduct*. Grand Rapids, MI: Eerdmans Publishing Co., 2001, pp. 114-119 and references therein.

[138] A. A. Hoekema, *Created in God's Image*. Grand Rapids, MI: Eerdmans Publishing Co., 1994, p. 27.

When Paul speaks of renewing the image of God, he is speaking of the process of sanctification. It is important for us to keep this in mind.

Going back to Eph. 4:24, we note the phase, "which after God is created," or rather "*who* was created after God." This corresponds to "after the image of him that created him" in Col. 3:10, and connotes the origin of the "new man." It is God's sovereign work. Both parallel passages make a strong allusion to Gen. 1:26-27, where God created man in his image. As the first man bore God's image, so does the new man.

In Eph. 4:24, Paul teaches us the true nature of the original image of God in which man was created. According to this text, it specifically consists of righteousness and holiness, the moral rectitude that pervaded all the faculties of Adam's soul in his original state. Paul characterizes the new man as being created "in righteousness and holiness of the truth." This was the moral perfection in which Adam most resembled God before the Fall. It was a state of righteousness.

The Grk term translated "righteousness" is δικαιοσύνῃ. Paul typically uses this term forensically as a legal term referring to God's righteousness and moral standard. God's righteousness is revealed to man in terms of his moral law. Righteousness is conformity to his moral law and will. Being renewed in righteousness is being restored to the original integrity Adam was created in − a moral integrity that governed the faculties of his soul, enabling him to walk with God, to commune with God and to worship God in righteousness.

The Grk term translated "holiness" (ὁσιότης) denotes piety towards God. Holiness is God's supreme perfection; both old and new testaments speak more about God's holiness than any other attribute. Holiness is the attribute of attributes; all of God's attributes are holy attributes. The fundamental idea of holiness is separation. God is completely separate from all moral evil or sin. Holiness describes God's absolute purity. God can have no communion with sin because it is completely contrary to his nature. God hates and abhors sin. God is light, and in him is no darkness at all. (1 Jn 1:5).

Every believer is called to an obedient life that imitates the holiness of God. The renewed Christian is commanded in Scripture, "Be ye holy for I [God] am holy" (1 Pet. 1:16). Holiness is living a life that is consecrated, devoted and faithful to God, having no desires outside of God and opposed to everything that is evil. This was part of the original integrity Adam was endowed with. It was the original state of his heart. He was created with a holy heart, separated unto God.

Lastly, Paul says the new man is being "created in righteousness and true holiness." In the original Grk, "true" is not an adjective but a noun in the genitive case meaning "of the truth."[139] In the KJV, we find only holiness is associated with "the truth." However, "the truth" stands in the same relationship to righteousness as it does to holiness. A better translation would be "in true righteousness and holiness."

Both righteousness and holiness are products of the truth; they are effects of the truth. The truth is the dynamic of the Christian life. Truth is spiritual knowledge, which sanctifies the heart.

John 17:16-17 [16] They are not of the world, even as I am not of the world. [17] Sanctify them through thy truth: thy word is truth.

Nothing can be more detrimental to the life of a Christian than to devalue truth and doctrine, and to regard doctrine as some evil and cold intellectualism. Truth is the basis of our sanctification.

It is plain from these two passages (Col. 3:9-10; Eph. 4:22-24) that true knowledge, righteousness and holiness are the main elements of the image of God in which man was originally created. These elements constitute the narrow view of the image of God, which was lost in the Fall.

---

[139] Grammatically, "truth" is a subjective genitive.

APOLOGETICAL IMPLICATIONS OF THE NARROW VIEW

The Noetic Effects of Sin

The noetic effects of sin refer to the effects the Fall and the defacement of the image of God had on the mind and intellectual faculty of man. Natural man's intellectual faculty has become totally depraved as the result of the Fall. He is born with a false theory of knowledge, readily exchanges the truth of God for "the lie" (Rom. 1:25) and lives in a world of self-deception. His thoughts are continually overcome by moral corruption (Gen. 6:5) and his reasoning is futile (1 Cor. 3:20; Rom. 1:21). The Bible characterizes natural man's depraved mind as having his understanding darkened (Eph. 4:18; Rom. 1:21) and walking in the vanity of his mind (Eph. 4:17). He is noetically blind and his reasoning ability has become totally depraved because he is spiritually dead.

The reality of the noetic effects of sin correlates directly to the unbeliever's inability to truly know anything. Consequently, one's apologetic method must take into account the total depravity of man's intellectual faculty. Presuppositional apologetics assumes the universal corruption of the unregenerate's mind. All unbelieving thought is under the power of the noetic effects of sin.

No Neutrality

Because of the defacement of the moral image of God, unregenerate man has become hostile to God in his mind (Rom. 8:7). He has become destitute of the truth because of his hatred of God; he is an enemy of God in his mind (Col. 1:21). As a result of his enmity against God, man cannot be neutral in his thinking.

The apologist must not appeal to any alleged neutrality of man's reasoning. Natural man is incapable of reasoning objectively without bias against God. Intellectual neutrality is impossible because of the depravity of man's heart. The unbeliever will exalt human reasoning as ultimate and claim intellectual autonomy in order to interpret the universe without reference to God. Under this guise, he thinks he can be objective in the interpretation of facts and reality. All the while, he hates God, is an enemy of God and habitually suppresses the truth of God. He has his own worldview to interpret reality and it is hostile to God. Christians must refuse to think or reason according to the secular mind-set of the world and their apostate epistemology.[140] Neutrality is a delusion. To assume neutrality would be to give up the ultimate and absolute standard for all truth and reality – the word of God.

Man's Suppression of the Truth

Because man is depraved in his mind and hostile to God, he must necessarily suppress the truth that is revealed to him in natural revelation. Unbelieving thought will not admit to a Creator-creature relationship where man is responsible for his sin and must one day give an account for it. Thus, he constantly suppresses the truth in unrighteousness (Rom. 1:18).

Romans 1:18 For the wrath of God is revealed from heaven against all ungodliness and unrighteousness of men, who hold the truth in unrighteousness.

Heaven reveals that God is angry with the wicked and his wrath abides upon them. Unregenerate man must run from this reality at all cost. To do this, he must live in a world of self-deception, continually suppressing the truth of God. Paul describes man's reaction against the clear revelation of God, "Who hold the truth in unrighteousness." The Grk verb for "hold" is κατεχόντων and literally means to "hold down" (from κατα – down, and εχω – to hold). It is a deliberate act of suppressing the truth of God. Man is not neutral or innocent in the matter; he wickedly and intentionally suppresses God's revelation in

---

[140] Epistemology is the theory of knowledge. It seeks to answer questions about the nature of knowledge, what we know and how we know it. See Chapter 10, *The Necessity of the Creator-creature Relationship for a Coherent Worldview*, for a brief discussion on epistemology.

unrighteousness. The present tense of the verb "to hold down" denotes continual action. The unregenerate are habitually suppressing "the truth" (τὴν ἀλήθειαν) about the existence, nature and moral character of God. It is truth that has been clearly revealed to them in creation (Ps. 19:1-6; Rom. 1:18-21, 32).

Conflict of Worldviews

Understanding the antithesis between the regenerate and the unregenerate worldviews is fundamental to presuppositional apologetics. Because of the defacement of the image of God in man and the consequent noetic effects of sin, the unbeliever invents a worldview[141] that facilitates the suppression of the truth of God. The unbeliever's system of thought is hostile to God. It is a worldview characterized by futile reasoning (Rom. 1: 21) that exalts itself against the knowledge of God (2 Cor. 10:5). Unregenerate man deliberately abandons the Creator-creature relationship in his presuppositions and makes himself autonomous, exalting human reasoning as ultimate. His worldview is necessarily antithetical to the Christian's worldview.

There is an irreconcilable antithesis between the regenerate and the unregenerate mind-sets. It is a clash between two completely different worldviews; two different sets of presuppositions are in collision with each other. One submits to the authority of God's word as a presuppositional commitment and the other doesn't. The two belief systems are irreconcilable because their basic assumptions differ. Both are totalitarian in nature. The Christian apologist must identify the utter epistemological futility of the unbeliever's reasoning and seek to expose it. The argument must be on the presuppositional level.

In the final analysis, the unbeliever must renounce his system of thought; his presuppositions must be altered. His mindset and

---

[141] A worldview is defined as the sum of one's presuppositions, which provide the framework to view and interpret the world and all reality. See Chapter 10, *The Necessity of the Creator-creature Relationship for a Coherent Worldview.*

worldview must be brought into captivity to the obedience of Christ (2 Cor. 10:5).

Restoration to True Knowledge

Only by the regenerating work of the Holy Spirit can unregenerate man be restored to true knowledge. By the sovereign grace of God and through the operation of the Spirit, man's mind is renewed and able to come to the true knowledge of God and reality (Eph. 4:23-24; Col. 3:9-10). The blindness and darkness of man's mind are removed in the work of regeneration; the eyes are opened to see the knowledge of God as it is in Jesus Christ. The hatred and bias against God is definitively broken. Hence, Christ is realized as the fountain "in whom are hid all the treasures of wisdom and knowledge" (Col. 2:3). This is why apologetics is necessarily evangelistic and must never be separated from the context of the gospel.

Because the success of apologetics is dependent upon the sovereign work of God illuminating the mind and restoring true knowledge, the Christian apologist must realize he is only God's instrument. Human effort and the most brilliant arguments will be of no avail unless God blesses. Prayer must sanctify the work of apologetics. Faithful Christians will win the battle for the truth of God on their knees.

9. THE NOETIC EFFECTS OF SIN AND AN APOSTATE *POU STO*

INTRODUCTION

The phrase, *noetic effects of sin*, is a theological term commonly used in the field of apologetics. The Webster dictionary defines the adjective *noetic* as existing or originating in the intellect, i.e., that which pertains to the mind and apprehended by reason. The meaning of *noetic* is derived from the Grk noun νοετικος, which has reference to perceiving with the mind. The prepositional phrase "of sin" indicates a negative influence. Thus, the noetic effects of sin are the negative effects that influence and limit man's intellect and reasoning capacity.

In systematic theology, the noetic effects of sin are usually categorized within the locus of anthropology, under the subheading of original sin. The noetic effects of sin were introduced into the human race as a consequence of Adam's original sin and his rebellion against the Creator. The Bible characterizes unregenerate man's depraved mind as groping around in darkness (Acts 17:27), having his understanding darkened (Eph. 4:18), his mind at enmity against God (Rom. 8:7), suppressing the truth in unrighteousness (Rom. 1:18), exchanging the truth of God for *the lie* (Rom. 1:25), walking in the vanity of his mind (Eph. 4:17), vain in his imaginations (Rom. 1:21), an enemy of God in his mind (Col. 1:21), having vain deceit (Col. 2:8), having vain thoughts (1 Cor. 3:20), ignorant (Eph. 4:18); yet all the while seeking to exalt himself against the knowledge of God (2 Cor. 10:5). Sadly, every person is born into this world blinded by the noetic effects of sin, having inherited a corrupt nature from Adam.

The crucial issue in apologetics is the noetic effects of inherent sin. The extent of man's noetic corruption determines his ability to understand reality and have true knowledge. From the Scripture references mentioned above, we understand that the natural man's epistemology, i.e., his theory of knowledge, is necessarily biased against God.[142] He is naturally hostile to God in his mind (Rom. 1:18-32). Hence, it should also be apparent that one's apologetic method is determined by his view of the Fall of Adam and the consequent noetic effects. The extent and degree of Adam's fall correlates directly to man's ability to know truth and reality. If one truly adheres to the biblical doctrine of total depravity, then presuppositionalism is the only consistent apologetic method. There is no alternative method that gives noetic depravity its proper place. All other methods deny the depravity of the mind and allow the unbeliever to remain the ultimate authority for determining truth.

This chapter is organized in three related sub-headings: *The Nature of Man, An Apostate Pou Sto* and *The Necessity of Presuppositional Apologetics*. The divisions are arranged in a progressive order that build upon each other. *The Nature of Man* expounds on what the noetic effects of sin are and their extent. *An Apostate Pou Sto* elaborates on the presuppositional commitments of the non-Christian resulting from noetic effects of sin. Finally, *The Necessity of Presuppositional Apologetics* addresses the only way man can consistently defend the faith in light of the unregenerate's worldview as corrupted by the noetic effects of sin.

---

[142] See Chapter 10, *The Necessity of the Creator-creature Relationship for a Coherent Worldview*, for a discussion on epistemology.

THE NATURE OF MAN

Original Righteousness

In the beginning, man was created in the image and likeness of God. Adam was created in a state of original righteousness to have perfect fellowship with God. He was created sinless and morally righteous (not merely innocent). All the faculties of his soul were made in conformity to the splendor of God's moral law. There was no corruption in body, soul or mind. Adam had a perfect knowledge of God's law and his duty toward God. He had an exquisite knowledge of God's works and gave names to all the beasts of the field and the fowls of the air according to their respective natures (Gen. 2:19-20). Through true knowledge of God, Adam lived in blessed communion with his Creator. ·

Within the intended Creator-creature relationship, God's revelation was the basis for all meaning and the interpretation of all facts. God gave Adam special revelation and directly revealed his will and law to him. Adam was not created to live by natural revelation alone. He was created to interpret reality in subjection to the absolute authority of God's revelation. God's revelation was Adam's ultimate reference point, his *pou sto*, from which he was to know God, and interpret the world he was created in.

As a creature, Adam's knowledge was derived from God. His knowledge was subordinate to and dependent upon God's revelation. God never intended Adam to be independent in his knowledge because nothing in the universe existed independently of God. Every fact in the universe had meaning by virtue of its relationship to God. To Adam, every single fact revealed God as its Creator. Thus, Adam knew the true meaning of each fact because God had previously interpreted it and revealed it to him.

Further, in paradise Adam had true knowledge of the relation of all the particulars to God's created universe.[143] He named the animals according to their nature and the place God had given them in his universe. Therefore, Adam's knowledge was *receptively reconstructive*,[144] that is, he truly knew things by thinking God's thoughts after Him.

Original Sin

Sadly, our first parents did not continue in the state wherein they were created. Being seduced by the subtlety and temptation of Satan, they sinned by eating the forbidden fruit. By sinning, they fell from their original righteousness and communion with God and became spiritually dead and wholly defiled in all the parts and faculties of soul and body.[145] More specifically, Adam and Eve lost the image of God as a consequence of the Fall. I use the term "image of God" in the narrow sense, which is normally taken to mean true knowledge, righteousness and holiness. This sense of God's image is based upon the New Testament teaching that Christ came to restore the defaced image of God in sinners to true knowledge, righteousness and holiness (Col. 3:10; Eph. 4:24).

The restoration of true knowledge spoken of in Col. 3:10 gives us an idea of the extent of the noetic effects of original sin. The apostle Paul writes, "And have put on the new man, which is renewed in knowledge after the image of him that created him." This passage speaks of regeneration and progressive sanctification. The implication is that Adam was originally in possession of the knowledge of which the apostle speaks. When the natural man is regenerated, he is restored in principle unto true knowledge. This renovation is said to be εἰς ἐπίγνωσιν, not *in* knowledge, much less *by* knowledge, but *unto*

---

[143] C. Van Til, *An Introduction to Systematic Theology*. Presbyterian and Reformed Publishing Co., 1974 edition, p. 25.

[144] A term coined by Cornelius Van Til.

[145] *The Westminster Confession of Faith*, Chapter VI, I-II.

knowledge.[146] The preposition επι prefixed to the noun "knowledge" intensifies the meaning and denotes full knowledge. The knowledge intended here is not mere cognition, but full, accurate, living and practical knowledge; such knowledge as is eternal life, so that this word also includes what Eph. 4:24 expresses by "righteousness and holiness of the truth."[147] This knowledge was lost in the Fall. It was the knowledge man originally possessed as being created in the image of God, a true and full knowledge in concert with moral perfection and righteousness. Thus, in Adam's fallen state, he lost possession of the true knowledge of God.

Adam sought after knowledge and meaning independently of God. While knowing God, he rebelled against him and denied the absolute and ultimate authority of God's revelation. Adam set aside the law of his Creator and became a law unto himself. He wanted to be autonomous and sought to interpret the universe without reference to God. He wanted to be his own authority and determine for himself what was true and what was false, what was right and what was wrong. Adam wanted to be as God, to judge good and evil and to be the standard of truth.

The consequent noetic effects due to Adam's sin are far reaching. All of Adam's posterity, descending from him by ordinary generation, have inherited his corrupted nature and perverted epistemology. Since the Fall of Adam, "there is none that understandeth" (Rom. 3:11); all have been noetically blinded. None can come to a true knowledge of God. Only by the regenerating work of the Holy Spirit can man be restored to true knowledge.

Total Depravity

Total depravity is a theological term that designates the pervasive character of man's inherited corruption from original sin. It is usually

---

[146] C. Hodge, *Systematic Theology*. Eerdmans Publishing Co., 1989, **2**:99.
[147] Ibid, p. 100.

thought of as the first point of the five points of Calvinism. However, in systematic theology, it is found in the locus of anthropology within the sub-division of original sin. Total depravity is both negative and positive, the absence of original righteousness and the positive presence of evil. Berkhof defines it as an inherent corruption that extends to every part of man's nature, to all the faculties and powers of both soul and body; and there is no spiritual good, i.e., good in relation to God, in the sinner at all, but only perversion.[148] The noetic effects of sin comprise only one aspect of total depravity.

When dealing with the noetic effects of sin, it is important to understand that man's intellectual faculty cannot be separated from his will and affections. Sin does not reside in any one faculty but has its seat in the heart. From the heart, the influence and operations of sin spread to the intellect, the will and the affections; in short, the entire man.[149] Hodge states, "The whole man, soul and body, the higher as well as the lower, the intellectual as well as the emotional faculties of the soul, is affected by the corruption of our nature derived from our first parents."[150] If the heart is corrupt, then the whole soul in all it's powers are corrupt.

Scripture does not make a broad distinction between the understanding and the heart, which is commonly made in philosophy. Scripture speaks of thoughts of the heart, the intents of the heart and the eyes of the heart. When one separates the intellectual faculty from the heart, it necessary becomes separated from one's moral character. Thus, man's intellect is imagined as neutral or without morality. This is the device of evidential apologetics and cannot be tolerated. Nothing can be more repugnant to the teaching of the Bible than the dissociation of moral character from knowledge. We know that every

---

[148] L. Berkhof, *Systematic Theology*. Eerdmans Publishing Co., 1988, pp. 246-247.

[149] Ibid, p. 233.

[150] C. Hodge, *Systematic Theology*, 2: 255.

affection of a rational creature includes an exercise of cognitive faculties and every exercise of our cognitive faculties (in relation to moral and religious subjects) includes the exercise of our moral nature.[151]

To further expand on the biblical teaching of total depravity concerning the noetic effects of sin, I will use, in part, an outline of Thomas Boston.[152] I have not found a better organization. Boston elucidates the corruption of man's understanding in six points, but I have condensed it into four for simplicity. Man's mind is: 1) naturally overwhelmed with gross darkness, 2) naturally biased to evil and opposed to spiritual truths, 3) naturally prone to lies and falsehoods and 4) naturally high-minded.

1. Scripture teaches us that the natural man is blind and in terrible darkness concerning spiritual things. Man's fallen nature gives rise to a most obdurate blindness, stupidity and opposition to the things of God.[153] The apostle John tells us that natural man is in *darkness* and cannot comprehend the light (John 1:5). Further, we are told in John 3:19 that man loves darkness rather than light because his deeds are evil. The apostle Paul describes carnal understanding as being darkened because of the blindness of their heart (Eph. 4:18). He refers to Christians before their conversion as being in a state of darkness (Eph. 5:8). In Paul's address to the Areopagus, he speaks of the philosophers as groping around in darkness (Acts 17:27). The apostle Peter speaks of the unconverted as blind and unable to see afar off (2 Pet. 1:9). Christ himself tells us that if thy eye be evil, thy whole body shall be full of darkness (Matt. 6:23). Thus, it is observed from Scripture that natural man's understanding is overwhelmed in gross darkness. The unregenerate man understands neither what he says or what he

---

[151] Ibid, **2**: 256.

[152] T. Boston, *Human Nature and Its Fourfold State*. Associated Publishers and Authors Inc., Sovereign Grace, pp. 30-39.

[153] L. Boettner, *The Reformed Doctrine of Predestination*. Presbyterian and Reformed Publishing Co., p. 63.

affirms (1 Tim 1:7). Therefore, he can in no wise approach God by his intelligence and reason.[154]

2. *The mind of the natural man is biased to evil and in opposition to spiritual truths.* The words of the prophet Jeremiah are plain concerning the imaginations of the carnal mind, "they are wise to do evil, but to do good they have no knowledge" (Jer. 4:22). In Romans 1:23 we are told that the natural mind is biased toward idolatry seeking to change the glory of the uncorruptible God into images. It is plain that this idolatry can be manufactured in more subtle and refined forms in the minds of men. The Bible also speaks of the eyes being full of adultery that cannot cease from sin (2 Peter 2:14). Evil and corruption stick like glue to the natural man's mind. Further, there is a strong aversion to spiritual truth as is seen in Rom 1:18, which describes the natural man as suppressing the truth in unrighteousness. The natural man is opposed to the knowledge of God and exalts himself in his own imaginations against it (2 Cor. 10:5). Further, Rom. 8:7 tells us that the carnal (natural) mind is enmity against God; for it is not subject to the law of God, neither indeed can be.

3. *The mind of the natural man has a proneness to lies and falsehoods.* All men are addicted to lying as soon as they are born (Ps. 58:3). The natural man because of his hatred of God has changed the truth of God into *the lie* (Rom. 1:25), and he will live his whole life according to *the lie* unless God regenerates him and converts his life. Indeed, every man is a liar (Rom. 3:4) and lives a lie. Where does this habitual falsehood come from? It comes from Satan, for he is the father of it. It was the devil that lied to our first parents, "Ye shall not surely die." Man has embraced it ever since.

4. *Man is naturally high-minded.* He exalts himself above the knowledge of God (2 Cor. 10:5). Intellectual pride of man originated with our first parents when they sought to be like God, knowing good

---

[154] H. Hoeksema, *Reformed Dogmatics*. Reformed Free Publishing Ass., 1985, p. 270.

and evil (Gen. 3:5). Since then man has lusted after autonomy in his thinking and every way of man is right in his own eyes (Prov. 21:2). Thus, man by exalting his ability to understand abases God in his thinking. The thoughts of man are full of pride, bursting with vanity and overflowing with haughtiness.

Therefore, man in his natural state is totally depraved in his mental faculties and unable to come to a true knowledge of God. Unregenerate man is totally biased against God. His understanding has been saturated with corruption. It is "Ichabod," for the glory has departed from it, and it is incapable of understanding the things of God.

Absolute Depravity

Scripture teaches that unregenerate man is totally depraved in his mental faculties and capacity to reason. Total depravity means that human depravity extends to every faculty of the soul: intellect, will and emotions. However, we must be careful not to misrepresent total depravity as meaning man is as bad as he can be. If this were true, there would be no restraint on sin and man would be a veritable devil. Man's mind is not fully and exclusively bent upon evil.[155] Although man hates God and is at enmity with God, this enmity does not come to full expression in this life. Common grace restrains the operations of sin. A distinction must be made then between *total* depravity and *absolute* depravity. Van Til makes a distinction that depravity can be absolute in principle, but not in its full expression.[156]

As a creature, natural man still bears a remnant of the image of God. In our previous discussion of original sin, we used the narrow sense of the image of God. However, the image of God is not to be restricted to just the original knowledge, righteousness and holiness,

---

[155] C. Van Til, *Common Grace and the Gospel*. Presbyterian and Reformed Publishing Co., 1972 edition, p. 165.

[156] Ibid, pp. 164, 196-197,

which was lost by sin.[157] In a broader sense the image of God includes elements that belong to the natural constitution of man. Fallen man is still a rational and moral creature. It is this image of God that makes man different from the beasts. As created in the image of God, man has a rational and moral nature, which he could not lose without ceasing to be man.[158] This part of the image of God has been terribly defaced by sin, but still remains in man even after his fall into sin. In Scripture, fallen man is still represented as the image bearer of God (Gen. 9:6; 1 Cor. 11:7, Jas. 3:9). Therefore, it is unwarranted to say that man has absolutely lost the image of God. Man still retains the ontological[159] image of God.

Because natural man is an image bearer of God, there is a sense of deity indelibly engraved upon his mind.[160] The apostle Paul stresses this point in the first chapter of Romans. Natural man knows God in spite of his intellectual depravity, and to some extent recognizes God and the world as His creation. Van Til refers to this as the *revelational pressure* of God on man.[161] So definite and inescapable is this sense of deity that, try as he may, man cannot escape knowing God. All men unavoidably know God and themselves as creatures of God.

However, being marred by sin and being set wholly against God, man seeks to constantly suppress this sense of deity, to hold down the truth in unrighteousness (Rom. 1:18). He daily changes the truth of God into *the lie*. Knowing God, man refuses to keep God in his remembrance (Rom. 1:28). His very intellect is constantly devising schemes by which he thinks he may overthrow God.

---

[157] L. Berkhof, *Systematic Theology,* p. 204.

[158] Ibid, p. 204.

[159] Constituting the very being and essence of man.

[160] J. Calvin, *Institutes of the Christian Religion.* The Westminster Press, 1960, 1:4

[161] C. Van Til, *An Introduction to Systematic Theology.* Presbyterian and Reformed Publishing Co., 1974 edition, p. 29. *Revelational Pressure* is a term coined by Cornelius Van Til.

When our first parents fell from the state wherein they were created, they made themselves the final and ultimate point of reference instead of God. Natural man lusts to be as God, to be the judge of good and evil and to be the standard of truth. Man in his rebellion against God presupposes that he is autonomous in his thinking. He wants to define and interpret reality apart from God. His sense of deity is colored, and to the jaundiced eye everything is yellow. Therefore, even when possessing a remnant image of God, natural man has no power of true interpretation. From the unregenerate man's point of reference, he can know nothing truly.[162] He is epistemologically bankrupt. Even "facts" and "logic," not based upon the creation doctrine, nor placed in the context of God's all embracing providence, are without relation to each other and therefore wholly meaningless.[163]

Views of the Noetic Effects of Sin by Various Reformed Theologians

It is admitted that the views of the selected theologians discussed herein are skewed toward the "Amsterdam tradition"[164] and the great Abraham Kuyper who was a pioneer in the area of presuppositional apologetics. According to Kuyper's own conviction, he was merely a copyist of Calvin and followed him in utter fidelity.[165] Therefore it is appropriate to include Calvin here as well, although Calvin came centuries before Kuyper. Van Til was born in the Netherlands and was a master of Kuyper's works. Van Til readily confesses that what he has advocated in *The Defense of the Faith* has in large measure been

---

[162] Ibid, p. 26.

[163] C. Van Til, *The Defense of the Faith*. Presbyterian and Reformed Publishing Co., 1967 edition, p. 230.

[164] Amsterdam tradition refers to the great Dutch theologians from the Free University in Amsterdam founded by Abraham Kuyper in 1880.

[165] H. R. Van Til, *The Calvinistic Concept of Culture*. Baker Academic, 2001, p. 117.

prepared under the influence of Kuyper.[166] Bahnsen was a student of Van Til's and was the main proponent of Vantilian apologetics. Reymond appears to be less related to the Amsterdam tradition but has been unquestionably influenced by Kuyper and Van Til. Their views on the noetic effects of sin follow below.

John Calvin

Calvin is very explicit regarding the depravity of the mind transmitted through original sin.[167] He states, "Whatever is in man, from the understanding to the will...has been defiled and crammed with concupiscence." To Calvin, the mind is given over to blindness and the heart to depravity. Impiety occupies the very citadel of the mind. "Our reason," says Calvin, "is overwhelmed by so many forms of deceptions, is subject to so many errors, dashes against so many obstacles, is in so many difficulties, that it is far from directing us aright. The reason of our mind, wherever it may turn is miserably subject to vanity, and our knowledge of this is detestable, by which, we miserably deceive ourselves."

I will quote a few comments from Calvin's *Institutes* on selected scriptural passages. Concerning 1 Cor. 1:18, Calvin refers to the apostle Paul as condemning the stupidity and vanity of all human reason and utterly reducing it to nothing. Quoting 1 Cor. 1:20 about God making foolish the wisdom of this world, he asks the question, "Shall we then attribute to it the keen insight by which man can penetrate to God and to the secret places of the Kingdom of Heaven? Away with such madness!" Concerning those who believe that man has impulses (though puny) to good, he again reveals the folly of men by asking questions. Calvin asks, "What shall we reply to the apostle who even denies that we are capable of conceiving anything (2 Cor. 3:5)? What shall we reply to the Lord, who through Moses declares

---

[166] C. Van Til, *The Defense of the Faith*, p. 263.

[167] J. Calvin, *Institutes of the Christian Religion*. The Westminster Press, 1960, 2:239-309.

that every imagination of man's heart is only evil (Gen. 8:21)?" Concerning man's darkened understanding and ignorance described in Eph. 4:17-23, Calvin says that the grace of Christ is the sole remedy that can free us from that blindness. Concerning the light of men in John 1:4-5, Calvin asserts that we are drunk with the false opinion of our own insight, and are thus extremely reluctant to admit that we are utterly blind and stupid in divine matters. These are examples of how Calvin interprets some of the key passages relating to the noetic effects of sin.

However, in all the condemnations of man's mental faculties due to the Fall, Calvin makes allowances for a remnant of human understanding and judgment. It is this that distinguishes man from beast. Reason is proper to our nature; it is a remaining trace of the image of God. The mind of man, though fallen and perverted, is nevertheless adorned with God's excellent gifts. But Calvin is quick to qualify reason as choked with dense ignorance due to the Fall. Man's mind cannot hold to the right path, but wanders through various errors and stumbles repeatedly, as if it were groping in darkness, until it strays away and finally disappears. It is incapable of seeking and finding truth. Concerning the philosophers, Calvin states, "The greatest geniuses are blinder than moles! Although they may chance to sprinkle their books with droplets of truth, how many monstrous lies defile them!" John Calvin very pointedly remarked that philosophers need to see that man is corrupt in every aspect of his being – the Fall pertains to man's mental operations as much as to his volition and emotions.[168]

---

[168] G. Bahnsen, *Always Ready*. Covenant Media Foundation & American Vision, 1996, p. 46.

Kuyper is articulate when expounding the noetic effects of sin.[169] He states that every theory of knowledge must accept the hard reality of the fact of sin. In discussing the "vanity of the mind" and "darkened understanding" of Eph. 4:17-18, he says it may fearlessly be stated that:

1) Falsehood in every sense and form is in the world.

2) There is unintentional mistake, in observation and memory, as well as in the processes of thought.

3) Self-delusion and self-deception are no less important factors in the processes of thought.

4) Evil resides in our imagination...so that fantasy and reality frequently pass into one another. The imagination itself is a deceitful condition that falsifies our self-consciousness.

5) Equally injurious are the influences, which this abnormal element [sin] in the condition of other minds exerts upon us, ideas and current expressions approved by the spirit of the times and instilled in us. In the face of the fact that these influences are fallacious, it becomes clear that our mind, which of itself lies ensnared in all manner of deceptions, is threatened to be entirely misled.

6) All sorts of wrong and sickly commotions bestir themselves in our body and work their effect in our spiritual dispositions.

7) Strong still is the influence of the sin-disorganized relationships of life, an influence, which makes itself especially felt with the social sciences.

8) Different parts of the content of our consciousness affect each other, and no one exists atomistically in his consciousness. The inaccuracies and false representations, which are gleaned from one

---

[169] A. Kuyper, *Principles of Sacred Theology*. Baker Book House, 1980, pp. 106-114.

realm of life affect injuriously again the similar mixed ideas, which are made from another domain. This evil multiplies...especially in one's worldview.

Kuyper also asserts that sin works upon our consciousness through an endless variety of moral motives. These moral differences, which are governed by our own self-interests, govern the results of our studies unconsciously and unknown to us.

Finally, there is also considerable noetic damage in forming the conception of the whole. One might have adequate knowledge of the parts of the cosmos, but cannot come to an adequate knowledge of the whole. The organic relation of the parts, which form the whole, present new questions as to the origin and purpose; questions as to an absolute being and non-cosmos. If there is no sense of God in the heart, then all science is impossible as long as sin confines you with your consciousness to the cosmos. Kuyper concludes his great chapter on *Sin and Science* by affirming that you cannot omit the fact of sin from your theory of knowledge. Ignorance wrought by sin is the most difficult obstacle standing in the way of all true science and knowledge. Thus, Kuyper asserts that every effort to prove the existence of God by so-called evidences must fail and has failed.

Yet, in all this, Kuyper observes that man has not lost his capacity to think logically; the *logica* has not been impaired by sin. However, he also observes that we are often the victims of a false and seemingly true logic, but in reality it is illogical reasoning. With respect to weighing, measuring and formal logic, Kuyper says, "Any man can deal with external matters effectively. A man's reasoning power has not been influenced by the fact of sin. The non-Christian can reason as logically as can the Christian." [170] The difference is the presuppositional starting point.

---

[170] C. Van Til, *The Defense of the Faith*, p. 289.

Van Til stresses the Creator-creature distinction in his writings because it is basic to all human knowledge.[171] Man cannot truly know anything apart from the Creator-creature distinction. Presuppositional apologetics makes this distinction; evidentialism does not.

When man fell, it was his attempt to do without God in every respect; he sought to interpret the universe without reference to his Creator. Fallen man made for himself a false ideal of knowledge, i.e., the absolute comprehension of knowledge. This was a direct result of denying the reality of his creaturehood. It is totally inconsistent with creaturehood that man would strive for comprehensive knowledge. If this could be obtained, it would wipe out the existence of God, and man would then be God. Man sought to destroy the distinction between absolute (God) and derivative (man) thought and tried to make them equally ultimate. Consequently, this is what brought man's woe upon himself.

Van Til asserts that man is ethically depraved. This lifts the whole question of knowledge out of its supposed intellectual or neutral atmosphere.[172] It becomes a matter of life and death. If man is ethically depraved, then he will fall into utter ruin unless he has true knowledge of God. Van Til writes, "When we say that sin is ethical we do not mean, however, that sin involved only the will of man and not also his intellect. Sin involves every aspect of man's personality." It should be noted that Van Til does not separate man's will from his intellect. All man's reactions, in every relation in which God has set him, were ethical and not merely intellectual; the intellectual itself is ethical.[173] The intellectual problem is caused by the moral problem, not the moral problem by the intellectual problem. The natural man stands in an absolute ethical antithesis to God. Therefore, he knows

---

[171] Ibid, p. 225.

[172] C. Van Til, *An Introduction to Systematic Theology*, pp. 25-27.

[173] C. Van Til, *The Defense of the Faith*, p. 46.

nothing truly as he ought to know. The natural man is not only basically mistaken in notions of religion and God, but also about atoms and laws of gravity. From this ultimate point of view, man knows nothing truly.

In regards to the interpretation of facts, Van Til writes that all the facts of the universe attest to God; they are all inter-related in their testimony. [174] Therefore, man always confronts God in every fact that he meets. The natural man assumes that he himself and the facts about him are not created, and therefore, he assumes what is basically false.[175] Everything he says about himself and the universe will be colored by this assumption. It is therefore impossible to grant that man is right in what he says about any fact. Facts and logic, not based upon the creation doctrine and not placed in the context of God's all embracing Providence, are without relation to one another and therefore wholly meaningless.[176]

The following is a brief summary of Van Til's position on the noetic effects of sin.[177] Unregenerate man daily changes the truth of God into a lie. He daily worships and serves the creature more than the Creator. He daily holds the truth in unrighteousness (Rom 1:18). He is spiritually dead (Eph. 2:1). He is filled with the spirit of error. He lives in a stupor (Rom. 11:8). To him the wisdom of God is foolishness. The truth about God is obnoxious to him and he closes his eyes and ears to those who give witness of the truth. He is, in short, utterly self-deceived.

Further, it must be stated that Van Til was aware of the fact that unbelievers have a great deal of knowledge about this world, which is true as far as it goes.[178] There is a sense in which we can and must

---

[174] Ibid, p. 297.

[175] Ibid, p. 224.

[176] Ibid, p. 230.

[177] Ibid, pp. 230-231.

[178] C. Van Til, *An Introduction to Systematic Theology*, pp. 26-30.

allow for the value of knowledge of non-Christians. However, this seems to be contradictory concerning what Van Til previously said about natural man – that he knows nothing truly. The natural man can have knowledge in the sense that God, through natural revelation, impresses his presence on man's consciousness. So definitely and inescapably has he done this that, try as he may, man cannot escape knowing God. This is what Paul stressed in the first two chapters of Romans. Man has a sense of deity indelibly engraved upon his heart, but this is the very thing that natural man seeks to suppress. Thus, by virtue of their creation in God's image, by virtue of the ineradicable sense of deity within them, and by virtue of God's restraining grace, those who hate God can in a restricted sense know God and do good. Being without God in the world, the natural man can know God in spite of himself. All men have a sense of deity, but it is colored by the noetic effects of sin. All men are either in covenant with Satan or in covenant with God. The former invariably seek to suppress (Rom. 1:18) and therefore always misinterpret the general sense of deity within them.

Greg Bahnsen

Bahnsen emphasized that the apologist must recognize the noetic effects of sin.[179] The Fall of man had *drastic* results in the world of thought and thus man's reasoning ability has become depraved. The whole creation is subject to vanity (Rom. 1:21; 8:20) and is in confusion and skeptical despair. Moral corruption has overcome man's thoughts (Gen. 6:5). Man exhaustively, continually and inescapably uses his mind for evil. Unregenerate man suppresses the truth in unrighteousness to embrace *the lie* (Rom. 1:18-25). He suppresses the truth to distort it into a naturalistic scheme, to preclude the interpretation of the God who makes things and events what they are. By holding down the truth about God, man's thinking and interpretative endeavors will, of necessity, be misdirected into error

---

[179] G. Bahnsen, *Always Ready*, pp. 45-48.

and foolishness. Man uses his reason to rise up in arrogant opposition to the knowledge of God (2 Cor. 10:5). To follow the intellectual outlook of those who are outside of a saving relationship is to have a vain mind and a darkened understanding (Eph. 4:17-18). Vain thinking is that which is not in accord with God's word. To Bahnsen, this is the essence of *neutralist* thinking and is characterized by intellectual futility and ignorance.

In Col. 2:3-8, Paul scorns a particular kind of philosophic thinking, which did not begin with the truth of God.[180] There is a kind of philosophy that takes its direction and finds its origin in the accepted principles of the world's intellectuals, in the traditions of men. This philosophy makes God's word void. The non-Christian thinks that his thinking process is normal; he thinks his mind is the final court of appeal in all matters of knowledge. Natural man believes he is the final reference point for all interpretation of fact. In other words, he has become epistemologically autonomous and a law unto himself. In contrast, Bahnsen promotes the reality that all the treasures of wisdom and knowledge are to be found in Christ (Col. 2:3). Thus, if man tries to arrive at truth apart from commitment to the epistemic authority of Jesus Christ, he would be robbed through vain philosophy and deluded by crafty deceit. For the wisdom of the world knows not God and to them the cross is foolishness (1 Cor.1:18-21).

Yet, despite the unregenerate's rejection of God's truth, he can come to know certain things.[181] Although man outwardly denies the truth of God, he is not inwardly devoid of a knowledge of God. He is actually double-minded. The unbeliever is still a creature made in God's image and living in God's created world. The knowledge that unregenerate man suppresses is the very knowledge by which he understands God's world. Man cannot escape the face of God, and

---

[180] Ibid, pp. 11-13.

[181] Ibid, pp. 37-40.

this is the foundation of the unregenerate's knowledge. Natural revelation is clear and inescapable. It reflects the mind and character of God.

Robert Reymond

To Reymond,[182] one of the basic and crucial questions that characterizes presuppositional apologetics is "What significance do the noetic effects of sin carry for man's ability to know God?" It is the noetic effects of sin that establish man's epistemology and his ability to know the world and man. The original transgression of man was far more than an act of willful rebellion by the creature against his Creator. It was man claiming the stance of autonomy and freedom from God his Creator. Man demanded to become his own authority and determine for himself what was true and what was false.[183] For man to test the claims of God's Word is an immoral act indicative of self-acclaimed autonomy, which can be assumed only upon apostate grounds.

After describing the transmission of original sin (Rom. 5:12-19), Reymond briefly expounds on various texts to establish the noetic effects of sin. From Rom. 3:10-18, he states that *none* understands God. From Rom 8:7-8 and Eph. 4:17-19, Reymond describes man as noetically hostile toward God; his thoughts refuse to be subject to God's laws (depravity) nor is he able to subject his thoughts to God (inability). By referencing 1 Cor. 2:11-14, he further establishes man's total inability to judge spiritual things properly. He notes the apostle Paul's disdain for depraved human wisdom. The unregenerate world cannot, by its wisdom, know God. From Rom. 1:18-32, he elaborates on how it is the nature of men to perpetuate their apostasy from God as men who suppress the truth through unrighteousness; they have an idolatrous preference for religious falsehood. The unbeliever's

---

[182] R. Reymond, *The Justification of Knowledge*. Presbyterian and Reformed Publishing Co., 1976, p. 6

[183] Ibid, pp. 15-24.

knowledge of God is thoroughly perverted, untrustworthy, and impotent to find God. Therefore, it is the total depravity and total inability of fallen man, which the Christian apologist must consciously keep in mind when he presents the truth claims of Christianity to the lost. A defective view of sin will result in a defective apologetic.

Reymond refers to man's final reference point for human predication as his *pou sto*.[184] As an out-working of the unregenerate man's religious *pou sto*, the unbeliever exchanges the truth of God for *the lie*. Thus when natural man operates epistemologically from this *pou sto* with his depraved mind and darkened understanding of the universe, *chance* becomes ultimate in finding the meaning of the universe. Epistemologically this means that unregenerate man knows nothing as he ought to know it, for he rejects the only sufficient ground which can justify any knowledge. He repudiates his sole *pou sto* for the justification of any and every human predication and thereby destroys theoretically even the possibility of knowledge. Reymond asserts that the noetic effects of sin most centrally and most tragically display themselves, resulting in man's ever-increasing theoretical isolationism from epistemological truth confronting him, namely, that if Christian theism were not true, he could discover no meaning anywhere, no less in his sciences and arts than in his religious commitments. Although man in his fallen state is a thinking and reasoning creature, he must use *borrowed capital* from Christian theism to be able to make sense of anything. Only the power of God in regeneration can restore a man noetically.

AN APOSTATE *POU STO*

The Grk mathematician Archimedes once boasted, "Give me a place where I may stand on and I will move the earth." Archimedes investigated the physical laws of the lever and it was to this mechanical device that he was referring to. From this saying came the

---

[184] Ibid, pp. 66-75.

Grk term *pou sto* which means "to stand on" referring to a basis of operation. In apologetics the term *pou sto* is employed epistemologically to mean a final point of reference for all human predication. The *pou sto*, the Archimedean point of reference, is one's ultimate authority from which he reasons. This final point of reference must ultimately rest in some mind, divine or human.[185]

The essence of the unregenerate *pou sto* is that man is assumed to be ultimate and autonomous. He seeks to interpret the universe without reference to God. In the Fall of Adam, man has rebelled against the law of his Creator and seeks in principle to be a law unto himself. Fallen man refuses to subject himself to the absolute authority of God and will be subject to none but himself. He believes he can obtain unto genuine knowledge independent of God's directives and standards. He therefore thinks of himself as the absolute reference point in all predication. The unbeliever thinks that his mind is the final court of appeal for all truth and knowledge. He thinks himself to be the judge for all interpretation of facts. He has no need of revelation. He is hostile to God, he hates God, and his presuppositions allow him to suppress the knowledge of God. The unbeliever has epistemologically become a law unto himself; he has become autonomous.[186] Natural man is epistemologically in rebellion against God.

To further characterize the apostate nature of the unbeliever's *pou sto*, we must directly compare it to the Christian's *pou sto*. To the Christian, God is his *pou sto* for knowledge and the final reference point for every human predication.[187] God has revealed himself to man in Scripture and the self-attesting Christ of Scripture is the epistemological basis for all reasoning. The Bible is the infallible word of God and is the ultimate standard of truth. Thus, to the Christian,

---

[185] C. Van Til, *The Defense of the Faith*, p. 215.

[186] G. Bahnsen, *Always Ready*, p. 46.

[187] R. Reymond, *The Justification of Knowledge*, p. 66.

Scripture is the absolute authority. This fundamental presupposition of Christianity is diametrically opposed to the non-Christian's *pou sto*. In fact, the unbeliever is by nature hostile to it.

As a consequence of the Fall of Adam and its accompanying noetic effects, fallen man possesses a *pou sto* antithetical to that of the Christian. The two systems differ because their basic assumptions and presuppositions differ.[188] The difference between the two systems of thought, believer and unbeliever, is fundamentally a clash between two worldviews – between ultimate presuppositional commitments and assumptions which are contrary to each other. Van Til refers to this as two opposing principles of interpretation.[189] The Christian principle of interpretation is based upon the assumption of God as the final and self-contained reference point. The non-Christian principle of interpretation is that man is self-contained and is the final reference point, i.e., that he is autonomous. There is a simple and all comprehensive *antithesis* between the knowledge concept of all non-Christian philosophies and the Christian view.[190] The two worldviews are in collision; one submits to the authority of God's word as a matter of presuppositional commitment, and the other to the autonomy of man.[191] Both are totalitarian in nature.

The following presuppositions characterize the unregenerate's *pou sto*. They are correlative to the unbeliever's fundamental presupposition, the autonomy of man, and define his worldview. It is apostate in its very nature.

1) Human reason is ultimate and man's knowledge is self-contained. Man possesses a wholly self-contained mind; his reason is the final judge of meaning.

---

[188] C. Van Til, *The Christian Theory of Knowledge*. Presbyterian and Reformed Publishing Co., 1969 ed., p. 15.

[189] Ibid, p. 44.

[190] C. Van Til, *The Defense of the Faith*, p. 47.

[191] G. Bahnsen, *Always Ready*, p. 68.

2) Human conscience is the ultimate point of reference in matters of ethics and morality. There is no absolute standard for morality.

3) Man's self-consciousness is ultimate.

4) Man is self-sufficient. All things can be interpreted without God. This means that the natural man denies his creaturehood and denies God's interpretation of his own creation.

5) Man is self-interpretive.

6) There is an ultimate non-rationality of facts. The non-Christian assumes that the facts of the universe are not created. They spring from chaos and are controlled by chance. Chance is ultimate. Facts are isolated events and interpreted from a non-rational principle of individuation. On such a basis the nature of any fact is different in all respects from all other facts.[192]

7) Man's logic is ultimate rationality. The power of logic determines what is possible and what is impossible in the universe of chance. The unbeliever bases his logic on fallacious premises and presuppositions.

8) Man can attain to comprehensive knowledge.

THE NECESSITY OF PRESUPPOSITIONAL APOLOGETICS

We have observed that the worldviews of the Christian and non-Christian are *antithetical*, operating from two different *pou sto*(s). The unbeliever opposes the Christian faith with a complete system of thought.[193] The apologist must recognize that it is not a debate about separate points and issues, but rather is a battle between two complete worldviews, which are contrary to each other. The unbeliever's antagonism is rooted in an overall philosophy. He is an enemy of God in his mind. The two philosophies, Christian and non-Christian, are

---

[192] C. Van Til, *The Defense of the Faith*, p. 216.
[193] G. Bahnsen, *Always Ready*, p. 67.

in collision. The task of the apologist is to vindicate the Christian philosophy of life against the various forms of the non-Christian philosophy.[194] Therefore, the only legitimate apologetic strategy calls for argumentation at the presuppositional level.

The source of the unbeliever's epistemological problem is that he has the wrong authoritative starting point in his system of thought. The unregenerate's philosophy at its epistemological base must be dismantled. The ultimate authority from which he reasons from must be questioned. Therefore, any effective method of apologetics must be presuppositional in its very nature. The unbeliever must renounce his hostile reasoning and embrace a new system of thought. His presuppositions must be altered.

The Christian must submit to the epistemic Lordship of Jesus Christ in his apologetic endeavors. He is called upon to tear down all reasonings and every high thing that exalts itself against the knowledge of God (2 Cor. 10:5). To surrender Christ as epistemic authority of all wisdom and knowledge is to be robbed by the vain philosophy of men (Col. 2:3-8). There is no neutral ground. The apologist cannot allow any legitimacy to the assumptions that underlie the non-Christian worldview. If the presuppositions of the unbeliever are not challenged then the truth of Christianity becomes subject to autonomous man. If we allow the legitimacy of natural man's assumption of himself as the ultimate reference point in interpretation, then we cannot deny his right to interpret Christianity from his *pou sto* as well. If the apologist cannot show the difference between the Christian and the non-Christian worldviews, then he cannot present any reason why the non-Christian should forsake his position. The two worldviews are in collision; we cannot ignore the epistemic antithesis between the Christian and the unbeliever. Nothing is neutral to the Christian. To quote Dr. Bahnsen, "Neutrality is nothing short of immorality."

---

[194] C. Van Til, *Christian Apologetics*, p. 1.

If the two worldviews are antithetical, where can the apologist find common ground or a point-of-contact? It is the sense of deity, the God consciousness that is innate in every man, that provides the point-of-contact. Every man possesses an inherent knowledge of God the Creator that he continually suppresses because of the noetic effects of sin. Although there is no neutral ground between the believer and the unbeliever, there is indeed an ever-present common ground. All men have in common the world created by God, controlled by God and constantly revealed by God. Therefore any area of life and any fact can be used as a point-of-contact.[195]

Lastly, and most importantly, any intellectual argument will not convince and convert the non-Christian. This takes the regenerating power of the Holy Spirit. The apologetical reasoning of the Christian is the means by which the Holy Spirit penetrates into the minds and hearts of unregenerate men. Only God can open the eyes of the blind. Therefore, the Christian must humbly and prayerfully approach the task of apologetics.

---

[195] Ibid, p. 43.

10. THE NECESSITY OF THE CREATOR-CREATURE DISTINCTION FOR A COHERENT WORLDVIEW

A worldview is defined as the sum of one's presuppositions, which provide the framework to view and interpret the world and all reality. There are three essential elements that comprise a worldview: *metaphysics*, *epistemology* and *ethics*. A worldview is only valid when all three elements are coherent. Christian theism is the only valid worldview; all others are incoherent and contradictory. Only by the presupposition of the Creator-creature relationship is coherency possible. The following examines each of the three essential worldview elements in the context of the Creator-creature relationship.

METAPHYSICS

Metaphysics deals with the ultimate nature of reality or being. Every person has a theory of being by which he understands himself and the world. Metaphysics seeks to answer such questions as what does it mean to exist? What is real? What is the nature of the universe? What is the nature of man?

When God revealed himself to Moses at the burning bush (Ex. 3:14), He revealed himself as the self-existent God, "I am that I am." The "to be" verb (hayah, הָיָה) is in the imperfect tense denoting a continuing reality. The verb is also repeated in order to emphasize God's eternal existence. Here, God is revealed as transcendent, self-existent and absolute. His being is completely independent of his creation. He alone is self-contained, self-sufficient and dependent upon nothing. It necessarily follows that all of creation is absolutely dependent upon God for its existence and being. God is the ultimate ground of reality; everything else derives from his creative power.

In Acts 17:24, when addressing the philosophers on Mars Hill, the apostle Paul declared the Creator as sovereign Lord and ruler of heaven and earth, "God that made the world and all things therein, seeing that he is Lord of heaven and earth, dwelleth not in temples made with hands." The Grk verb translated "he is" (ὑπάρχω) denotes a pre-existent state prior to creation and continued existence after creation.[196] It implies both the transcendence and immanence of God. For God to pre-exist, transcendent to his creation, was an entirely foreign concept to the Athenians. By quoting one of their poets, Paul concludes, "In him we live, and move and have our being" (Acts 17:28). That is the foundation of all reality. All things have their meaning in God alone, for it is God alone who defines what reality is. The Creator-creature distinction is clearly disclosed in natural revelation, yet held in contempt by unregenerate man and habitually suppressed (Rom. 1:18). Natural man refuses to recognize himself as a creature of God. The Christian engaged in apologetics must be ready to challenge the metaphysical element of the unbeliever's worldview. Unless the unbeliever interprets this world as God-created and God-governed, he cannot know the true meaning of anything. He will end up in futile reasoning as Paul articulates in Rom. 1:21, "But became vain in their imaginations, and their foolish heart was darkened."

EPISTEMOLOGY

Epistemology is the study of the nature of human knowledge. It asks what we know and how we know it. As discussed above, the Creator-creature relationship reveals that there are two levels of existence: God's transcendent existence as absolute and self-contained, and man's existence as derivative and dependent of God's existence. This is especially true in the realm of knowledge. God's

---

[196] W. E. Vine, *Expository Dictionary of New Testament Words*, pp. 61 & 116.

knowledge is absolutely comprehensive and self-contained. By virtue of the Creator-creature distinction, man's knowledge is necessarily derivative of God's knowledge. Thus, as finite creatures we are absolutely dependent upon God for all truth and meaning. We live in a God-created and God-defined universe; every fact is a created fact, pre-interpreted and defined by God. Every fact has its meaning by virtue of its relationship to the Creator, and no fact exists independently of God. All created things are pre-conceived and pre-interpreted by God from eternity; thus, there are not brute facts.

As creatures we are to give the same meaning to everything that the Creator has given to it.[197] This is the basis of true knowledge. Man must replicate God's thinking to truly know something. In other words, we are to think God's thoughts after him.[198] Only in the context of the Creator-creature distinction can man gain a true knowledge of who he is and the universe in which he lives.

Within the Creator-creature relationship, God has infallibly revealed himself to man in his inscripturated Word. Scripture is the absolute standard of truth because God is its author and there is no higher authority. It is the ultimate authority for all meaning and interpretation of facts. It is the starting point of all our thinking, and the standard by which we judge all things.[199] The Bible is the absolute reference point from which man can know God and interpret the world he was created in. When man thinks God's thoughts after him, he is submitting to the absolute authority of God's revelation, which is the only possible ground for true knowledge. To think autonomously, i.e., to assume man's ability to reason as ultimate, is immoral and

---

[197] C. Van Til, *An Introduction to Systematic Theology*. Phillipsburg, NJ: Presbyterian and Reformed Publishing Co., 1974, p. 171.

[198] This saying is attributed to the 16th century astronomer, Johannes Kepler, who wrote in regards to the mathematical harmony of the planets, "I was merely thinking God's thoughts after him."

[199] G. Bahnsen, Greg L., *Always Ready*. Texarkan, TX: Covenant Media Foundation, 1996, p. 25.

sinful. This is an attempt to redefine meaning apart from God and his infallible Word.

From the above stated *revelational epistemology* it is important to understand the relationship between natural revelation and special revelation. The two forms of revelation must be seen as presupposing and supplementing one another.[200] They both come to man with absolute authority. Together they form the complete revelation of God. However, natural revelation was never meant to function by itself. It is insufficient without its complement of special revelation. As Bahnsen puts it, "Man reads general revelation through the spectacles of special revelation."[201]

ETHICS

Ethics concerns man's conduct and deals with moral standards and responsibilities. God has written his moral law in the heart of every person, and his conscience bears witness to it (Rom. 2:14-15). Every person was created with a sense of deity by which he understands the judgment of God (Rom. 1:18, 21, 32). It is an inward witness, in the very constitution of man, which is inescapable. The unbeliever knows he is culpable to God for breaking his law, and is without excuse (Rom. 1:21). He is confronted with the moral witness of God every time he looks up into the heavens, "For the wrath of God is revealed from heaven against all ungodliness and unrighteousness of men." God's moral character has been revealed.

The unbeliever denies the Creator-creature relationship for ethical reasons. To admit this relationship is to make himself accountable to God. There is an ethical motivation for adhering to the philosophies of this world. Unregenerate man must adopt

---

[200] C. Van Til, "Nature and Scripture" in *God's Infallible Word*. Phillipsburg, NJ: Presbyterian and Reformed Publishing Co., 1974, p. 171.

[201] G. Bahnsen, *Presuppositional Apologetics*. Powder Springs, GA: American Vision Press & Nacogdoches, TX: Covenant Media Press, 2008, p. 275.

presuppositions and a worldview that facilitate the suppression of the knowledge of God (Rom. 1:18). The unbeliever will abandon his Creator-creature relationship in intellectual defiance in order to make himself autonomous. He wants to be a law unto himself. The Creator-creature relationship disclosed in natural revelation brings man face-to-face with God and establishes an ethical relationship. The Creator has revealed his perfect moral character in his moral law,[202] which is written in the heart and conscience of every man (Rom. 2:14-15). God alone is the absolute moral standard, and he alone defines what is right or wrong. As the image bearer of God, man is obligated to conform to the moral character of his Creator. The reality of this ethical relationship is the source of man's rebellion and hatred of God. He must suppress it at all cost.

CONCLUSION

The essence of the unregenerate's incoherent worldview is this; man is assumed to be autonomous and epistemologically a law unto himself. Natural man seeks to be his own ultimate reference point. He believes he can obtain unto genuine knowledge independent of God's revelation. He seeks to interpret the universe without reference to God, making himself the final authority for all interpretation of facts. Arrogantly, natural man believes he has no need of divine revelation. Therefore, the unbeliever lives in a world of false assumptions and false pretentions. His reasoning ends in futility because he will not admit to the Creator-creature distinction.

On the other hand, the Christian lives in the reality of the triune God as revealed in nature and Scripture. God's revelation is the ultimate authority and standard for all reasoning. God's word is the

---

[202] The moral law of God has been codified and summarized in the Ten Commandments (Ex. 20:1-17). It is the expression of God's holy and righteousness character.

indisputable and unquestionable starting point; there is no higher criterion by virtue of the Creator-creature relationship.

11. A BRIEF COMPARISON BETWEEN PRESUPPOSITIONAL AND EVIDENTIAL APOLOGETICS

1. Presuppositionalism reasons from Scripture, evidentialism reasons to Scripture. The difference is *a priori* versus *a posteriori* reasoning.

Presuppositional apologetics is based upon *a priori*[203] reasoning, arguing from the cause to the effect. It argues from presuppositions (cause) to its logical conclusions (effects). It is therefore deductive. It holds that there are certain preconditions of knowledge innate in man that are prerequisite before one can understand anything. These presuppositions comprise one's worldview and form the basis of knowledge and experience.

Evidential apologetics is based upon *a posteriori*[204] reasoning, arguing from the effect to the cause. It seeks to understand the first principles by the effect. It is not deductive reasoning but rather inductive. It reasons from particulars to first causes by way of inference. Therefore, at best, it is only an inference. In scientific terms, this means one can prove the truth of Christianity only as a probability.

This is the fundamental difference between presuppositional and evidential apologetics. Presuppositional apologetics reasons *from* Scripture. Evidential apologetics reasons *to* Scripture.

2. In evidential apologetics, Christianity is defended from an assortment of isolated facts (historical, archeological or scientific facts). In presuppositional

---

[203] *A priori* is derived from the Latin *prius* meaning first, as in first principles.

[204] *A posteriori* is derived from the Latin *posterius* meaning subsequent or following.

apologetics, Christian theism is to be defended as a unit, as a belief-system. To the evidentialist, the confirmation of the Christian faith stands on the accumulated weight of all the evidences. Each fact stands on its own merit according the philosophy of empiricism and the so-called scientific method.

In presuppositional apologetics, one does not try to defend the faith by historical, archeological or scientific facts. It is useless to try to defend the faith by only a discussion of facts. Why? Nobody interprets facts without a set of assumptions and presuppositions. All men have presuppositions comprising a precondition of knowledge prior to the interpretation of any fact. Facts are interpreted by one's belief-system, i.e., one's worldview. We all have a belief-system by which we interpret facts. For example, to interpret a fact of history, such as the resurrection, requires a philosophy of history. A philosophy of history is determined by the presuppositions that comprise one's worldview. Presuppositional apologetics goes right to the heart of the matter and challenges the unregenerate's philosophy of history. It challenges the unbeliever's worldview by which he interprets history. The apologist must not be side-tracked by a single isolated fact, but defend the Christian's worldview, the entire system of truth as revealed in the Holy Scriptures. Christian theism is to be defended as a unit, as a belief-system. The defense of our faith must never compromise the content of our faith. It is not a defense against details but of principle, an exposition and vindication of the Christian worldview.[205]

3. In presuppositional apologetics, the word of God is held as ultimate. In evidential apologetics, man's reasoning is held as ultimate. Only in presuppositional apologetics is God's word held as absolute in authority and the standard for all truth and knowledge.

We are to presuppose God's word and the authority of Christ in all our thinking, making it foundational to all knowledge (1 Pet. 3:15).

---

[205] James Orr, *The Christian View of God and The World.* Grand Rapids, MI: Kregel Publications, 1989, p. 4.

We must be committed to Christ in the world of thought. We must bow to the Lordship of Christ in every area of life, and that includes scholarship and academics. The Christian is obligated to presuppose the word of Christ in every area of knowledge. It seems dogmatic and uncompromising. It is, and the Christian should not be ashamed of this fact. This is not unreasonable.

Presuppositions are a matter of faith. A presupposition is an assumption in one's reasoning. It is a pre-condition for knowledge. It is not something that you prove, but rather it is where one begins his reasoning. It is the starting point for one's reasoning. A worldview is made up of the sum total of one's presuppositions.

Augustine's motto (which Anselm later adopted) was *credo ut intelligam,* "I believe in order that I may understand." Here we find an insight into presuppositionalism. Belief precedes understanding. Faith in God and the revelation of his inspired and infallible Word precedes the understanding of everything else. The writer to the Hebrews writes, "Through faith we understand that the worlds were framed by the word of God, so that things which are seen were not made of things which do appear" (Heb. 11:3).

Man is by nature a presuppositionalist, i.e., he thinks and acts from his presuppositions.[206] The presuppositions that man espouses form his worldview, the belief-system by which he interprets the meaning of the universe. They form the very foundation by which man understands and evaluates the world he lives in and everything contained in it. They form the basis of an all-inclusive view of reality. Therefore, the defense of the faith is unavoidably a presuppositional matter.

Hence, the starting point of reasoning for the presuppositional apologist is always the word of God. All reasoning must be based

---

[206] W. R. Downing, *An Introduction to Biblical Epistemology.* Morgan Hill, CA: PIRS Publications, 1998, p. 59.

upon God's word from the very start. The fundamental presupposition of Christian theism is the existence of the triune God who has revealed himself in Scripture. *The Bible is the Word of God.* The Bible never attempts to prove the existence of God, it always assumes it; "in the beginning God made the heavens and earth" (Gen. 1:1).

4. Evidential Apologetics holds to a very dangerous assumption of man's ability to be a competent judge and interpreter of facts. Presuppositional Apologetics assumes the inability of man to rightly interpret any fact because of the depravity of his mind. To the evidentialist, man is neutral and he is capable to objectively look at the facts. This assumes man is ultimate and autonomous in his reasoning. It is the basis of the unbeliever's worldview. Employing this erroneous assumption forces the Christian to adopt the unbeliever's worldview in order to argue for Christianity. Truth cannot be established by presupposing a lie.

On the other hand, presuppositional apologetics assumes the universal corruption of the unregenerate's mind. The Scriptures clearly teach that fallen man's heart is wicked from birth, "Behold, I was shapen in iniquity, and in sin did my mother conceive me" (Ps. 51:5). "The heart *is* deceitful above all *things* and desperately wicked: who can know it?" (Jer. 17:9). The Bible speaks of the unbeliever's understanding as being darkened (Eph. 4:18), his mind being at enmity against God (Rom. 8:7), being vain in his reasoning (Rom. 1:21) and walking in the vanity of his mind (Eph. 4:17). He is an enemy of God in his mind (Col. 1:21). Further, man's mind has been blinded by the God of this world (2 Cor. 4:4). Apologetics must not ignore the noetic effects of sin.

Natural man's mind is by no means neutral; it terribly suffers from the noetic effects of sin. The unbeliever cannot and will not be objective, or unbiased in his reasoning. Romans 1:18 tells us just how man will interpret God's natural revelation placed before him, "For the wrath of God is revealed from heaven against all ungodliness and unrighteousness of men, who hold the truth in unrighteousness." He will habitually suppress the truth. In doing so, he will seek to exalt himself against the knowledge of God (2 Cor. 10:5). Therefore the unbeliever has an inherent bias against God and he will not be neutral in interpreting any facts of history, archeology, cosmology or science.

God's word and not man's reason is ultimate. God's word stands in judgment over all and is to be judged by no one.

5. *The evidentialist must first prove the truth and reliability of Scripture before he can use it authoritatively. The presuppositionalist holds Scripture as ultimate, and therefore it does not need to be corroborated.* To the evidentialist, Scripture becomes a hypothesis to be proven by evidences and not embraced as the actual truth of God. It must be subjected to independent human reasoning. The truth of Scripture becomes only a probability. Therefore, Christianity, at best, is only probably true.

The presuppositionalist holds Scripture as ultimate; it is the absolute standard, not subject to anything external of itself. God is its author. It is self-attesting; it carries its own inherent evidences. God alone is the only adequate witness to himself. Man is not the judge.

6. *In presuppositionalism, there is an antithesis between the believer and unbeliever's worldviews. In evidentialism, a capitulation is made to adopt the worldly philosophy of secular empiricism and the ultimacy of man's reasoning.*

The evidentialist capitulates to the worldly philosophy of atheistic empiricism and the autonomy of man's reasoning. He assumes that man's rational faculties are neutral. The reliability of the word of God must first be proven by empirical methods.

The presuppositionalist is cognizant of the irreconcilable antithesis between the regenerate and the unregenerate mind-sets. It is a clash between two completely different worldviews, two different sets of presuppositions and two different systems of thought in collision with each other. One submits to the authority of God's word as a presuppositional commitment, and the other doesn't. The unbeliever's system of thought is according to the tradition of this world, and he is an enemy of God in his mind. The impossibility of a neutral approach to reasoning and facts must be admitted. The two worldviews constitute opposing theories of knowledge. Each worldview has its presuppositions about reality, knowledge and ethics. Therefore, worldviews and presuppositions must be critiqued in the enterprise of apologetics.

12. THE INADEQUACY OF EVIDENTIALISM

The evidential approach to apologetics would argue that the perceived order of the universe evidences a Designer. All that is needed for the enterprise of apologetics is scientific evidence and human rationality. This approach is inherently flawed because it promotes an alleged autonomy of human reasoning and strips Scripture of its authority. Even if one becomes convinced of the rationality of intelligent design, it does not follow that his *designer* is the God of the Bible.

A number of brilliant scientists and philosophers have adopted theistic[207] explanations to the rational order of the universe with absolutely no commitment to the God of Scripture. The following are quotations that illustrate this point:[208]

> Every one who is seriously engaged in the pursuit of science becomes convinced that the laws of nature manifest the existence of a spirit vastly superior to that of men, and one in the face of which we with our modest powers must feel humble. (Albert Einstein)

> God is a mathematician of a very high order and He used advanced mathematics in constructing the universe. (Paul A. M. Dirac)

> When thus reflecting I feel compelled to look to a First Cause having an intelligent mind in some degree analogous to that of man; and I deserve to be called a Theist. (Charles Darwin)

---

[207] Theism as distinguished from Christian theism; the belief in one god as creator of the universe, intervening and sustaining its order, but not necessarily a personal god. Divine revelation is denied.

[208] Quotations taken from Anthony Flew's *There is a God: How the World's Most Notorious Atheist Changed His Mind*. New York, NY: HarperCollins Publishers, 2007, pp. 102-110.

We shall be rationally warranted in concluding that it is God – the God of the theistic account – who creates the laws by imposing the regularities on the world as regularities. (John Foster)

In all of the above examples, the theism adopted by these men was not Christian theism. The gods they invented to explain the rationality of the laws of nature was not the God of the Bible but of their own imagination. When you reason from presuppositions independent of God's word, you will draw conclusions independent of God's word. When the Christian apologist argues strictly from evidences independent of Scripture, he capitulates to the unbeliever's worldview that interprets scientific data independently of Scripture. The Christian must always hold Scripture as the absolute standard of truth and knowledge. All reasoning must be based upon this preeminent presupposition. Evidences must be maintained as supplemental to God's word.

EVOLUTION

AND

PRESUPPOSITIONAL APOLOGETICS

13. Creation or Evolution: A Matter of Faith (Heb. 11:3)

Hebrews 11:3 Through faith we understand that the worlds were framed by the word of God, so that things which are seen were not made of things which do appear

Introduction

In September 2011, immediately following the GOP presidential debate in California, Chris Matthews, the tough host of MSNBC's Hardball, interviewed Rick Santorum, who was one of the participants in the debate. During the interview he asked Santorum, "Do you believe in evolution?" Santorum responded, "I believe that we are created by a living and loving God…. For evolution to explain the creation of human beings from nothing…absolutely not, I don't believe that."

Sadly, the nature of Matthews' question reflected the atheistic prejudice of our society today, a bias that unjustly stigmatizes belief in creation as irrational and stupid. It was a ploy to discredit the intelligence of Rick Santorum and to make him look like a religious fanatic. Chris Matthews admitted the reason for asking the question, "Because that always opens up a can of worms for your party." But to Rick Santorum, it was a matter of faith. He believed in creation and didn't believe in evolution. Whether he understood the philosophical undertones, I don't know, but it was a good answer because it addressed both creation and evolution as matters of faith. For indeed, they are both religious beliefs based upon religious presuppositions. The difference of the Christian's view is the presupposition of the absolute authority of Scripture.

As a scientist,[209] I am qualified to state that evolution[210] is not an empirical science. It cannot be demonstrated by observation, nor proven by experimentation. The transmutation of one distinct species into another distinct species has never been observed because it is beyond the limits of experimentation – no human can live long enough to observe it. It is impossible to verify because it cannot be tested. Therefore, evolution cannot even be classified as a theory because by definition a theory must be testable. Evolution is simply unprovable. It is but a speculative philosophy, a faith projection back into time.

Yet despite the fact that evolution is not an empirical science, it is hailed and exalted today as scientific dogma. It reigns supreme as the prevailing creed of our universities. It is an untouchable doctrine. To question evolution is to call down the curse of academia and to be labeled an ignoramus. Professors have lost tenure for merely using the term "intelligent design." Not only has evolution seized our universities; it has also trickled down to every aspect of our society. It is the deceitful propaganda of an atheistic society.

The evolutionist condemns the biblical account of creation because it is believed as a matter of faith and not based upon scientific fact. The Christian readily admits that it is a matter of faith but would take issue with their wholesale hijacking of science. Scientific fact and the interpretation of it are two different things. The observation of any fact never stands alone; it must be interpreted by a philosophy, a *worldview*[211] that forms the basis of one's interpretation. To the chagrin

---

[209] Dr. Nelson received his Ph.D. in chemistry from Arizona State University. He is the author of numerous scientific papers and inventor of eight patents. He has studied DNA chemistry for over 30 years. Currently, he is CEO and President of a small biotech company in the San Francisco Bay Area.

[210] The use of the terms "evolution" and "evolutionist" refer to atheistic evolution, which is the primary sense of the word used in modern day science. Theistic evolution is not addressed in this chapter.

[211] A *worldview* can be defined as the sum of one's presuppositions, which provide the framework to view and interpret the world and all reality.

of the evolutionist, the Christian can equally make the charge that belief in evolution is a matter of faith, a pantheistic religion by which the facts of science are interpreted. The clash is between two different worldviews, each held to by faith.

This chapter will evaluate the religious nature of both worldviews through an exegetical exposition of Hebrews 11:3:

> Through faith we understand that the worlds were framed by the word of God, so that things which are seen were not made of things which do appear.

The above text is very important to Christian apologetics because it establishes the crucial relationship between faith and knowledge and articulates what we understand by faith. It lends itself to a simple outline: 1) *How We Understand,* and 2) *What We Understand.*

HOW WE UNDERSTAND

Hebrews 11:3 begins with the statement, "through faith we understand." In the original Grk, the noun "faith" (πίστει) is in the instrumental case.[212] It denotes that by means of faith we understand. The verb for "understand" is νοέω, which relates to use of the mind (νοός). It means to perceive with the mind and signifies an intellectual apprehension.[213] Grammatically, it is in the present tense (νοοῦμεν) indicating continuous action. By means of faith, we continue to understand. Faith is the means and understanding is the result.

Credo ut intelligam is a Latin phrase that conveys accurately the sense of "through faith we understand." It means, "I believe in order that I may understand." This became the motto of Anselm (*c.* 1033-1109) and was based on the teaching of Augustine (*c.* 354-430).[214] It

---

[212] Each example of faith in Hebrews 11 is formally introduced by πίστει (by faith). It is used linguistically as an anaphora and occurs 17 times in succession after v. 3.

[213] BDAG, p. 818.

[214] Augustine, *On Free Will*, 1.4 referring to Isa. 7:9 and *Tract XXVII* on John 6:34; Anselm, *Proslogion 1*.

summarizes the proper relationship between faith and knowledge. Faith in the triune God and the revelation of his inspired Word precedes the understanding of everything else. We believe the word of God in order that we might understand the universe and all of reality. Belief must precede understanding.

In our text, the writer to the Hebrews assumes that human reasoning is insufficient to provide a right understanding of the created universe. Human reason is not and has never been ultimate for man. Mere human reason can never fathom the origin and existence of the universe. Without the light of divine revelation, it is incomprehensible. Solving this problem does not lie in the scope of experience, empiricism or the scientific method. It is revealed in Scripture and apprehended by faith.

When the author of Hebrews wrote, "By faith we understand;" he was asserting the proper relationship between faith and knowledge. He stated that faith is a precondition for true knowledge. We must go back to the first man, Adam, to more fully understand this statement. Being made in the image of God (Gen. 1:26-27), Adam was to interpret the world he was created in by the divine revelation given him. God's word was his absolute standard and reference point for all knowledge and reality. As a mere creature of God, man can never think of his mind as autonomous but must recognize total dependency on the Creator for true understanding. God alone defines what reality is, giving absolute meaning to his creation. He is the ultimate interpreter of his creation.

All things have their meaning in God. No fact in the universe exists independently of God; every fact has its meaning by virtue of its relationship to the Creator. We can only know the true meaning of something because God has previously interpreted it and revealed it to us in Scripture. For us to understand, or have true knowledge of something, is simply to think God's thoughts after him. Human reasoning was designed by God to serve faith. *By faith we understand.*

From the very beginning man was constituted a faith-creature, i.e., a presuppositionalist that thinks and acts from his presuppositions, which are held to by faith.[215] They are the spectacles by which he sees, interprets and evaluates the world he lives in and everything contained in it. The sum total of the presuppositions man espouses forms a belief-system (worldview) by which he attempts to understand the meaning of the universe and all of reality. When Adam and Eve doubted God's word and autonomously divorced human reasoning from God's revelation, the result was the Fall of man. The human race plunged into the depths of sin. The fact that natural man continues to seek after intellectual autonomy, exalting human reasoning as ultimate, reveals his utter rebellion against God.

Presuppositions are a matter of faith.[216] We know the universe was created, not because the evidences prove it, but because the word of God declares it. The opening verse of the Bible begins with, "In the beginning God created the heavens and the earth." The Bible never seeks to prove the existence of God nor creation. It is presupposed. Evidences can never be used to prove creation because man can never come to know the Creator by rational argumentation outside of God's revelation. At best, scientific evidences can only be supplemental to the word of God. They are only valid when God's word is presupposed as ultimate. Therefore, the defense of the faith is unavoidably a presuppositional issue.

The fundamental presupposition of Christianity is the existence of the triune God who has revealed himself in Scripture. *The Bible is the word of God.* The word of God is held as ultimate by faith. As the absolute standard of truth, it cannot be verified by anything external to itself because there is no higher authority to credential it. It is self-

---

215 W. R. Downing, *An Introduction to Biblical Epistemology*. Morgan Hill, CA: PIRS Publications, 1998, p. 59.

216 By definition a presupposition is not something you prove; it is an assumption in one's reasoning. It is the starting point where one begins his reasoning from and is assumed to be true by faith.

attesting because God is its author, and God alone is the only adequate witness to himself. God is Absolute. Therefore, the starting point of all reasoning must begin with God's word. The presuppositionalist is committed to reason *FROM* the word of God, and never *TO* the word of God as the evidentialist does. Reasoning *TO* the word of God assumes a higher authority than God, which is tantamount to holding man's reasoning as ultimate. Every Christian is obligated to presuppose the word of God in every area of thought (2 Cor. 10:5).

WHAT WE UNDERSTAND

The author of Hebrews states, "By faith we understand that the worlds were framed by the word of God." The Grk term for "the worlds" (τοὺς αἰῶνας) literally means "the ages." It not only has reference to time[217] but also depicts a spatial concept.[218] In the context, it refers comprehensively to the entire realm of space and time. In other words, it denotes the universe and all that has being in it. Our text articulates three realities we understand by faith: *the order*, *the cause* and *the material* of the universe. It is a statement that takes us back to Genesis 1 and presupposes the absolute authority of Scripture.

The Order of the Universe

Heb. 11:3 affirms that the worlds "were framed," i.e., placed in perfect order by God himself. The Grk verb used for "framed" (καταρτίζω) means to put together or to fit together. It denotes a perfect and complete ordering. The passive voice of the verb indicates that the universe was acted upon by something external and completely independent, and hence, assumes a transcendent Creator. God is absolutely distinct from his creation. He alone is absolutely

---

[217] TDNT 1:197. When used in the singular, αἰών can refer to a long period of time. In the plural τοὺς αἰῶνας can mean eternity as in Mt. 6:13; Lk. 1:33, Rev. 1:25; 9:5; 11:36, 2 Cor. 11:31; Heb. 13:8. The context must determine the meaning.

[218] BDAG, p. 33.

independent, self-existent, infinite and eternal. It necessarily follows that His creation is finite, temporal and wholly dependent on Him for its very existence. Therefore, all pantheistic[219] theories of the existence of the universe (including evolution) must be rejected because they deny the transcendence of God the Creator.

Further, the perfect tense of the verb "framed" (κατηρτίσθαι) indicates the universe was not only created in perfect order but continues in an undiminished state of order. It is God who upholds the intricate order and impeccable uniformity of the universe. The Bible says God "upholds all things by the word of his power" (Heb. 1:3) and "in him all things consist" (Col. 1:17), i.e., they are in a perpetual state of coherence.[220] The God of Scripture, the true and living God, continues to govern and maintain the exquisite order of the universe through his divine Providence.

Without question, the order of the universe reveals a transcendent Creator who fashioned and maintains this world in infinite wisdom, knowledge and power. As the Psalmist says, "The heavens declare the glory of God; and the firmament sheweth his handiwork" (Ps. 19:1). All of creation is revelational of God. The apostle Paul writes, "For the invisible things of him [God] from the creation of the world are clearly seen, being understood by the things that are made, even his eternal power and Godhead" (Rom. 1:20). Indeed, the glory of God's divine attributes are "clearly seen" in his creation. Yet, unregenerate man in his bias against God suppresses

---

[219] The term *pantheism* derives from two Grk words, *pan* (παν) meaning all, and *theos* (θεός) meaning God. It is a philosophy that identifies God and the universe; all is God, and God is all. God and nature are identical. It denies the transcendence of God, refusing to recognize Him as distinct from his creation. Evolution is necessarily a pantheistic philosophy.

[220] In Col. 1:17 the Grk verb translated "consist" is συνιστάω and means "to hold together" or "to cohere." The perfect tense denotes a continual state of coherence. God maintains and preserves his creation. He is the principle of cohesion in the universe. "Thus, the universe is a cosmos and not a chaos" (J. B. Lightfoot).

this reality in unrighteousness (Rom. 1:18). He is without excuse according to the word of God (Rom. 1:20).

Let us consider the created order of the universe and the subject of evolution. When the evolutionist denies the existence of the Creator, he is faced with a metaphysical quagmire regarding the order of the universe. The whole philosophy of *naturalism*[221] hinges on the uniformity of nature and its laws, and there can be no science without the laws of nature.[222] But how is it that the laws of nature even exist? Where did they come from? When did they come into existence? The evolutionist, because he denies the Creator, is forced to ascribe an inherent deity to nature in order to account for its uniformity. Nature and its laws are given divine status and ascribed attributes of God. The evolutionist creates a new reality in his vain reasoning, adopting a worldview that worships and serves creation rather than the Creator (Rom. 1:25). Make no mistake about it; evolution is a pantheistic philosophy in which nature and god are one. It exchanges the truth of God the Creator for a lie. God is not the Creator; he is nature itself.

The following is a brief critique of the evolutionist's worldview in regards to natural order, which clearly reveals the religious nature of his philosophy. All evolutionists are naturalistic philosophers. To the evolutionist, the universe is presupposed to be a closed system, i.e., it is an independent and self-contained being (divine attributes) having its own powers and laws. Its absolute independence and self-containment are presuppositions held to by faith. Being self-contained, the universe functions according to the laws intrinsic within itself. These laws are referred to as the laws of nature. To the evolutionist, natural law

---

[221] *Naturalism* is a metaphysical philosophy that presupposes the universe to be a closed system in which only natural laws and forces operate. All phenomena can only be explained mechanistically in terms of natural causes and laws. *Evolution* is a form of naturalism that centers on the origin of species.

[222] The laws of nature (natural law) simply mean the regularity and symmetry of nature. Examples are the law of gravity, Boyle's law, Newton's first law of motion, and the law of conservation of energy. These laws are universal and mathematically precise.

possesses the divine attributes of 1) *sovereignty*, 2) *immutability*, 3) *eternality* and 4) *self-determination*. Again, these are presuppositions held to by faith.

1) Naturalism presupposes that nature is governed entirely by natural law. The laws of nature are *sovereign*; they cannot be broken nor can they be violated. Every part of existence and every aspect of the universe is considered to be obedient to the laws of nature. Miracles do not and cannot occur because the laws of nature cannot be infringed.[223] Anything supernatural is an absurdity because the sovereignty of natural law is absolute. Hence, to the evolutionist, the supernatural inspiration of the Bible and any account of a miracle therein, are absolute falsehoods.

2) Naturalism ascribes the divine attribute of *immutability* to natural law. If the laws of nature could change, phenomena would be unpredictable and the entire enterprise of science impossible. Without a religious commitment to the immutability of natural law, there could be no science. Naturalism absolutely depends upon the immutable god of natural law to make sense out of anything.

3) Naturalism ascribes the divine attribute of *eternality* to natural law. Proponents of naturalism believe the laws of nature had no beginning. They were not created but existed from eternity. This is a metaphysical reality they hold to by faith.

4) Naturalism ascribes the divine attribute of *self-determination* to natural law. To the Christian, only the triune God of Scripture is self-determinant; the universe derives its order from the determinant purpose and will of God. However, to the naturalist, the sovereign, immutable, eternal and self-deterministic god of natural law is the cause of the intricate order and design of nature. It is inherently self-organizing. Natural law, functioning in an endless chain of cause and effect, becomes the guiding purpose that brings about a mystically

---

[223] See Chapter 16, *A Biblical View of Miracles*.

determined goal of universal order. [224] Ultimately, natural law becomes the governor of a plan that orchestrates the budding of life.

To explain the self-determination of natural law, evolutionists make nature to be some kind of mystical person. They personify their pseudo-determinism of natural law with the term "mother-nature," who is an intelligent person making choices, liking this or that, getting mad, etc. They also speak of nature as a composer, a poet or a playwright. Evolution doesn't get rid of teleological and intelligent design but simply re-introduces it in a metaphorical way. In evolution, the very term "natural selection" implies an intelligent personality that selects. Nature is the designer rather than God. Thus, by personifying nature, they can impose deterministic qualities to natural law.

This contradicts their presupposition concerning the mechanism of natural law, which they characterize as unconscious, impersonal, non-intelligent and non-teleological. To assign personal attributes to nature is to violate their own worldview. It is a deceitful attempt to cover up the incongruities of their theory. To the evolutionist, self-organization is a divine capacity inherent in matter; things design themselves.

Further, the great contradiction of evolution is its doctrine of chance, which is one of the main pillars of their philosophy. They say the universe is a universe of chance. Everything evolved and came into being by randomness, but randomness is the very antithesis of order. The preeminent presupposition of naturalism is the order of the universe, its uniformity and natural law. This is what defines the self-contained system they call the universe. According to their own philosophical presuppositions, chance can only operate within the confines of absolute order. Chance must be built upon irrefutable order, but an ordered chance is no chance at all. It is an oxymoron and an irrational absurdity.

---

[224] A. Kuyper, "Evolution" in *Calvin Theological Journal*, 31:11-50 (April, 1996).

The Cause of the Universe

Next, we consider *the cause* of the world's framing. The author to the Hebrews states, "the worlds were framed by the word of God." In the Grk, the phrase "by the word of God" is ῥήματι θεοῦ. The word ῥήματι denotes that which is spoken or uttered. Thus ῥήματι θεου is God's utterance. God framed the worlds by his command. He summoned space, time and matter into existence by divine fiat.

In Rom. 4:17, the apostle Paul reveals something of the nature of God. He says of God, "who quickeneth the dead, and calleth those things which be not as though they were." In other words, God calls into being that which does not exist. Now, it is true, that Paul is not speaking of the creation of the world in Rom. 4:17, but rather of the hope that Abraham would have a son. However, this description of God can be applied in general to the very nature of God; he summons into being that which does not exist. By God's sovereign will, he called the universe into existence. This is the cause of creation and *the framing of the worlds*.

The first chapter of Genesis vividly describes the cause of creation, "And God said, Let there be light: and there was light" (Gen. 1:3). That was the first day of creation, and the five subsequent days of creation are all prefaced with "and God said."[225] By uttering *the word of his power*, God called all things into being. Ps. 33:8-9 says, "Let all the earth fear the LORD: let all the inhabitants of the world stand in awe of him. For he spake, and it was done; he commanded, and it stood fast."

Ultimately, God's will was the cause of the universe. The origin of the universe flows out of God's eternal counsel and omnipotent will. He does all things after the counsel of his own will. All of creation was but the execution of His will, and its purpose was for His glory. Romans 11:36 says, "For of Him and through Him and to Him are all

---

[225] See Chapter 15 for a discussion of "Six Day Creation."

things, to whom be glory forever. Amen." And again, "All things were created by him and for him" (Col. 1:17).

Embarrassingly, the postulate of evolution is devoid of a cause for the universe. The best it can offer is the Big Bang Theory. Evolutionists try to mislead us on the origin of the universe by taking us back 15 billion years in time to what they say was the "Big Bang," where all the matter of the universe was condensed into a single, infinitesimal point (infinite in mass) and then exploded with such immensity and at roughly the speed of light that the universe was created. That was the beginning of space and time and according to this theory, the universe has been expanding ever since. However, the Big Bang Theory is not an explanation of the cause of the universe. It is but a meaningless description of an endless chain of cause and effect devoid of a first cause. If the universe does not have a first cause, it must necessarily be self-existent.

Again, we see the evolutionist ascribing divinity to the universe in order to avoid incoherency in their explanation of its cause. To the evolutionist, the universe exists only for itself without ultimate cause or purpose. Nothing existed outside of it that could have been its cause. Nothing existed before it that could have been its cause. Therefore, the evolutionist must ascribe the divine attribute of self-existence to the universe. It is a faith commitment.

Recently, the host of the new television series *Cosmos: A Spacetime Odyssey*, astrophysicist Dr. Neil deGrasse Tyson began the first episode by declaring an article of faith, "The cosmos is all that is or ever was or ever will be." As a religious statement, it is comparable to Christ's declaration in Rev. 1:9, "I am Alpha and Omega, the beginning and the ending, saith the Lord, which is, and which was, and which is to come, the Almighty."

The Material of the Universe

Finally, in the latter part of Heb. 11:3, we are told, "so that things which are seen were not made of things which do appear." The Grk verb translated "made" is γίνομαι and denotes coming into existence or coming into being. In the original language, the negative adverb "not" (μὴ) is placed before the participle "appear." The better sense is "that which is seen was made out of things which do *not* appear." Also, in the Grk, we find the phrase εἰς τo occurs with the perfect infinitive of γίνομαι (to come into existence), a grammatical construction that denotes actual result. The things "which are seen" with our eyes came into existence out of things invisible and are the *result* of things that do not appear. This directly implies creation *ex nihilo*, creation out of nothing. *Ex nihilo* refers to the material world and the absolute absence of any pre-existent material. Before the beginning, there was nothing outside of God, and hence, there was no pre-existent material from which He would construct the universe. We understand this to be infallibly true by faith. The material that this universe consists of is not eternal but had a beginning, and this beginning can only be explained by the creative power of God.

Again, let us critique the evolutionist's worldview. First, we need to understand what *matter* is. Matter is the technical term for the substance that makes up the physical universe. It includes all physical entities such as light and energy, elements, atoms, protons and neutrons, sub-atomic particles and etc. – all these make up what we call matter. The common definition of matter in science is "any substance that has mass and occupies space." The universe is defined as the sum total of all matter and energy.

Secondly, evolution is part of a materialistic philosophy where *matter* is ultimate reality. To them, matter is the only objective reality, and hence, everything in the universe is derived from matter. Matter is sacred; for all reality exists totally within the realm of the material universe. By faith, the evolutionist believes there exists only one substance – matter – and everything in the universe is ultimately explicable in terms of material properties and interactions.

But where did the initial material of the universe come from? This is the first great dilemma of the theory of evolution that neither science nor philosophy can solve. The explicitness of Heb. 11:3 concerning creation out of what is *invisible* suggests that the writer had other philosophical views in mind he desired to repudiate. Creation *ex nihilo* was contrary to the ancient philosophers and is indeed contrary to modern day philosophy and science. There is a philosophical maxim, which is absolutely necessary for the idea of science; *out of nothing comes nothing (ex nihilo nihil fit)* or *out of nothing, nothing can be made.* This axiom is universal and non-negotiable in science. However, evolutionists arrogantly point us to the Big Bang Theory and think they have given us a sufficient answer. The Big Bang Theory presupposes the pre-existence of matter; you cannot have a "big bang" without matter already existing. The Big Bang Theory only explains what happened to matter, not where matter came from. So from the very get-go, evolutionists have a philosophical dilemma.

There are only two possible explanations for the existence of matter. Either the material that the physical universe is composed of was created and had a beginning, or it is self-existent and possesses the divine attribute of eternality. Therefore, it is necessary for evolutionists to fabricate another pantheistic deity, a metaphysical presupposition, in order to avoid making their worldview incoherent. They must ascribe to *matter* the divine attribute of eternality. Outside of creation, there is no other rational explanation; it is a presupposition held to by faith. It is noteworthy that Stephen Hawking readily admits, "An expanding universe [the Big Bang Theory] does not preclude a creator." This admission reveals skepticism about the eternality of matter. The late atheistic philosopher Antony Flew said, "Why should we not simply accept the existence of the universe, as theists simply accept the existence of their God."[226] Flew concedes it is a matter of faith.

The British philosopher Herbert Spencer, a renowned proponent of evolution in the 19th century, has rightly defined atheism as the religious presupposition of the eternality and self-existence of matter and force. Faith commitment to the self-existence of matter necessarily makes evolution an atheistic religion because it excludes the existence of any personal God that transcends the physical universe. With this presupposition alone, the Creator-God of Scripture is completely shut out of all reality. By faith, the evolutionist believes in the eternality of matter; it is a religious commitment. The bottom line is, evolution is not scientific, but rather a religious worldview masquerading as science.

CONCLUSION

When God revealed himself to Moses at the burning bush (Ex. 3:14), he revealed himself as the self-existent God, "I am that I am."[227] In the Hebrew, the "to be" verb (hayah, הָיָה) is in the imperfect tense denoting a continuing reality. God's timeless and eternal existence is emphasized by the repetition of the verb. As self-existent and absolute, God's being is completely independent of his creation. He alone is eternal, self-contained, self-sufficient and dependent upon nothing. He is the transcendent Creator. It necessarily follows that all of creation is wholly dependent upon him for its existence and being. It is God alone who governs the universe and "upholds all things by the word of his power" (Heb. 1:3). He is the ultimate ground of reality; everything else derives from his creative power. The Bible says that man "lives and moves and has his being" in God (Acts 17:28). The God of Scripture is the Creator of heaven and earth.

---

[226] Antony Flew, *Stephen Hawking and the Mind of God* (http://www.infidels.org/ library/modern/antony_flew/hawking.html).

[227] See P. S. Nelson, "Essential Texts for a Biblical Approach to Apologetics (4) Romans 1:18-21" in *PIRSpective*, Vol. 2, Issue 2.

The doctrine of creation asserted in Heb. 11:3 establishes a Creator-creature relationship between God and man. This reality brings man face-to-face with God. If God is Creator, then we are subject to him as his creatures. There is an ethical relationship to him. Man becomes accountable to God for his sin. Man becomes accountable to God for breaking His moral law and stands guilty before God without excuse (Rom. 1:20). He knows he is under the judgment of God (Rom. 1:32). When man studies the universe, the wrath of God is revealed to him. The apostle Paul writes, "For the wrath of God is revealed from heaven against all ungodliness and unrighteousness of men" (Rom. 1:18). This is inescapable because man is made in the image God, and a sense of deity is indelibly inscribed upon his heart.[228] Evolutionists are confronted with the witness of God every time they look up into the heavens. "The heavens declare the glory of God" (Ps. 19:1).

Therefore, there is an ethical motivation for adhering to the philosophy of evolution. Evolutionists must suppress the truth of the Creator-creature distinction (Rom. 1:18). They must deny Biblical creation at all costs. For to admit it, is to make oneself accountable to God. They would seek to deny the Creator, so they don't have to be accountable to him and face the reality of sin. Evolution is not science; it is an atheistic worldview that seeks to deny the God of creation. It is not an objective approach to scientific facts; there is no neutrality about it.

Not too long ago, Stephen Hawking, hailed as one of the most brilliant men in the world, made a very profound assessment of the existence of the universe: "If we can find the answer to that [why we and the universe exist] it would be the triumph of human reason – for then we should know the mind of God."[229] I have news for Dr.

---

[228] See P. S. Nelson, "Essential Texts for a Biblical Approach to Apologetics (6). Romans 1:18-21" in *PIRSpective*, Vol. 3, Issue 3.

[229] Stephen Hawking, *A Brief History of Time*. Bantam, 1988, p. 193.

Hawking; we can know the mind of God and we can think God's thoughts after him, for he has revealed himself to us in his word. Do you believe in the God of the Bible or in the pantheistic gods of evolution?

14. THE RELIGION OF EVOLUTION
(ROM. 1:25)

Romans 1:25 Who changed the truth of God into a lie, and worshipped and served the creature more than the Creator, who is blessed for ever. Amen.

INTRODUCTION

As a scientist, I am qualified to assert the fact that evolution is not an empirical science. It cannot be proven by experimentation, it cannot be demonstrated by observation, it cannot be tested and it cannot be verified. It is unproved and unprovable. The transmutation of one distinct species into another distinct species has never been observed and never will be because man cannot live a million years attempting to verify it. It is impossible to observe. Therefore, evolution cannot even be classified as a theory, because by definition a theory must be testable. It is but a speculative philosophy, a projection back into time. It is a wishful extrapolation outside of the realm of experimentation. But more to the point, it is an attempt to reconstruct history in order to do away with God. As Richard Dawkins boasts, "Darwin made it possible to be an intellectually fulfilled atheist."[230]

Yet despite the fact that evolution is not an empirical science, it is hailed and exalted today as scientific dogma. Evolution is untouchable in the academic world. It reigns supreme in our universities. It is the sacred cow that cannot be questioned. To do so is to call down the curse and scorn of all of academia. To question evolution is to be labeled an ignoramus and a religious fanatic. Brilliant scientists have

---

[230] Richard Dawkins, *The Blind Watchmaker*. New York: Norton, 1986, pp. 6-7.

lost their careers, their academic tenure and have been blackballed from the scientific community by the mere use of the term "intelligent design." This extreme hatred of any theory other than evolution is very conspicuous. It reveals that there is a moral rebellion against God in the heart of man.

If evolution is not an empirical science, then what is it? It is a religious philosophy based upon religious presuppositions, which are held to by faith. It is a worldview, a belief system, with atheistic presuppositions, as we shall see. The philosophy of evolution is none other than a religious belief.

The philosophy of evolution is a direct assault upon the biblical doctrine of creation. We are told in Romans 1:18-32 how unregenerate man suppresses and "holds down" the clear revelation of the Creator. In v. 25 we find that man willfully creates a new reality in his vain reasoning, adopting a worldview that worships and serves creation rather than the Creator. The apostle Paul tells us the result of unregenerate man's vain reasoning:

> **Romans 1:25** [25] Who changed the truth of God into a lie, and worshipped and served the creature more than the Creator, who is blessed forever. Amen.

The prepositional phrase "more than the Creator" (παρὰ τὸν κτίσαντα) uses the preposition παρα which denotes a position "alongside of" or "parallel to" as its basic sense.[231] The use of this preposition indicates that man deliberately side steps the Creator to avoid the truth. The verb "changed" (μεταλλάσσω) is more accurately translated "exchanged"; "Who exchanged the truth of God for *the* lie." [232]

---

[231] S. E. Porter, *Idioms of the Greek New Testament*. Sheffield, England: Sheffield Academic Press, reprint 1999, p. 166.

[232] "Lie" possesses a definite article in the Grk text.

When the apostle Paul wrote his epistle to the Romans, do not think that he was ignorant of ancient Greek philosophy.[233] Greek philosophy had existed for hundreds of years before the apostle Paul. His masterful defense of Christianity on Mars Hill before the Areopagus demonstrated a firm grasp on Greek philosophy. Paul grew up in Tarsus, in the Roman province of Cilicia, which was one of the three university cities of the world. He no doubt heard the Greek philosophers teaching and debating their philosophy daily in the marketplace. Paul was exposed to a liberal, classical education, which included the various Greek philosophies. He was accomplished in Greek rhetoric. F. W. Farrar remarks, "...we find upwards of fifty specimens of thirty Greek rhetorical figures in St. Paul."[234] As a student of Gamaliel (Acts 22:3), his rabbinic education certainly included Greek philosophy as part of its curriculum. Therefore, Paul was very familiar with Greek philosophy, and he could quote the philosophers verbatim (Acts 17:28; 1 Cor. 15:33; Tit. 1:12).[235]

Further, one must understand that the philosophy of evolution is not a new philosophy. Charles Darwin did not invent this philosophy. It dates back to the pre-socratic philosophers (Socrates born 469 B.C.) of Anaximander (610-546 B.C.), Democritus [236] (460-370 B.C.), Empedocles (490-430 B.C.), Heraclitus [237] (535-474 B.C.) and

---

[233] P. S. Nelson and W. R. Downing, *Classroom Lecture Notes: An Introduction to Biblical Apologetics*. Morgan Hill, CA, PIRS Publications, 2004, pp. 38-39.

[234] F. W. Farrar, *The Life and Work of St. Paul*. New York: E. P. Dutton & Company, Vol. I, p. 629.

[235] Paul quoted or referred to Epimenides, Menander, Aratus, and Cleanthes.

[236] Plato (c. 427 — c. 347 B.C). objected to the mechanistic purposelessness of the atomism of Democritus. He argued that atoms just crashing into other atoms could never produce the beauty and form of the world. In the *Timaeus*, (28B – 29A) Plato insisted that the cosmos was not eternal but was created, although its creator framed it after an eternal, unchanging model.

[237] Heraclitus developed the metaphysic of constant flux. He believed that the nature of all existence is change. Perpetual change is the foundation of evolution

Leucippus[238] (mid 5th century B.C.). The philosophies of materialism, atomism, naturalism and developmental philosophy (evolution) all existed at the time of the apostle Paul and had been around for hundreds of years.

In Rom. 1:25, Paul says that unregenerate reasoning changes the truth of God into a lie. As previously mentioned, the Grk term for "change" is μεταλλάσσω and more accurately means "to exchange." The unbeliever possesses a true knowledge of the Creator but deliberately exchanges it for the lie. What the unbeliever knows about God is seen in Rom. 1:20-21:

> **Romans 1:20-21** [20] For the invisible things of him from the creation of the world are clearly seen, being understood by the things that are made, even his eternal power and Godhead; so that they are without excuse: [21] Because that, when they knew God, they glorified him not as God, neither were thankful; but became vain in their imaginations, and their foolish heart was darkened.

They exchanged the truth of an omnipotent, sovereign and eternal Creator for the lie. The result of this lie was idolatry, to worship and serve the creation (τὸν κτίσαντα)[239] rather than the Creator.

This is a very accurate description of the philosophy of evolution. For evolution is a pantheistic philosophy, in which nature and god are one. Nature is given divine status and is ascribed the attributes of God. Nature possesses and exhibits qualities that can only be attributed to God. To the evolutionist, God is not the Creator; he is nature itself. By this immanentist interpretation of the universe, the

---

(time and chance), which is further developed in the field of developmental philosophy.

[238] Atomism was developed by Leucippus and his pupil Democritus. Atomism is a philosophy that believes the ultimate constituents of the universe are simple, minute, indivisible, and indestructible particles, i.e., atoms. They are the basic components of the entire universe.

[239] Although κτίσις is often translated "creature," there are at least six passages where it is rightly translated "creation." It can denote the act of creating or the product of creating. It's meaning in Rom. 1:20 as "creation" gives good context to the same rendering in v. 25.

evolutionist ends up worshiping the creation rather than the Creator. This is the lie that has deceived untold millions and permeates our culture today.

Evolution is a naturalistic philosophy derived from religious presuppositions and faith commitments. The theory depends upon metaphysical presuppositions regarding the structure of reality. Darwin's argument for evolution was based upon a set of faith assumptions, assumptions corresponding to the philosophy of naturalism. Richard Dawkins, the notorious proponent of evolution, asserted that evolution is the main supporting pillar in the temple of naturalism.[240]

The following is an examination of the religion of evolution and the deities of naturalism.

THE ULTIMATE BEING OF MATTER: SELF-EXISTENT AND ETERNAL

In naturalism, *matter* has ultimate being; it is absolutely independent and eternally self-sustaining.[241] In other words, to the evolutionist, matter is self-existent, which is a quality that can only be ascribed to God. To presuppose the self-existence of matter is a faith commitment. It is a presuppositional commitment that believes all reality exists totally within the realm of the material universe. Nothing exists or transcends the material universe, not even God. The material cosmos with all its forces is ultimate reality.

Do you realize that if matter was not created as the evolutionist argues, then there is no other explanation but self-existence? If it was not created, if it did not have a beginning, then it must be self-existent.

---

[240] Richard Dawkins, *The Blind Watchmaker*. New York: Norton, 1986, pp. 6-7.

[241] G. Bahnsen, *Journal of Christian Reconstruction*. Covenant Media Foundation, Summer 1974, I:1

Hence, to be consistent, the evolutionist must ascribe the divine attribute of eternality to matter.

What do we mean by matter? Matter is the substance that makes up the physical universe. Matter denotes all physical entities such as particles, light and energy: elements, atoms, protons, neutrons, sub-atomic particles; all of these make up what we would call matter. In science, the common definition of matter is any substance that has mass and occupies space. The universe is defined as the sum total of all matter and energy.

Evolutionists try to mislead us on the origin of matter by taking us back 15 billion years in time to what they say was the "Big Bang." All the matter of the universe was condensed into a single, infinitesimal point (infinitesimally small and infinitely dense) and then exploded with such immensity and at roughly the speed of light that the universe was created. That was the beginning of space and time, and according to this theory, the universe has been expanding ever since.

But this only begs the question, where did the initial material come from? The Big Bang Theory presupposes the pre-existence of matter. You cannot have a "big bang" without matter already existing. The Big Bang Theory only explains what happened to matter, not where matter came from. So from the very get-go, evolutionists and naturalists have a dilemma. Yet, some think they have given us a sufficient answer for the beginning of the universe. They think, if the Big Bang was not the beginning, it will at least do until a beginning comes along.

It is necessary for evolutionists to create a god in order to avoid irrationality. They are forced to make a metaphysical presupposition on the self-existence of matter. The material that the physical universe is composed of must either be self-existent, possessing the divine attribute of eternality, or it had to be created out of nothing.[242] For evolutionists know, as Stephen Hawking admits, "an expanding universe does not preclude a creator." The atheistic philosopher Antony Flew admits it's a matter of faith, "Why should we not simply accept the existence of the universe, as theists simply accept the existence of their God, as being ultimately unexplained and inexplicably brute fact."[243]

In the religion of evolution, matter is deified. The divine attribute of eternality is ascribed to matter. Belief in such a god presupposes that matter is ultimate reality. Matter is the only objective reality. Matter is sacred; it is worshiped as the source of all reality. Everything in the universe is derived from matter. Hence, there exists only one substance – matter – and everything in the universe is ultimately explicable in terms of material properties and interactions. The only way the evolutionist can explain the existence of matter is to deify it.

This one presupposition alone makes naturalism an atheistic religion because it excludes the existence of any personal God that transcends the physical universe. The British philosopher Herbert Spencer, a renowned proponent of evolution in the 19th century, has rightly defined atheism as the religious presupposition of the eternality and self-existence of matter and force. With this presupposition, the Creator-God of Scripture is completely shut out of all reality. To hold to this presupposition is to be an atheist. The belief that matter is self-existent is an atheistic philosophy. Alvin Plantinga, a contemporary theistic philosopher, has condemned naturalism as being even stronger that atheism.

---

[242] There are some that believe matter was self-created and spontaneously emerged out of nothing, space and time emerging out of mathematical points. See John Byl, *The Divine Challenge* (Carlisle, PA: The Banner of Truth Trust, 2004, p. 46). It is a philosophical axiom, that out of nothing comes nothing. This axiom is universal and non-negotiable in science. It is a philosophical maxim. It is impossible for something to come out nothing. That would be a logical fallacy and the height of irrationality. For something to come out of nothing presupposes creation.

[243] Anthony Flew, *Stephen Hawking and the Mind of God*, 1996.

The word of God reveals to us that the being of God is absolute. He alone is self-existent and transcends his creation. He is absolutely independent, and all of creation is entirely dependent upon him for their existence. When God revealed himself to Moses at the burning bush (Ex. 3:14), he revealed himself as the self-existent God; "I am that I am."[244] The "to be" verb (hayah, הָיָה) is in the imperfect tense denoting a continuing reality. God's timeless and eternal existence is emphasized by the repetition of this verb. As self-existent and absolute, God's being is completely independent of his creation. He alone is self-contained, self-sufficient and dependent upon nothing.

It necessarily follows that all of creation is wholly dependent upon God for its existence and being. Man owes his very existence to God. He "lives, and moves and has his being" in God (Acts 17:28). Though natural man may hate to admit it, he is absolutely dependent upon God for all things. God governs and "upholds all things by the word of his power" (Heb. 1:3). Calvin stated that our very being is nothing else than subsistence in God alone. God is the ultimate ground of reality; everything else derives from his creative power. All things have their meaning in God alone; God alone defines reality.

Where did matter come from? It was created by the self-existent God of Scripture. The opening verse of the Bible makes that very clear, "In the beginning God created the heaven and the earth." God, the Creator, fashioned this world in His infinite wisdom, knowledge and power. He spoke it into existence by his fiat decree.

Hebrews 11:3 Through faith we understand that the worlds were framed by the word of God (ῥήματι θεου), so that things which are seen were not made of things which do appear.

In the above text, we see that God framed the worlds by his command. He brought matter into existence by his ῥήματι θεοῦ – the utterance of God (Heb. 11:3). This is a description of creation *ex nihilo*,

---

[244] See P. S. Nelson, *PIRSpective*. Morgan Hill, CA: PIRS Publications, 2009, Vol. 2, Issue 2.

creation out of nothing. *So that things which are seen were not made of things which do appear.* The only way that something can come out of nothing is by the omnipotent hand of the Creator. The Christian presupposes matter exists because God created it. It is the only rational explanation for matter's existence. We understand this by faith.

ABSOLUTE INDEPENDENCE:
SELF-CONTAINMENT OF THE UNIVERSE

Having presupposed the self-existence and the eternality of matter by faith, the evolutionist must also presuppose the absolute independence of the universe. According to his religious belief, nothing above or outside the universe exists. There is nothing that transcends the cosmos; there is nothing external to it. The cosmos is all that is or ever was or ever will be. By faith, the evolutionist believes there can be no external influence on this system called the universe. It exists as God does in perfect independence.

Further, fundamental to naturalism and the philosophy of evolution is the assumption that the universe is self-contained. If the universe is absolutely independent (a divine attribute), it necessarily must be self-contained. If self-contained, it necessarily is self-sufficient and self-sustaining. The universe exists by itself and derives all meaning and purpose from itself. It sustains itself and needs nothing outside of itself. This is a big leap of faith. Such presuppositions of the universe cannot be proved neither tested; it is a religious commitment. So once again, we find the evolutionist deifying the universe to maintain his religious worldview.

Science likes to use the term "a closed system." By a closed system, the evolutionist maintains that the universe is an entirely self-contained system. It is absolutely independent; nothing can transcend the realm of nature. This is the pre-eminent presupposition of naturalism.

The following quotation from Stephen Hawking illustrates the religious nature of a self-contained universe:

> So long as the universe had a beginning, we could suppose it had a creator. But if the universe is really self-contained, having no boundary or edge, it would have neither beginning nor end, it would simply be. What place, then for a creator?[245]

The analogy of a "box" can be used to illustrate the self-contained universe. Everything that happens within the box can only be explained or caused by things that exist within the box. Nothing can enter in from outside to disturb anything within the box. This includes God! God is excluded from the box; he can't get in. Naturalism is closed to any supernatural intervention. As an article of faith, God cannot intervene. God is shut out of the system. This is a presupposition held to by faith. Naturalism is not neutral or objective by any means. It is a faith commitment made prior to investigation of any observable fact.

With the religious presupposition of a self-contained universe, all miracles are excluded. Only natural processes exist. That which is supernatural is non-existent. All cause and effect exists only within the box. Nothing outside of the box can affect anything inside the box. It cannot be changed or acted upon by anything outside of itself. Therefore, anything supernatural is impossible by virtue of this faith commitment.

Do you understand the ramifications of this? An evolutionist will not and cannot accept a miracle. This denial is a religious commitment held to by faith. If one is able to prove a miracle by scientific evidences, the evolutionist may admit to the extraordinary phenomenon but will not admit to anything supernatural. He will simply say that there is some natural law that has not been discovered yet. But in due time, we will discover the natural law that caused the extraordinary phenomenon. As to whether it is supernatural, that

---

[245] Stephen Hawking, *A Brief History of Time*. Bantam, 1988, pp. 156-157.

would apostatize their faith in the self-contained universe. They worship the god of self-containment, which is an attribute that only God possesses.

To put things in perspective, below I have quoted A.W. Pink's comment on Gen. 1:1 regarding the solitude of God before creation:

> "In the beginning, God." There was a time, if "time" could be called, when God, in the unity of His nature (though subsisting equally in three Divine Persons), dwelt all alone. "In the beginning, God." There was no heaven, where His glory is now particularly manifested. There was no earth to engage His attention. There were no angels to hymn His praises; no universe to be upheld by the word of His power. There was nothing, no one, but God; and that, not for a day, a year, or an age, but "from everlasting." During a past eternity, God was alone: self-contained, self-sufficient, self-satisfied; in need of nothing.[246]

You see, only God is self-existent, self-contained and self-sufficient in and of himself. He far transcends this universe. He is absolute.

THE LAWS OF NATURE: SOVEREIGN, IMMUTABLE AND DETERMINISTIC

To the evolutionist, the universe, as an independent and self-contained being, has its own powers and laws. The universe functions according to the laws intrinsic within itself. These laws are referred to as the laws of nature; they comprise the laws of physics, the laws of chemistry, etc. The evolutionist believes that natural law is absolute. Thus, he ascribes attributes of deity to the laws of nature.

Natural law is ascribed the divine attribute of *sovereignty*. It is presupposed that nature is governed entirely by natural law. The laws of nature are essentially divine principles that govern the universe. Every part of existence and every aspect of the universe are considered to be in obedience to the laws of nature. Nature is sovereignly ruled by natural law.

---

[246] A. W. Pink, *The Attributes of God*.

These laws cannot be broken nor violated. In fact, the definition of a miracle is the violation of natural law. This was the philosopher David Hume's definition. Since natural law cannot be violated, miracles are absolutely impossible. For an evolutionist to believe a miracle, he would have to tear down his gods of self-existence of matter, self-containment of the universe, and the sovereign and immutable god of natural law.

Evolutionists also ascribe the divine attribute of *immutability* to natural law. The laws of physics are unchangeable. Without this religious commitment, there could be no uniformity in nature, and without uniformity in nature, the enterprise of science would be impossible. Naturalism absolutely depends upon the immutable god of natural law to make sense out of anything because the very order of nature is determined by natural law.

Another divine attribute ascribed to natural law is *self-determination*. The universe functions only by cause and effect, which are dictated by the laws of nature. Natural law becomes the driving force of cause and effect. This deterministic supposition is one in which the universe is no more than a chain of events following one after another according to the law of cause and effect.[247] The only processes and mechanisms that exist are natural laws. Nothing can interfere with the determinism of natural law.

It is the god of self-determinism that caused the intricate order and design of nature. Nature is self-organizing. There is a direction and progression toward order.[248] In evolution, higher life forms are evolved from lower life forms. It is a faith commitment to natural law. Although the naturalist would claim that natural law works without

---

[247] Wikipedia, *Causality*.

[248] The self-determining order of the universe is diametrically opposed to the 2nd Law of Thermodynamics, which states that universe is spontaneously moving toward a state of maximum entropy (disorder). This should be an obvious contradiction to the evolutionist – order evolving from disorder, resulting in negative entropy.

purpose, i.e., it is non-teleological, he inconsistently ascribes the attributes of design and purpose to it.

Evolutionists say that the determinism of natural law is an impersonal, mechanically blind process. Yet, they make nature to be some kind of person. They deify nature as an intelligent person with purpose, order and design. Nature assumes personal qualities. They speak of nature as a composer, a poet or a play-write. The very term "natural selection" assumes a personality that selects. The theory of evolution requires personification of the natural order. Presupposing the god of self-determinism justifies this. Evolution doesn't get rid of teleological and intelligent design but simply re-introduces it in a metaphorical way. Nature is the personal designer rather than God.

In summary, there are three divine attributes the evolutionist ascribes to natural law: absolute sovereignty, immutability and determinacy.

CONCLUSION

In this chapter, we have exposed the religious nature of evolution. Evolution is a religious philosophy based upon many metaphysical presuppositions, which are faith commitments about reality and existence. The evolutionist has whittled out a god of his own imagination. It is the god of nature. Numerous attributes of God are ascribed to nature. Let me tell you, it takes a lot of faith to be an evolutionist. The evolutionist *worships and serves creation rather than the creator*. It is a very vivid example of Rom. 1:25.

The first step in presuppositional apologetics is to back our opponents up to their own presuppositions and expose the inconsistency and incoherency of their worldview. Most people you talk to about evolution, and most scientists for that matter, are ignorant of the religious presuppositions of their worldview. They think that science is objective, and Christianity is but blind faith and fanaticism. They think Christianity is anything but rational. Show them their religion and their pantheistic faith commitments, which reveals they are really the ones who are practicing blind faith. You will surprise them for they really haven't given it much thought at all. They think that evolution is an objective science and have no idea of the religious faith commitments involved. Then invite them over to a Christian's worldview, the theistic worldview based upon the infallible word of God, and show them how it is the only worldview that can truly make sense of anything.

15. Six Day Creation: Long or Short Days (Gen. 1)

Introduction

The previous chapter on "The Religion of Evolution" critiqued naturalism and the various divine attributes that evolutionists ascribe to nature. One of the topics not discussed was theistic evolution. Theistic evolutionists believe that evolution occurred, but God was involved in the process. It is a religious version of evolution. God providentially guided and supernaturally intervened to direct the process of evolution. He used evolution as the instrument for the development of humans and to bring Adam into existence.

Theistic evolutionists generally side with the atheistic evolutionist's teaching that mankind slowly evolved from primitive life forms by means of animal evolutionary stages through long epochs of time. They teach that a race of subhuman men lived thousands of years before Adam was born. God then selected Adam from among this race, breathed the breath of God into him, and thus, rendered him no longer an animal but a man.

Theistic evolution is a futile attempt to harmonize the theory of evolution with the Bible. It is a forced interpretation of Scripture designed to comply with certain presuppositions, which are held to by faith. It is a prime example of the danger of reasoning *to* scripture rather than *from* scripture. Theistic evolutionists assume the reality of evolution, and therefore, interpret the Bible based on that presupposition.

As evolutionists, they believe in a very old earth, i.e., billions of years old. The time allegedly needed to evolve man from some primordial soup. The argument for theistic evolution depends upon an allegorical interpretation of the length of the six days of creation mentioned in Genesis 1. Theistic evolutionists interpret each day as a long epoch of time, a long geological age. Hence, they must interpret Genesis 1 as allegorical.

FRAMEWORK HYPOTHESIS

The argument all boils down to the interpretation of the six days. Short days or long days? Literal or allegorical? As you can imagine, theistic evolutionists have to skew their interpretation of Genesis chapter one. They do this by a dangerous hermeneutical method known as the *Framework Hypothesis*.

The *Framework Hypothesis* assumes a topical arrangement of Genesis 1 rather than a chronological arrangement. It is a complete restructuring of the Genesis account of creation. Proponents of this hypothesis flat out deny the chronological arrangement, rejecting the sequence of immediate and instantaneous fiat acts. They say that Moses merely provided an artistic expression of the truth of divine creation. Thus, they interpret Genesis 1 artistically rather than chronologically.

ARGUMENT FOR A LITERAL 24-HOUR DAY[249]

However, there is an obvious chronological structure revealed in Genesis 1. It is a record of history and not a poetic description of the work of God. Since the argument for theistic evolution stands or falls on the meaning of the term "day," I want to present eight arguments for a literal 24-hour day interpretation of the six days of creation.

1. The primary meaning of the Hebrew word "yom" which is translated "day." The word "yom" (יוֹם) in its singular, dual and plural forms is

---

[249] R. Reymond, *Contending for the Faith*. Scotland: Christian Focus Publications, 2005 pp. 39-51; L. Berkoff, *Systematic Theology*, p. 154-155; K. Gentry, *Reformed Theology and Six Day Creation*.

used 2,225 times in the O.T. It is admitted that the word can have various meanings. However, the primary meaning of the word is a natural 24-hour day. The overwhelming usage of this term refers to a normal day. It is a good rule in exegesis not to depart from the primary meaning of the word unless it is required by the context. The word should be taken in its obvious sense, and the obvious sense and primary meaning is a literal 24-hour day. Robert Dabney said in regards to Genesis 1, "The narrative seems historical, and not symbolic; and hence the strong initial presumption is, that all its parts are to be taken in their obvious sense."[250]

2. Each day is qualified as "evening and morning." Each day is described as being composed of its natural parts, evening and morning. Outside of Genesis 1, the words "morning" and "evening" occur together 37 times. In each instance it speaks of a normal 24-hour day.

3. Each day possesses a numerical adjective (first, second, third, etc.). In Moses' writings, there are 119 occurrences where *yom* is used in conjunction with a numerical adjective. In each case, *yom* means a literal day. There are another 357 occurrences of *yom* having a numerical adjective in the rest of the O.T. Again, in each case, it denotes a literal day. Now, if you take the qualification of each day composed of "evening and morning," along with its numerical adjective, the obvious conclusion is that *yom* denotes a literal 24-hour day.

4. In Gen. 1:3-5, light is separated from darkness. This implies a rotating earth and a regular day. The repeated references to darkness of night further corroborate a normal solar day. We are plainly told in v. 5 that the light was called day and the darkness was called night, and that each day had one period of light-darkness.

---

[250] R. L. Dabney, *Lectures in Systematic Theology.* Zondervan, 1972 reprint, pp. 254-55.

5. The word yom, used for created days four through six, occurs after the creation of the sun and the moon. The sun was to rule the day, and the moon to rule the night.

> **Genesis 1:16** And God made two great lights; the greater light to rule the day, and the lesser light to rule the night: he made the stars also.

There is no question that this is referring to ordinary days. There is absolutely no dispute that days 4-6 are literal days. In days 4-6, the word *yom* and the phraseology used to qualify it ("evening and morning" plus the numerical adjective) are identical to that used in days 1-3.

6. Genesis 1:14 distinguishes between days, years and seasons.

> **Genesis 1:14** And God said, Let there be lights in the firmament of the heaven to divide the day from the night; and let them be for signs, and for seasons, and for days, and years.

With this threefold distinction, clearly, days mean literal days, years mean years, and seasons mean seasons.

7. The argument from the analogy of Scripture. Scripture interprets scripture, and the sense of a text is known by the other texts that speak more clearly. In Ex. 20:9-11 (the fourth commandment) Israel is commanded to labor six days and rest on the seventh because Jehovah made heaven and earth in six days and rested on the seventh day.

> **Exodus 20:9-11** Six days shalt thou labour, and do all thy work: [10] But the seventh day is the sabbath of the LORD thy God: in it thou shalt not do any work, thou, nor thy son, nor thy daughter, thy manservant, nor thy maidservant, nor thy cattle, nor thy stranger that is within thy gates: [11] For in six days the LORD made heaven and earth, the sea, and all that in them is, and rested the seventh day: wherefore the LORD blessed the sabbath day, and hallowed it.

Here, man's six-day workweek is tied to the six days of creation, the original creation workweek. God's creating the world and its creatures in six days and resting on the seventh is the ground of his sanctifying the Sabbath day.[251] Moses is certainly referring to literal

---

[251] Ibid.

days in the fourth commandment. Sound hermeneutics would require that *yom* in the days of creation be taken in the same sense.

8. Finally, in Exodus 20:11, the creation week is spoken of as involving six literal days.

Exodus 20:11 For in six days the LORD made heaven and earth, the sea, and all that in them is, and rested the seventh day: wherefore the LORD blessed the sabbath day, and hallowed it.

"Days" is plural (*yammim*, יָמִים). Of the 858 instances of the plural "days" in the O.T., there is never any other meaning than ordinary days. "Ages" is never expressed as the plural *yammim*. Moses could have easily used another term *ōlam*, which means an age or period of indeterminate duration, if he wanted to mean epochs of time.

CONCLUSION

From the weight of the biblical data presented above, it is an inescapable conclusion that the six days of creation are literal 24-hour days. Indeed, Genesis 1 is an historical narrative, not an allegory.

16. A BIBLICAL VIEW OF MIRACLES

Miracles occupy an important place in the Bible. If you believe the Bible to be the inerrant, infallible word of God, then, of necessity, you believe in miracles. Christianity is a supernatural religion. The very heart of the Christian faith is based upon the miracles of the incarnation of the Son of God and his resurrection from the dead. Not to believe in miracles is to deny the inspiration of the Bible, and therefore, to deny the faith. We believe in miracles! It is one of the most fundamental presuppositions of the Christian's worldview. Without miracles we have no Christianity.

In this chapter we will investigate what miracles are and their purposes. I want to approach this subject by considering three definitions of a miracle: *biblical, theological* and *philosophical*.

A BIBLICAL DEFINITION

The biblical definition of miracles is comprised of three basic elements that are reflected in three distinct Greek words in the N.T. The Grk words are δύναμις (powers), σημεῖον (signs) and τέρας (wonders). Various combinations of these words are used to describe a miracle in Scripture. These terms describe the distinctive features of miracles and form the basis from which we will derive our biblical definition of miracles.

In the New Testament, there are three texts where all three Greek words are used together: Acts 2:22, 2 Cor. 12:12 and Heb. 2:3-4.

Acts 2:22 [22] Ye men of Israel, hear these words; Jesus of Nazareth, a man approved of God among you by miracles (δύναμις) and wonders (τέρας) and signs (σημεῖον), which God did by him in the midst of you, as ye yourselves also know:

2 Corinthians 12:12 [12] Truly the signs (σημεῖον) of an apostle were wrought among you in all patience, by signs (σημεῖον) and wonders (τέρας) and mighty works (δύναμις).

Hebrews 2:3-4 [3] How shall we escape, if we neglect so great salvation; which at the first began to be spoken by the Lord, and was confirmed unto us by them that heard him; [4] God also bearing them witness, both with signs (σημεῖον) and wonders (τέρας), and with divers miracles (δύναμις), and gifts of the Holy Ghost, according to his own will?

I want to look at each of the three Grk terms for our study.

Powers

The Grk word for "powers" is δύναμις. "Powers" describe the cause of miracles. A miracle is the manifestation of God's power. This same word is also translated as *wonderful works* and *mighty works*. *Power* (δύναμις) points to the divine power, the source of the miraculous phenomenon. It is specifically the word used for the inherent power of God.

God created all things out of nothing by his infinite wisdom, and he rules his creation by the word of his power. Every moment the universe exists, God is governing by the word of his power and according to his sovereign will. We call this God's providence. A miracle is simply an extraordinary act of God's providence, as compared to an ordinary act of providence. Miracles are greater manifestations of God's power in contrast to the things that are seen in the ordinary course of nature.

It is noteworthy that the same Grk word used to describe a miracle (δύναμις) is also used to describe salvation. God saves lost sinners by his almighty power. It is no less a miracle. The gospel of Christ is the power of God unto salvation.

Romans 1:16 [16] For I am not ashamed of the gospel of Christ: for it is the power (δύναμις) of God unto salvation to every one that believeth; to the Jew first, and also to the Grk.

When you pray for God to save a sinner, you are praying for a miracle. If God is able to create this universe out of nothing, to raise the dead, to cause the lame to walk, to give sight to the blind and to give hearing to the deaf, is he not also able to change one's wicked heart? Is he not able to create a new heart? Martin Luther said, "Conversion is the greatest of all miracles." It is the supernatural work of the Spirit of God that regenerates, converts, sanctifies and applies the redemptive work of Christ to the believer.

Signs

The Grk word for "signs" is σημεῖον. This term describes the purpose of a miracle. Miracles are called *signs* because they are designed to teach. The term *sign* denotes that the miracle has a purpose and a spiritual lesson to convey. A *sign* points to a spiritual truth of which the miracle is only the outward expression. A miracle is not pointless; it is a revelation of God. A miracle is not arbitrary, but has a definite purpose. The word *signs* tells us the purpose of miracles; they confirm God's message and his messengers.

All the miracles of Christ and his disciples occurred in order to confirm and bear witness to divine truth. Miracles are inseparable from revelation. They serve to mark and credential God's revelation. Furthermore, they authenticate the bearers of divine revelation. Note the following four things about the purpose of Christ's miracles.

Christ's Miracles Were a Means of Self-Disclosure

Christ's miracles made his divine glory visible. His miracles were an external glory that manifested his internal glory; the divine glory that was veiled in his humanity. Miracles glorified him as the Son of God (John 11:4).

Christ's miracles were different from the miracles of the prophets and apostles. God performed miracles through them as his instruments. But Christ's miracles were manifestations of his divinity and his own inherent power. They were inseparable from Jesus Christ himself.

> **John 2:11** [11] This beginning of miracles did Jesus in Cana of Galilee, and manifested forth his glory; and his disciples believed on him.

> **John 11:4** [4] When Jesus heard that, he said, This sickness is not unto death, but for the glory of God, that the Son of God might be glorified thereby.

Miracles Credentialed Christ as the Messiah

The prophecies that Christ fulfilled through miracles were proof that he was the Messiah. They identified him as the Messiah. When the disciples of John the Baptist came to Christ and asked him if he was the Christ or should they look for another, what was his answer? The answer is found in Luke 7:22-23:

> **Luke 7:22-23** [22] Then Jesus answering said unto them, Go your way, and tell John what things ye have seen and heard; how that the blind see, the lame walk, the lepers are cleansed, the deaf hear, the dead are raised, to the poor the gospel is preached. [23] And blessed is he, whosoever shall not be offended in me.

This is a quotation of the Messianic prophesy of Isaiah 35:5-6. Christ's miracles testified to the fact that he was the Messiah prophesied about.[252] Jesus expected John's disciples to understand this.

> **Isaiah 35:5-6** [5] Then the eyes of the blind shall be opened, and the ears of the deaf shall be unstopped. [6] Then shall the lame *man* leap as an hart, and the tongue of the dumb sing: for in the wilderness shall waters break out, and streams in the desert.

Miracles Credentialed Christ's Divine Authority

Miracles confirmed that Christ came from God with God's authority. A miracle is for the confirmation of divine authority. Christ's miracles credentialed Him as the authoritative bearer of special revelation.

---

[252] See also Mark 7:27 in the healing of one that was deaf and dumb.

238

John 3:2 [2] The same came to Jesus by night, and said unto him, Rabbi, we know that thou art a teacher come from God: for no man can do these miracles that thou doest, except God be with him.

Acts 2:22 [22] Ye men of Israel, hear these words; Jesus of Nazareth, a man approved of God among you by miracles and wonders and signs, which God did by him in the midst of you, as ye yourselves also know:

Christ's Miracles Were a Witness to Redemptive Truth

A miracle not only authenticates the bearer of the message, but the very message itself. As *signs* (σημεῖον), miracles are always connected to a message. There is an inseparable connection of miracles with special revelation. Christ's miracles authenticated his gospel message. This is indeed the primary purpose of a miracle – to authenticate the message! For without doctrinal truth miracles avail nothing.[253] They are nothing more than spectacles.

Hebrews 2:3-4 [3] How shall we escape, if we neglect so great salvation; which at the first began to be spoken by the Lord, and was confirmed unto us by them that heard him; [4] God also bearing them witness, both with signs and wonders, and with divers miracles, and gifts of the Holy Ghost, according to his own will?

Acts 14:3 [3] Long time therefore abode they speaking boldly in the Lord, which gave testimony unto the word of his grace, and granted signs and wonders to be done by their hands.

Mark 16:20 [20] And they went forth, and preached every where, the Lord working with them, and confirming the word with signs following. Amen

Wonders

The term "wonders" describes the effect miracles have on the observer. The meaning of the English word "miracle" is derived from the Latin *miraculum* which denotes wonder, i.e., that which excites wonder.[254]

---

[253] R. C. Trench, *Notes on the Miracles of Our Lord*. Grand Rapids, MI: Baker Book House, 1992 reprint, p. 21.

[254] C. Hodge, *Systematic Theology* (Eerdmans Publishing Co., 1989 reprint), Vol. 1; Webster's Dictionary

The Grk word for "wonders" is τέρας. It is found only in the plural and always accompanying the term "signs" (σημεῖον). The word means "a marvel." This refers to the attention-getting aspect of miracles. A miracle is designed to call the attention of the observers or of those who experience the miracle, to astound them and to startle them. Miracles are to elicit awe, to astonish and excite wonder. This is the obvious function of a miracle.

A miracle demands the awed attention of men, to make men think on things they would otherwise not think about. It arrests their attention so that they may contemplate the things of God. A miracle is designed to open the eyes in order to consider the meaning and purpose of the miracle. See Mark 7:31-37.

> **Mark 7:37** And were beyond measure astonished, saying, He hath done all things well: he maketh both the deaf to hear, and the dumb to speak.

However, a miracle is never to be considered as simply "a wonder." Christ never performed miracles strictly to elicit awe. That would make miracles without meaning and purpose. It would be strictly for entertainment value at that point. It would have no ethical value.

The Grk word τέρας (wonders) used to describe miracles in the N.T. is never used alone. Each time it occurs with the term *signs* (σημεῖον), it always has reference to the meaning and purpose of the miracle. In the N.T., a miracle can be described as a *sign* alone, it can be described as a *power* (δύναμις) alone referring to God's power, but it is never described as a *wonder* alone.

A miracle must not be construed as some freak display of power. Miracles are not performed arbitrarily. They are not mere wonders and exhibitions of power just to amaze the spectators.[255]

---

[255] L. Berkhof, *Systematic Theology*. Grand Rapids, MI: Eerdmans Publishing Co., 1988 reprint, p. 177.

Without debating the validity of modern day miracles and the charismatic movement, I do question the motive for their experience. It seems to be sensationalism. There is no message behind the miracle. It is for entertainment and amusement. It is for arousing the spectators to awe, but there is no message or meaning. The focus is on the alleged supernatural phenomenon. It is purely existential. It's no different than a magician show.

Summary

In summary, these three terms, *powers, signs* and *wonders*, describe for us three distinct features by which we are to understand what a miracle is. If we synthesize the meanings of the three terms, we can formulate a biblical definition of miracles: *A miracle is an act of God's power revealing his glory, purposing to credential God's message or messenger and designed to arrest the attention of the observer.*

But this is only a description of the properties or characteristics of a miracle. To take this further, we must harmonize all the separate accounts of biblical miracles into a unified framework. They are not isolated facts of Scripture but rather express a harmonized system. They must be connected to what we know about God, and the relationship God has to his created universe.

A THEOLOGICAL DEFINITION

The theological definition of a miracle is *an extraordinary act of God's providence.* It is an act of God that is out of the ordinary government of his creation. When we speak of natural processes, we are speaking of ever-repeating processes, everyday workings; these are ordinary acts of God's providence. They are common occurrences. God uses the laws of nature to govern common occurrences. Miracles are extraordinary. They are extremely rare acts of God, which are not common to human experience. This is the distinction we must make in regards to a miracle.

The sprouting of a kernel of corn is no less marvelous than the feeding of five thousand with five loaves of bread. The difference is that feeding the five thousand is extraordinary. The birth of a baby is no less spectacular than the raising of the dead by Christ. The difference is that raising the dead is extraordinary. The rising of the sun is no less amazing than turning water into wine, etc. The point I am making is there is no intrinsic difference between an extraordinary act of God and an ordinary act of God. They are both expressions of God's sovereign will and the ordering of His creation.

Accordingly, a miracle is distinguished as an *immediate* act of God's providence. This distinction excludes secondary causes that operate according to natural law. It would not be a miracle if it were brought about by causes according to natural law. An immediate act of God's providence is referred to as an "absolute miracle." Thus, we would define an absolute miracle as *the immediate efficiency of God's extraordinary providence*. The healing of the deaf and dumb man was an account of an absolute miracle.

God's providence presupposes a Creator-creature relationship. His created universe and creatures are subject to Him and his laws. All the laws of nature, such as the law of gravity and the laws of thermodynamics, etc., are subject to God's absolute rule. He created this universe and he governs it. All things are subject to him. In governing his created universe, he hath foreordained whatsoever comes to pass including miracles. God the Creator is the sovereign Governor of his creation. All of his creation serves him for his glory.

He rules and governs his creation by the word of his power. He preserves and governs all his creatures and all their actions. He preserves and governs everything in his created universe including the seemingly random fall of a leaf or the spin of an electron; everything in the minutest detail has been decreed from eternity. If but one event, one spin of an electron, or one collision of a molecule happened by chance, then God would no longer be sovereign, no longer be in absolute control and no longer be omniscient. He would not be God.

This brings me to another aspect of a theological definition of a miracle. A miracle is simply *an act of God's sovereign will*. It is God executing his eternal purposes, which necessarily requires governing his created universe. A miracle is *an act of God's government over his creation*.

The Creator-creature distinction is the foundation of all true knowledge. To deny the Creator-creature distinction, which is what secular science does, is to be ignorant of reality. To deny God's sovereign will and providential governance is to be void of the true meaning of anything.

A Christian does not interpret an act of nature (an observable fact) with the same set of presuppositions as the non-Christian. The philosophy espoused by modern-day science is in rebellion to the Creator-creature relationship. Their worldview is in collision with the Christian worldview; it is not neutral and will never admit to a miracle. This needs to be taken into account in the work of apologetics. The antithesis of the Creator-creature worldview must be pushed.

A PHILOSOPHICAL DEFINITION

The world of unbelieving thought does not hold God's word as the standard of truth. The Bible is not their authority for true knowledge. So how does the modern-day scientist view miracles?

They are forced to define miracles rationalistically and philosophically. The classic philosophical definition of a miracle is *a violation of the laws of nature*. However, we must immediately assert that a miracle is not a violation of natural law.[256] This is David Hume's

---

[256] W. Chantry, *Signs of the Apostles*; R. C. Trench, *Notes on the Miracles of Our Lord*; R. Nash, *Faith & Reason*.

definition of a miracle and presupposes an anti-Christian worldview. [257] We must be careful not to construe a miracle as something contrary to nature, or that which works against nature. This is a completely erroneous and an unbiblical perspective.

The term *natural law* does not reflect God's sovereign government of the universe. Only laws of God exist for us. It is meaningless to speak of God violating natural law when all of natural law is under his governance to begin with. The laws of nature are simply the expression of God's will. The laws of nature are not rules that prescribe how God must act; God is not subject to his own creation. In God's providence, he preserves and governs all things by the word of his power. Therefore, we can only speak of a miracle as being above and beyond natural law but never a violation of natural law.

Natural processes do not exist apart from God. The world is not an independent mechanism of natural law. On the contrary, God created uniformity in nature, which we call natural law. The laws of nature are uniform because God wills it, and they remain uniform because God wills it. God created all natural processes in his infinite wisdom. He rules and governs over all natural processes.

Now this is diametrically opposed to modern science and naturalism. By their presuppositions of what nature is, science can never admit to a miracle. Naturalism presupposes the universe is a closed system. To the scientist, the universe is like a box. Everything that happens within the box can only be explained or caused by things that exist within the box. By their presuppositions, the box must be self-sufficient and self-contained. The only processes and mechanisms that can exist within the box are natural laws. Nothing supernatural can occur. All things must be explained only by the so-called natural laws contained within the box.

---

[257] D. Hume, *An Enquiry Concerning Human Understanding*.

God is excluded from the box, its a closed system; by definition, he can't get in. Therefore, to the scientist, miracles cannot exist. This is a fundamental presupposition of their worldview. You cannot prove this to them; they are wholly biased against it. It's their belief system and they are not neutral on the matter. However, science may admit to a strange phenomenon that they do not understand and cannot explain. For example, they may admit to the raising of the dead, but it is not because they acknowledge the possibility of a miracle. From their presuppositions, they simply write it off as a natural phenomenon that has not yet been discovered. But in due time, and with the advancement of science, eventually, it will be fully explained by natural law. They will simply have to expand their limits upon what is possible.

Therefore, the scientist is shut out from reality by his own presuppositions because he cannot view this world as under the providential care of God. He can never come to a right understanding of the world around him. Only the Christian can properly interpret nature because he presupposes that God preserves and governs his creation by the word of his power. Only the Christian has a true understanding of reality.

OBSERVATIONS

Observation 1: The rejection or belief in miracles (and more importantly biblical miracles) is based upon a faith commitment to one's presuppositions and worldview. To Christians, miracles are a very coherent element of their belief system. Miracles are consistent with a Christian's worldview. If the Bible is true and the God of the Bible exists, then it is preposterous not to believe in miracles.

Observation 2. We are no longer living in an era of miracles. They ceased with the apostles and the close of the cannon of Scripture. The special revelation that miracles were given to authenticate is complete.

Do miracles exist today? Of course, God is sovereign and free to do whatever he pleases. We cannot put limitations on God. However, miracles do not occur in the same way they did during our Lord's earthly life and the apostles. But don't get me wrong. God still manifests his glory through miracles and sometimes answers our prayers miraculously, but not through the alleged gifts of *miracles* or *charismata*.[258] These miraculous gifts were given to the apostles and to a few they laid hands on in order to credential special revelation. The time of the apostles' witness was an epoch of miracles. That epoch has passed away.

Although the Bible contains many accounts of miracles, it is not a continuous book of miracles. There are periods in biblical history that do not contain any record of a miracle. We find only four epochs of miracles in the Bible: 1) the time of Moses and Joshua, 2) Elijah, Elisha and the prophets, 3) the ministry of Christ and 4) the Apostles. These are cycles of miracles connected with special periods in the history of redemption.[259] The major purpose of miracles was to authenticate each of these stages of progressive revelation. The special revelation they were given to authenticate is complete, i.e., the cannon of Scripture has been completed. There is no further need of special revelation (2 Tim. 3:16-17).

> **2 Timothy 3:16-17** [16] All scripture is given by inspiration of God, and is profitable for doctrine, for reproof, for correction, for instruction in righteousness: [17] That the man of God may be perfect, throughly furnished unto all good works.

The primary purpose of miracles has been fulfilled because the cannon of Scripture is closed. God has given us a full, complete and sufficient revelation in the Old and New Testaments of Scripture. Therefore, God no longer needs to credential a messenger with apostolic authority because we already have a complete revelation. Hence, the primary purpose of miracles is fulfilled.

---

[258] The Grk term for "gifts."
[259] Berkhof, L., *Systematic Theology*, p. 117.

The gifts (χαρίσματα) of miracles (δυνάμεις, 1 Cor. 12:28), i.e., the signs and wonders by which God credentialed the Apostles (Heb. 2:3-4; Acts 14:3) no longer exist today. What does this say about the modern day Charismatic movement and the tendencies of Christendom today? Many claim the gift of healing, the gift of prophecy and supernatural knowledge from God. Such gifts presuppose a continuing revelation and the insufficiency of Scripture. It is adding to the word of God.

Make no mistake about it. When charismatics prophesy, it is allegedly with the inspiration and divine authority of God. To them, it is the very revelation of God and carries the same authority as Scripture. These so-called gifts are usually accompanied with miracles such as tongues and healings. But do tongues and healing credential their message? Not one iota! If Scripture is complete, if Scripture is sufficient, then these prophecies are false. They have no divine authority.

Isaiah 8:20 To the law and to the testimony: if they speak not according to this word, *it is* because *there is* no light in them.

The charismatic movement is diverting professing Christians from the authority, completeness and sufficiency of the word of God. People are directed away from the truth to seek an experience. They seek a second work of grace that will solve all their spiritual problems. Oh, they think that if they could have these miraculous gifts and extraordinary experiences, they could be more spiritual. They are deceived because they think they can be immediately sanctified into a higher spiritual life. If you talk to any charismatic Christian and they find out you do not speak in tongues, you are immediately perceived as a lesser Christian, a second rate Christian.

The doctrine of biblical sanctification and true spiritual maturity is swept under the carpet. What ever happened to the mortification of sin? Where are the greater gifts of faith, hope and love? Who is seeking to be sanctified with the fruit of the Spirit: love, joy, peace, longsuffering, gentleness, goodness and faith? One can bypass all this and enter into a higher spiritual life by an ecstatic experience. Receive the baptism of the Holy Spirit they say! Speak in tongues! Prophesy! This is nothing but a thirst for sensationalism. It is an existentialism that seeks to bypass God's ordained means for sanctification.

> **Matthew 7:21-23** [21] Not every one that saith unto me, Lord, Lord, shall enter into the kingdom of heaven; but he that doeth the will of my Father which is in heaven. [22] Many will say to me in that day, Lord, Lord, have we not prophesied in thy name? and in thy name have cast out devils? and in thy name done many wonderful works? [23] And then will I profess unto them, I never knew you: depart from me, ye that work iniquity.

SELECTED BIBLIOGRAPHY FOR PRESUPPOSITIONAL APOLOGETICS

Bahnsen, G., *Always Ready: Directions for Defending the Faith.* Texarkana, AR: Covenant Media Foundation, 1996

————, *Presuppositional Apologetics.* Powder Springs, GA: American Vision Press, 2008.

————, *Pushing the Antithesis.* Powder Springs, GA: American Vision Press, 2007.

————, *Van Til's Apologetic: Readings and Analysis.* Phillipsburg, NJ: Presbyterian and Reformed Publishing Company, 1998.

Calvin, J., *Institutes of the Christian Religion.* Translated by F. L. Battles and edited by J. T. Mcneill. Philadelphia, Penn.: The Westminster Press, 1960.

Carnell, E. J., *Christian Commitment: An Apologetic.* New York, NY: The MacMillan Company, 1957.

————, *An Introduction to Christian Apologetics.* Grand Rapids, MI: Wm. B. Eerdmans Publishing Company, 1970.

————, *The Case for Biblical Christianity.* Grand Rapids, MI: Wm. B. Eerdmans Publishing Company, 1969.

Clark, G., *A Christian View of Men and Things.* Jefferson, MD: The Trinity Foundation, 1991.

————, *An Introduction to Christian Philosophy.* Jefferson, MD: The Trinity Foundation, 1993.

————, *Religion, Reason, and Revelation.* Jefferson, MD: The Trinity Foundation, 1995.

_____, *The Philosophy of Science and Belief in God*. Jefferson, MD: The Trinity Foundation, 1987.

Craig, W. L., Habermas, G.R., Frame, J.M., Clark, K.J., and Feinberg, P.D, *Five Views on Apologetics*. Grand Rapids, MI: Zondervan, 2000.

Downing, W. R., *An Introduction to Biblical Epistemology*. P.I.R.S. Publications, 1998.

Frame, J., *Apologetics to the Glory of God*. Phillipsburg, NJ: Presbyterian and Reformed Publishing Co., 1994.

_____, *Cornelius Van Til: An Analysis of His Thought*. Phillipsburg, NJ: Presbyterian and Reformed Publishing Co., 1995.

Geisler, N., *Christian Apologetics*. Grand Rapids, Michigan: Baker Book House, 1976. (This work teaches evidential apologetics).

Gerstner, J., *Reasons for Faith*. Morgan, PA: Soli Deo Gloria Publications, 1995 (Reprint). (This work teaches evidential apologetics).

Greehan, E. R. (Ed.), *Jerusalem and Athens*. Phillipsburg, NJ: Presbyterian and Reformed Publishing Co., 1980.

Kuyper, A., *Lectures on Calvinism*. Grand Rapids, MI: Wm. B. Eerdmans Publishing Company, 1994. Chapter IV entitled "Calvinism and Science."

_____, *Principles of Sacred Theology*. Grand Rapids, MI: Baker Book House, 1980.

McManis, C. B., *Biblical Apologetics*. Bloomington, IN: Xlibris Publishing, 2012.

Nash, R. H., *Faith & Reason: Searching for a Rational Faith*. Grand Rapids, Michigan: Zondervan Publishing House, 1988.

Oliphint, K. S., *The Battle Belongs to the Lord*. Phillipsburg, NJ: Presbyterian and Reformed Publishing Co., 2003.

_____, *Covenantal Apologetics*, Wheaton, IL: Crossway, 2013.

_____, *Reasons for Faith*. Phillipsburg, NJ: Presbyterian and Reformed Publishing Co., 2006.

_____, *Revelation and Reason*. Phillipsburg, NJ: Presbyterian and Reformed Publishing Co., 2007.

Orr, James, *The Christian View of God and the World*. Grand Rapids, MI: Kregel Publications, 1989. (Reprint of Scribner's 1887 3rd edition).

Pratt, R., *Every Though Captive*. Phillipsburg, NJ: Presbyterian and Reformed Publishing Co., 1994.

Ramm, B., *The Christian View of Science and the Scripture*. Grand Rapids, MI: Wm. B. Eerdmans Publishing Company, 1955.

_____, *Protestant Christian Evidences*. Chicago: Moody Press, 1953.

Reymond, R. L., *The Justification of Knowledge*, P.I.R.S. Publications, 1998 (Reprint).

Rushdoony, R. J., *By What Standard?* Philadelphia: Presbyterian and Reformed Publishing Co., 1958.

_____, *The Mythology of Science*. Nutley, NJ: The Craig Press, 1968.

_____, *The Word of Flux*. Fairfax, VA: The Thoburn Press, 1975.

Sproul, R. C., Gerstner, J., and Lindsley, A., *Classical Apologetics*. Grand Rapids: Zondervan Publishing House, 1984. (This work teaches evidential apologetics).

Sproul, R. C., *Not A Chance: The Myth of Chance in Modern Science & Cosmology*. Grand Rapids, MI: Baker Book House, 1994.

Van Til, C., *Christian Apologetics*. Phillipsburg, NJ: Presbyterian and Reformed Publishing Co., 2003. (2nd Ed., William Edgar editor).

_____, *The Defense of the Faith*. Phillipsburg, NJ: Presbyterian and Reformed Publishing Co., 2008. (4th Ed., K. Scott Oliphint editor).

_____, *Introduction to Systematic Theology*. Phillipsburg, NJ: Presbyterian and Reformed Publishing Co., 2007. (2nd Ed., William Edgar editor).

_____, *Christian Theory of Knowledge*. Phillipsburg, NJ: Presbyterian and Reformed Publishing Co., 1969.

_____, *Christian Theistic Evidences*. Volume VI of the Series "In Defense of the Faith." Phillipsburg, NJ: Presbyterian and Reformed Publishing Co.

_____, *Common Grace and the Gospel*. Phillipsburg, NJ: Presbyterian and Reformed Publishing Co., 1972.

_____, *The Doctrine of Scripture*. Volume I of the Series "In Defense of the Faith." Phillipsburg, NJ: Presbyterian and Reformed Publishing Co, 1969.

_____, *Survey of Christian Epistemology*. Volume II of the Series "In Defense of the Faith." Phillipsburg, NJ: Presbyterian and Reformed Publishing Co, 1969.

Various authors (compilation of excerpts), *The Risen Christ Conquers Mars Hill*. Birmingham, AL: Solid Ground Christian Books, 2013.

Warfield, B. B., *The Inspiration and Authority of the Bible*. Philadelphia: Presbyterian and Reformed Publishing Co., 1948.